Shadowline®
image
www.ShadowlineOnline.com

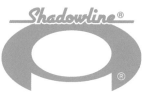

FIVE WEAPONS: TYLER'S REVENGE

FIRST PRINTING:
August, 2014

ISBN: 978-1-63215-028-8

Published by Image Comics, Inc. Office of publication: 2001 Center St. Sixth Floor, Berkeley, CA 94704.

CREATED, WRITTEN, ILLUSTRATED and LETTERED BY
JIMMIE ROBINSON

COLORED BY
PAUL LITTLE

EDITED BY
LAURA TAVISHATI

MARC LOMBARDI
COMMUNICATIONS
JIM VALENTINO
PUBLISHER/BOOK DESIGN

SPECIAL THANKS TO
GAIL FOLLANSBEE

A

PRODUCTION

IMAGE COMICS, INC.
Robert Kirkman – Chief Operating Officer
Erik Larsen – Chief Financial Officer
® **Todd McFarlane** – President
Marc Silvestri – Chief Executive Officer
Jim Valentino – Vice-President

Eric Stephenson – Publisher
Ron Richards – Director of Business Development
Jennifer de Guzman – Director of Trade Book Sales
Kat Salazar – Director of PR & Marketing
Jeremy Sullivan – Director of Digital Sales
Emilio Bautista – Sales Assistant
Branwyn Bigglestone – Senior Accounts Manager
Emily Miller – Accounts Manager
Jessica Ambriz – Administrative Assistant
Tyler Shainline – Events Coordinator
David Brothers – Content Manager
Jonathan Chan – Production Manager
Drew Gill – Art Director
Meredith Wallace – Print Manager
Monica Garcia – Senior Production Artist
Jenna Savage – Production Artist
Addison Duke – Production Artist
Tricia Ramos – Production Assistant
IMAGECOMICS.COM

"For my daughters, Jessica and Arielle."

Jimmie Robinson

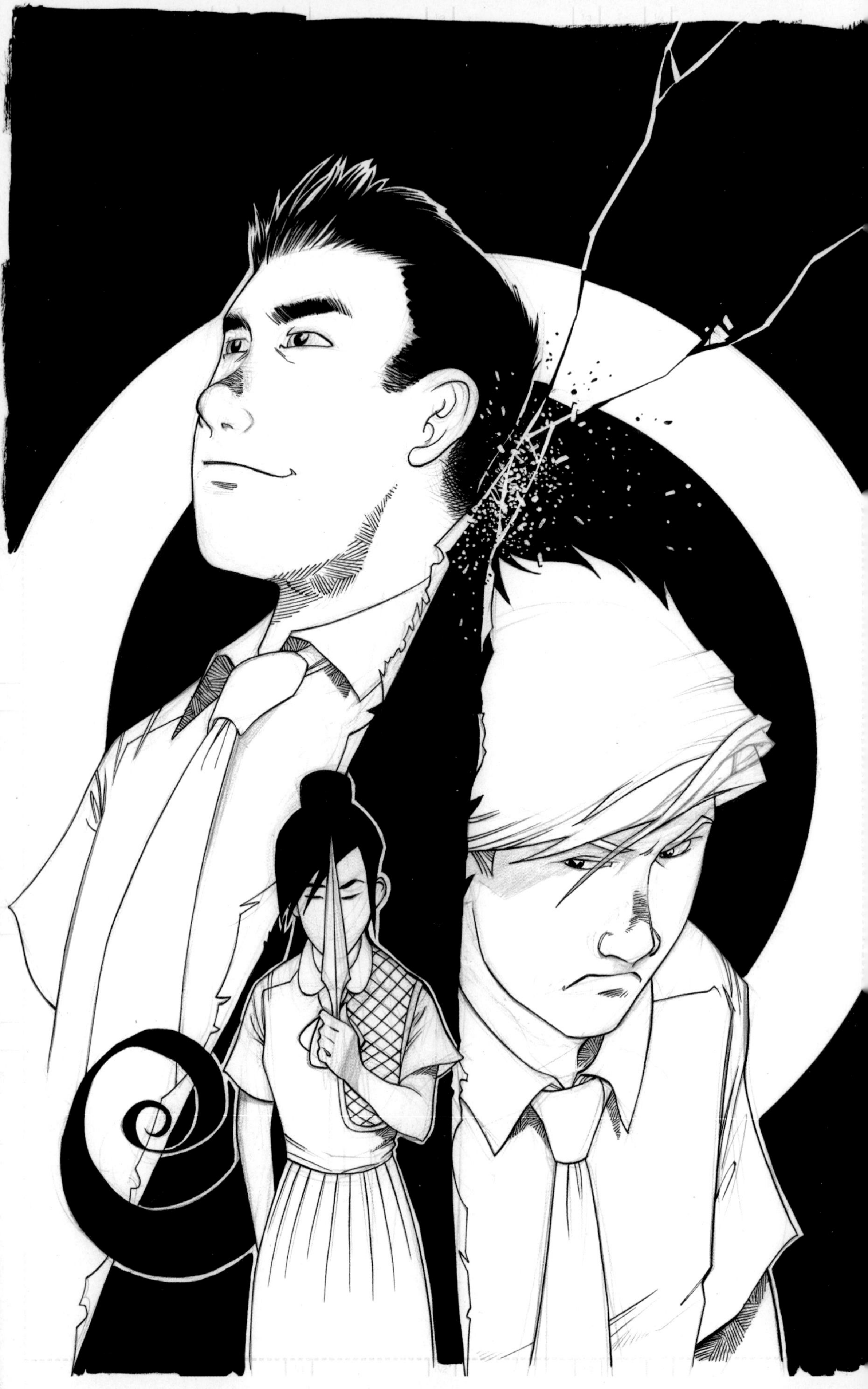

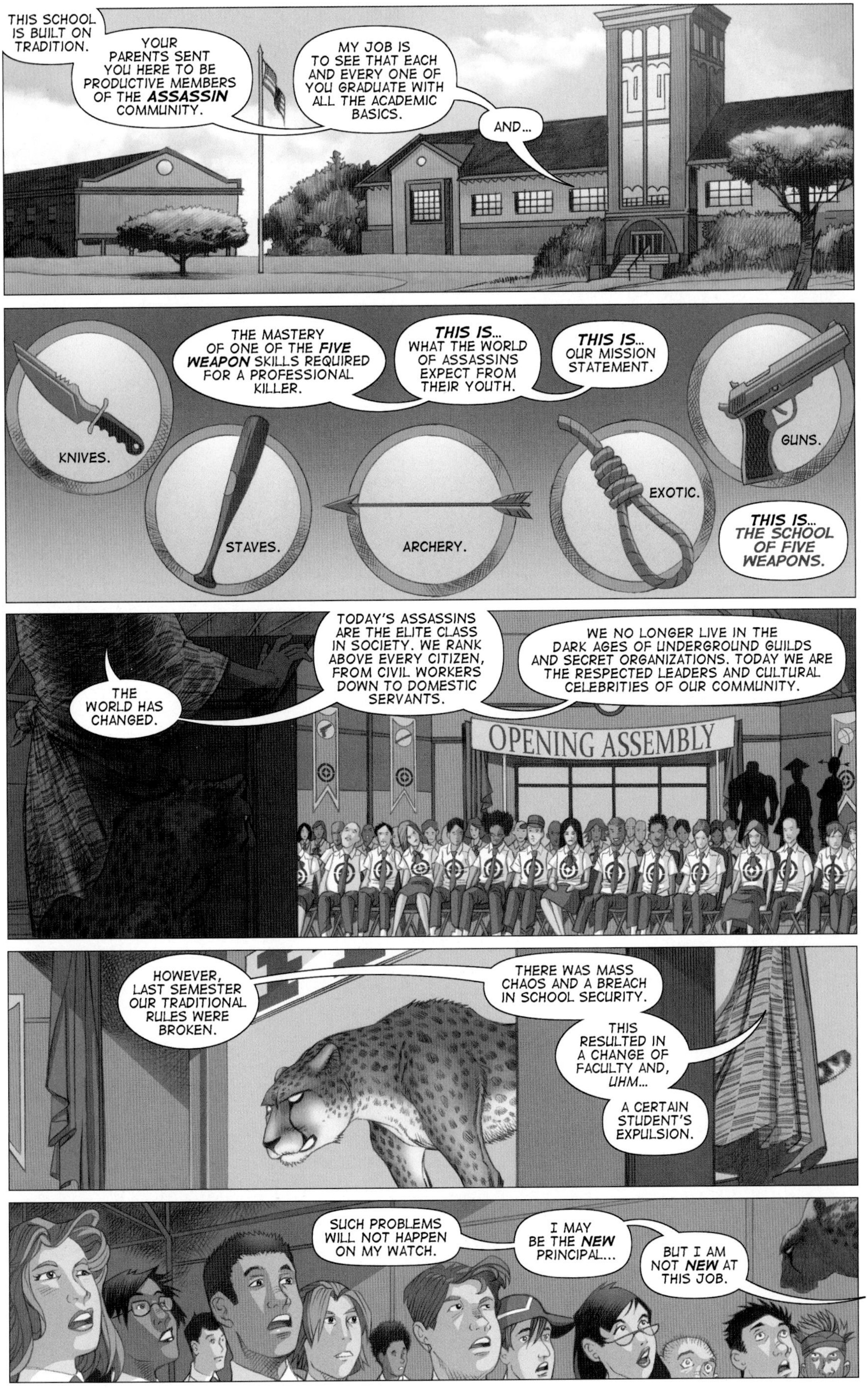

THIS SCHOOL IS BUILT ON TRADITION.
YOUR PARENTS SENT YOU HERE TO BE PRODUCTIVE MEMBERS OF THE ASSASSIN COMMUNITY.
MY JOB IS TO SEE THAT EACH AND EVERY ONE OF YOU GRADUATE WITH ALL THE ACADEMIC BASICS.
AND...
THE MASTERY OF ONE OF THE FIVE WEAPON SKILLS REQUIRED FOR A PROFESSIONAL KILLER.
THIS IS... WHAT THE WORLD OF ASSASSINS EXPECT FROM THEIR YOUTH.
THIS IS... OUR MISSION STATEMENT.
KNIVES.
STAVES.
ARCHERY.
EXOTIC.
GUNS.
THIS IS... THE SCHOOL OF FIVE WEAPONS.
THE WORLD HAS CHANGED.
TODAY'S ASSASSINS ARE THE ELITE CLASS IN SOCIETY. WE RANK ABOVE EVERY CITIZEN, FROM CIVIL WORKERS DOWN TO DOMESTIC SERVANTS.
WE NO LONGER LIVE IN THE DARK AGES OF UNDERGROUND GUILDS AND SECRET ORGANIZATIONS. TODAY WE ARE THE RESPECTED LEADERS AND CULTURAL CELEBRITIES OF OUR COMMUNITY.
OPENING ASSEMBLY
HOWEVER, LAST SEMESTER OUR TRADITIONAL RULES WERE BROKEN.
THERE WAS MASS CHAOS AND A BREACH IN SCHOOL SECURITY.
THIS RESULTED IN A CHANGE OF FACULTY AND, UHM...
A CERTAIN STUDENT'S EXPULSION.
SUCH PROBLEMS WILL NOT HAPPEN ON MY WATCH.
I MAY BE THE NEW PRINCIPAL...
BUT I AM NOT NEW AT THIS JOB.

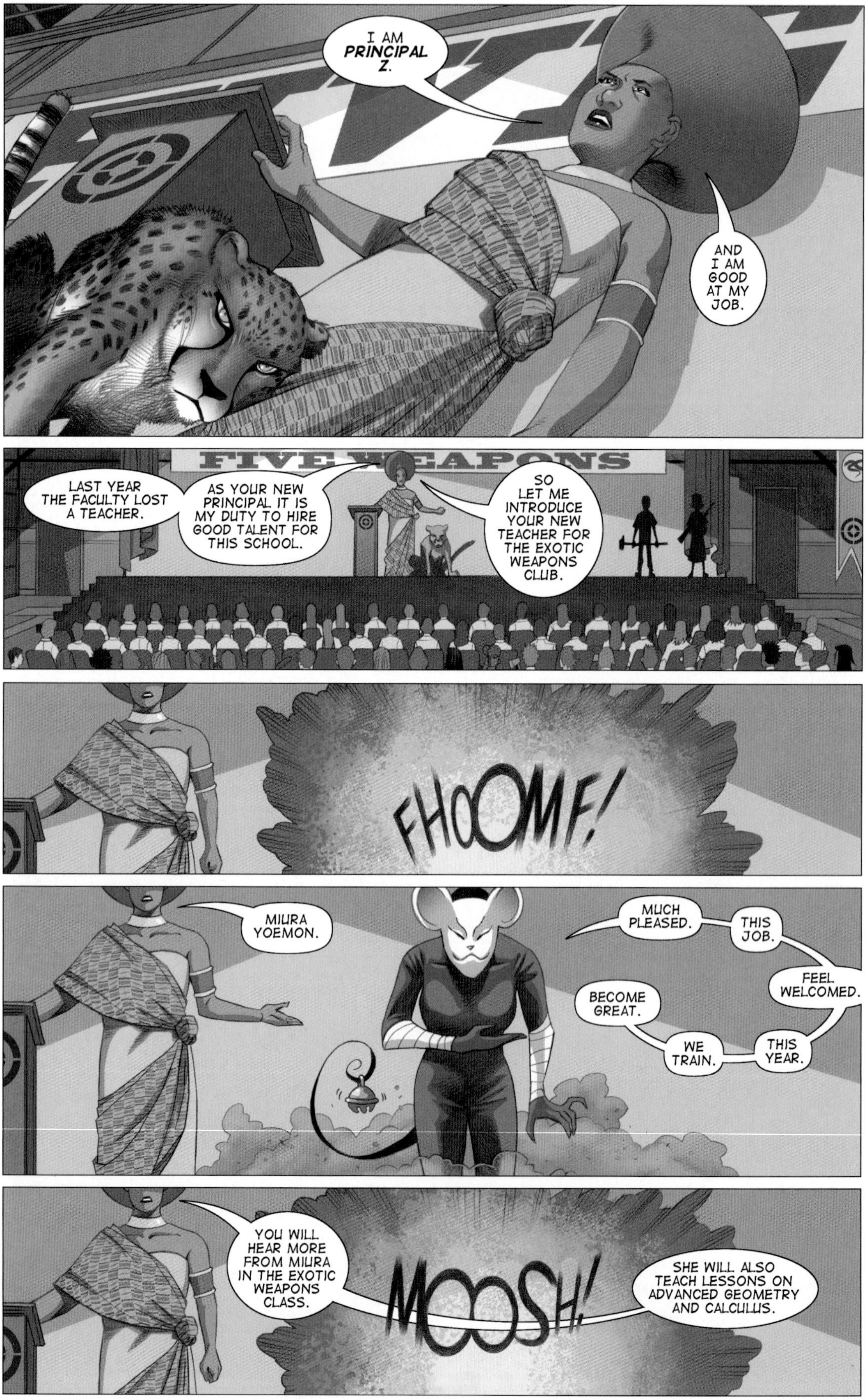
I AM PRINCIPAL Z.
AND I AM GOOD AT MY JOB.
FIVE WEAPONS
LAST YEAR THE FACULTY LOST A TEACHER.
AS YOUR NEW PRINCIPAL IT IS MY DUTY TO HIRE GOOD TALENT FOR THIS SCHOOL.
SO LET ME INTRODUCE YOUR NEW TEACHER FOR THE EXOTIC WEAPONS CLUB.
FHOOMF!
MIURA YOEMON.
MUCH PLEASED.
THIS JOB.
FEEL WELCOMED.
THIS YEAR.
WE TRAIN.
BECOME GREAT.
YOU WILL HEAR MORE FROM MIURA IN THE EXOTIC WEAPONS CLASS.
MOOSH!
SHE WILL ALSO TEACH LESSONS ON ADVANCED GEOMETRY AND CALCULUS.

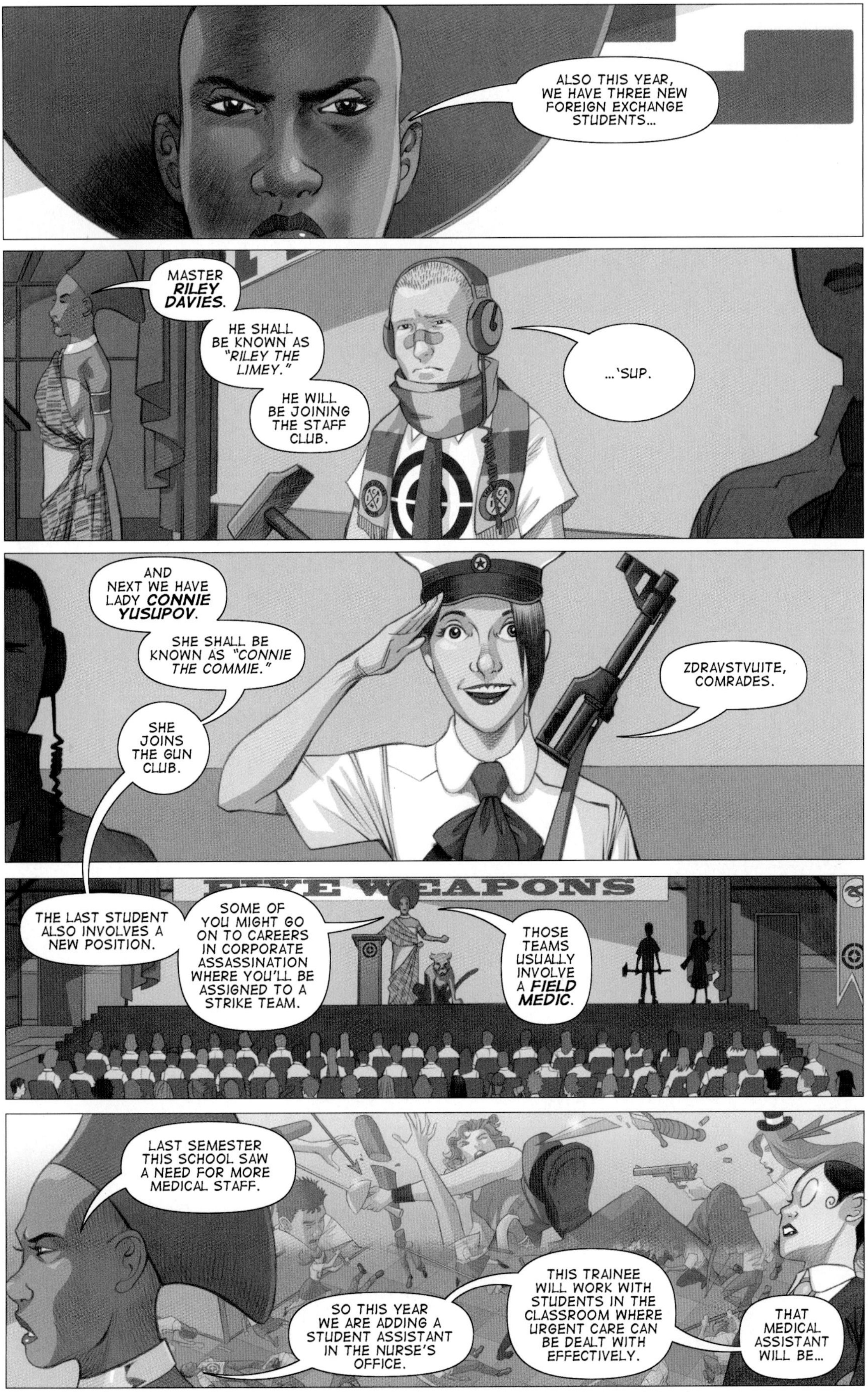
ALSO THIS YEAR, WE HAVE THREE NEW FOREIGN EXCHANGE STUDENTS...
MASTER **RILEY DAVIES**.
HE SHALL BE KNOWN AS *"RILEY THE LIMEY."*
HE WILL BE JOINING THE STAFF CLUB.
...'SUP.
AND NEXT WE HAVE LADY **CONNIE YUSUPOV**.
SHE SHALL BE KNOWN AS *"CONNIE THE COMMIE."*
SHE JOINS THE GUN CLUB.
ZDRAVSTVUITE, COMRADES.
FIVE WEAPONS
THE LAST STUDENT ALSO INVOLVES A NEW POSITION.
SOME OF YOU MIGHT GO ON TO CAREERS IN CORPORATE ASSASSINATION WHERE YOU'LL BE ASSIGNED TO A STRIKE TEAM.
THOSE TEAMS USUALLY INVOLVE A **FIELD MEDIC**.
LAST SEMESTER THIS SCHOOL SAW A NEED FOR MORE MEDICAL STAFF.
SO THIS YEAR WE ARE ADDING A STUDENT ASSISTANT IN THE NURSE'S OFFICE.
THIS TRAINEE WILL WORK WITH STUDENTS IN THE CLASSROOM WHERE URGENT CARE CAN BE DEALT WITH EFFECTIVELY.
THAT MEDICAL ASSISTANT WILL BE...

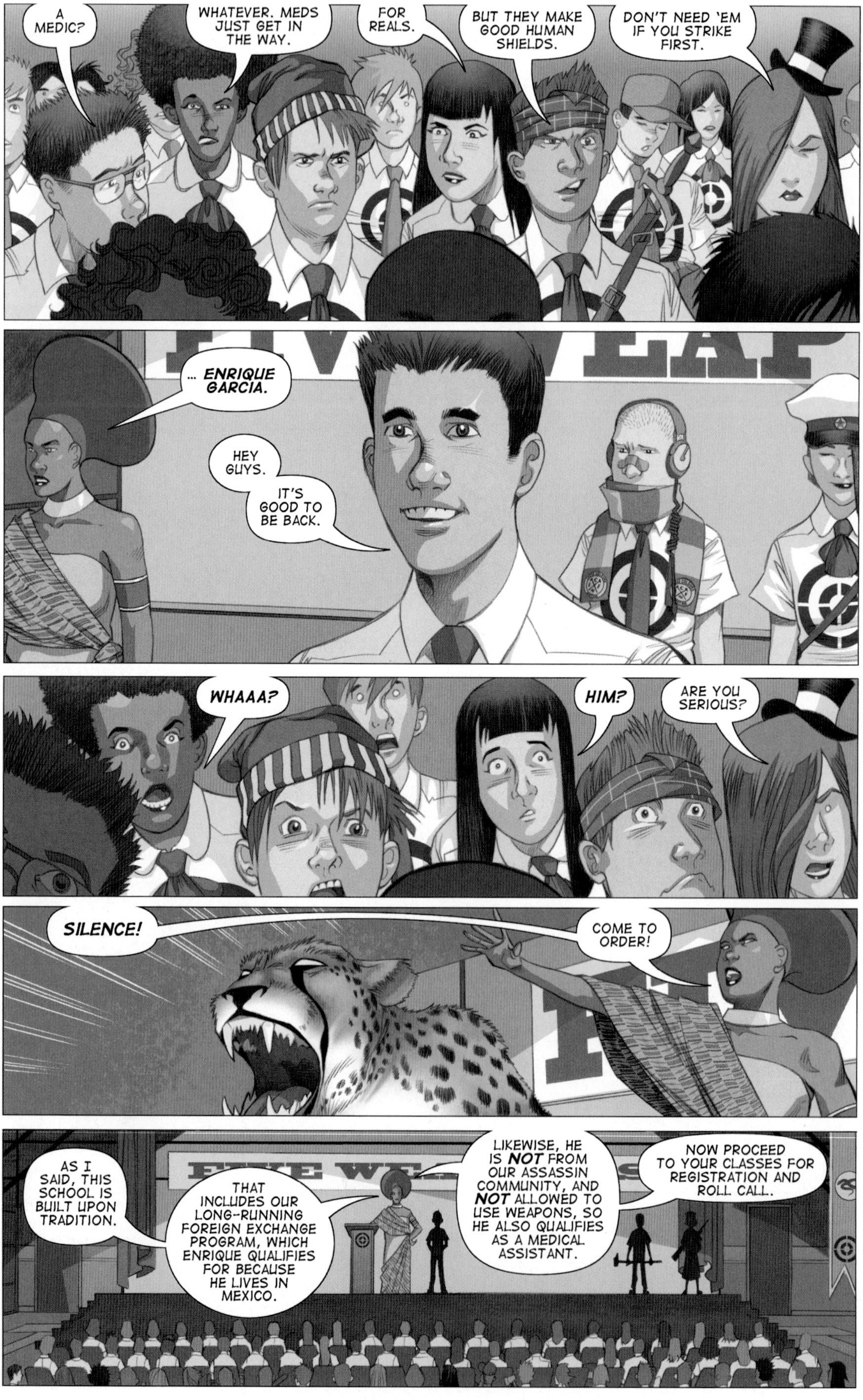
A MEDIC?
WHATEVER. MEDS JUST GET IN THE WAY.
FOR REALS.
BUT THEY MAKE GOOD HUMAN SHIELDS.
DON'T NEED 'EM IF YOU STRIKE FIRST.
... ENRIQUE GARCIA.
HEY GUYS.
IT'S GOOD TO BE BACK.
WHAAA?
HIM?
ARE YOU SERIOUS?
SILENCE!
COME TO ORDER!
AS I SAID, THIS SCHOOL IS BUILT UPON TRADITION.
THAT INCLUDES OUR LONG-RUNNING FOREIGN EXCHANGE PROGRAM, WHICH ENRIQUE QUALIFIES FOR BECAUSE HE LIVES IN MEXICO.
LIKEWISE, HE IS NOT FROM OUR ASSASSIN COMMUNITY, AND NOT ALLOWED TO USE WEAPONS, SO HE ALSO QUALIFIES AS A MEDICAL ASSISTANT.
NOW PROCEED TO YOUR CLASSES FOR REGISTRATION AND ROLL CALL.

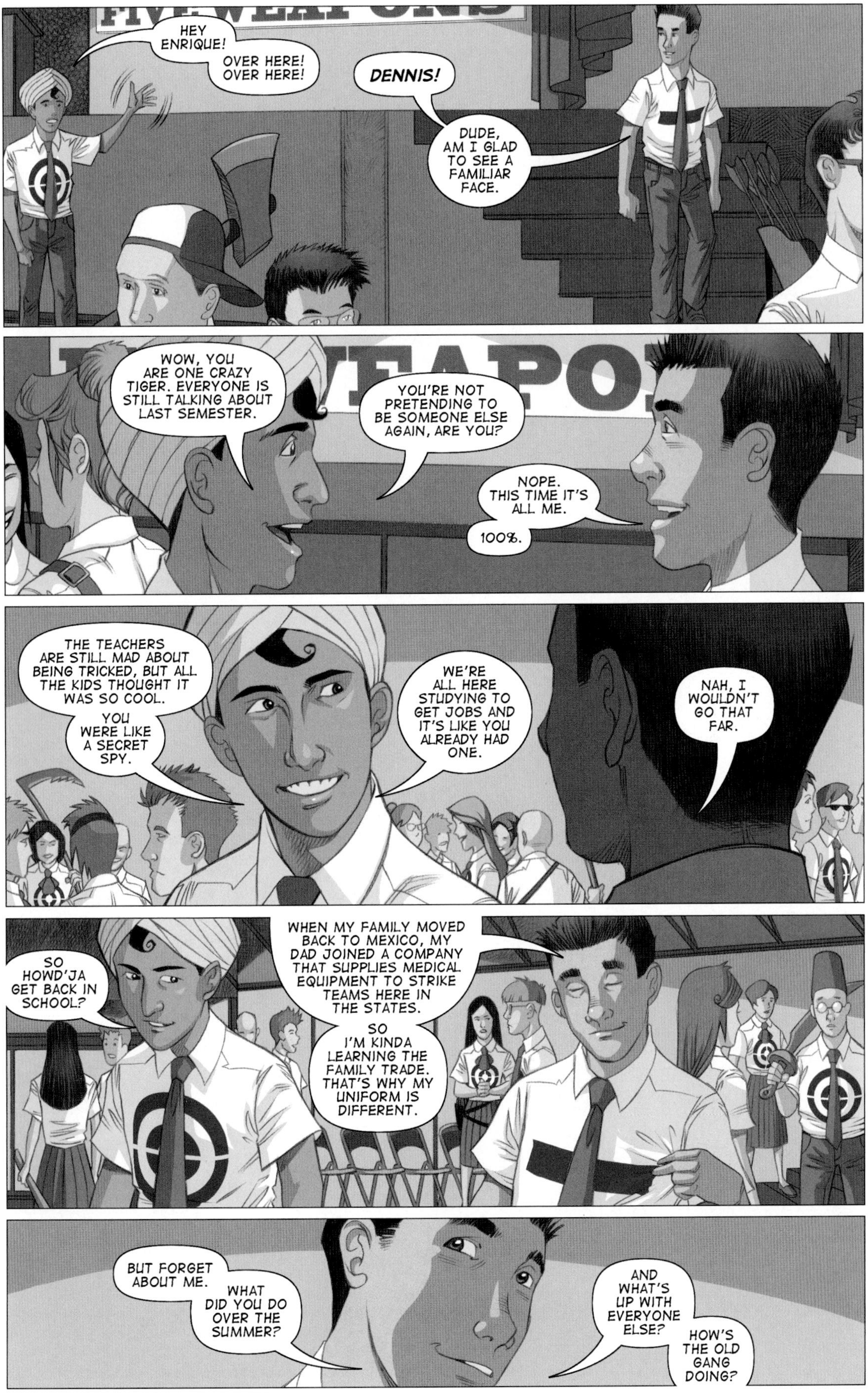
FIVE WEAPONS
HEY ENRIQUE!
OVER HERE! OVER HERE!
DENNIS!
DUDE, AM I GLAD TO SEE A FAMILIAR FACE.
WOW, YOU ARE ONE CRAZY TIGER. EVERYONE IS STILL TALKING ABOUT LAST SEMESTER.
YOU'RE NOT PRETENDING TO BE SOMEONE ELSE AGAIN, ARE YOU?
NOPE. THIS TIME IT'S ALL ME.
100%.
THE TEACHERS ARE STILL MAD ABOUT BEING TRICKED, BUT ALL THE KIDS THOUGHT IT WAS SO COOL.
YOU WERE LIKE A SECRET SPY.
WE'RE ALL HERE STUDYING TO GET JOBS AND IT'S LIKE YOU ALREADY HAD ONE.
NAH, I WOULDN'T GO THAT FAR.
SO HOWD'JA GET BACK IN SCHOOL?
WHEN MY FAMILY MOVED BACK TO MEXICO, MY DAD JOINED A COMPANY THAT SUPPLIES MEDICAL EQUIPMENT TO STRIKE TEAMS HERE IN THE STATES.
SO I'M KINDA LEARNING THE FAMILY TRADE. THAT'S WHY MY UNIFORM IS DIFFERENT.
BUT FORGET ABOUT ME.
WHAT DID YOU DO OVER THE SUMMER?
AND WHAT'S UP WITH EVERYONE ELSE?
HOW'S THE OLD GANG DOING?

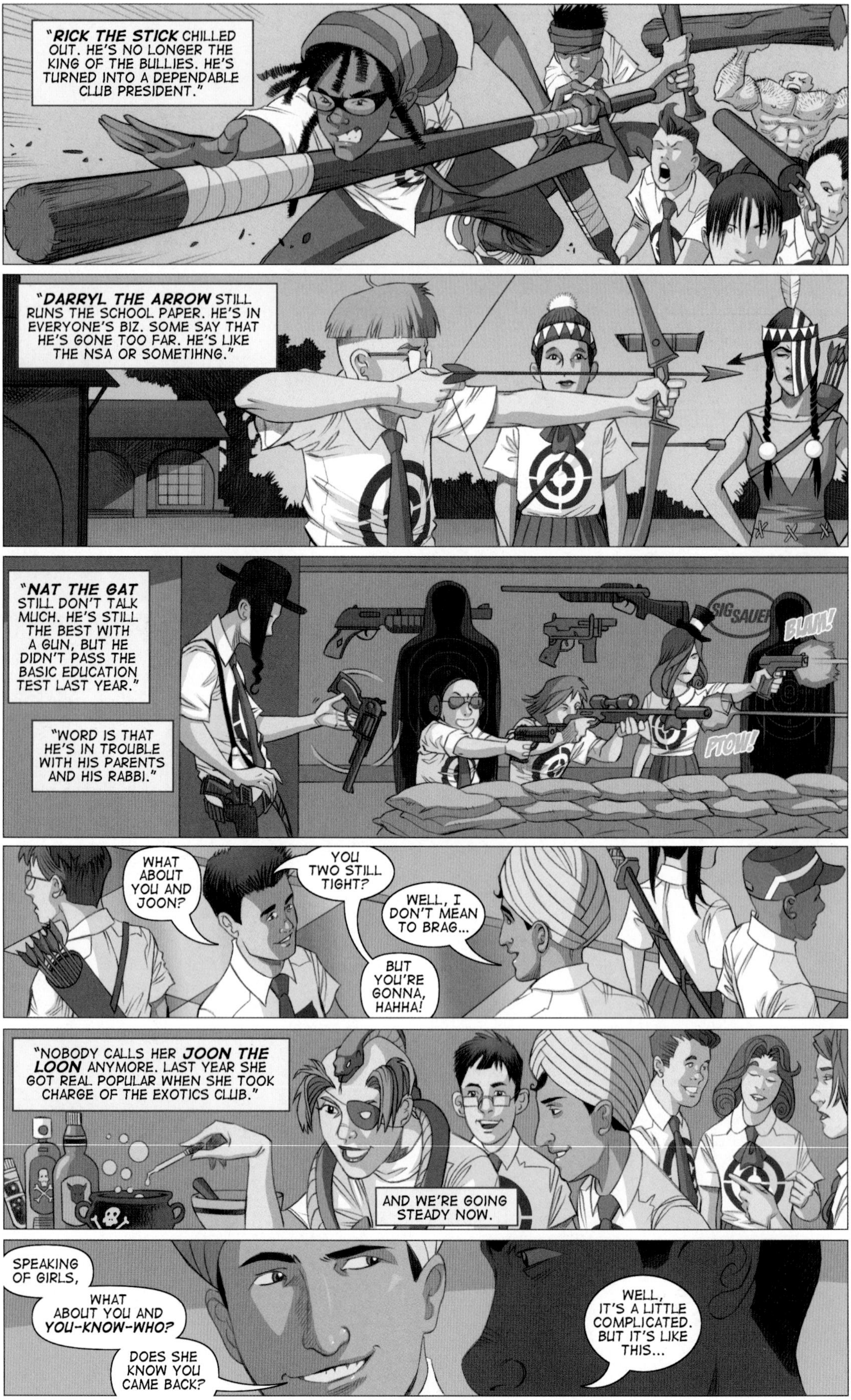
"RICK THE STICK CHILLED OUT. HE'S NO LONGER THE KING OF THE BULLIES. HE'S TURNED INTO A DEPENDABLE CLUB PRESIDENT."
"DARRYL THE ARROW STILL RUNS THE SCHOOL PAPER. HE'S IN EVERYONE'S BIZ. SOME SAY THAT HE'S GONE TOO FAR. HE'S LIKE THE NSA OR SOMETIHNG."
"NAT THE GAT STILL DON'T TALK MUCH. HE'S STILL THE BEST WITH A GUN, BUT HE DIDN'T PASS THE BASIC EDUCATION TEST LAST YEAR."
"WORD IS THAT HE'S IN TROUBLE WITH HIS PARENTS AND HIS RABBI."
SIG SAUER
BLAM!
PTOW!
WHAT ABOUT YOU AND JOON?
YOU TWO STILL TIGHT?
WELL, I DON'T MEAN TO BRAG...
BUT YOU'RE GONNA, HAHHA!
"NOBODY CALLS HER JOON THE LOON ANYMORE. LAST YEAR SHE GOT REAL POPULAR WHEN SHE TOOK CHARGE OF THE EXOTICS CLUB."
AND WE'RE GOING STEADY NOW.
SPEAKING OF GIRLS,
WHAT ABOUT YOU AND YOU-KNOW-WHO?
DOES SHE KNOW YOU CAME BACK?
WELL, IT'S A LITTLE COMPLICATED. BUT IT'S LIKE THIS...

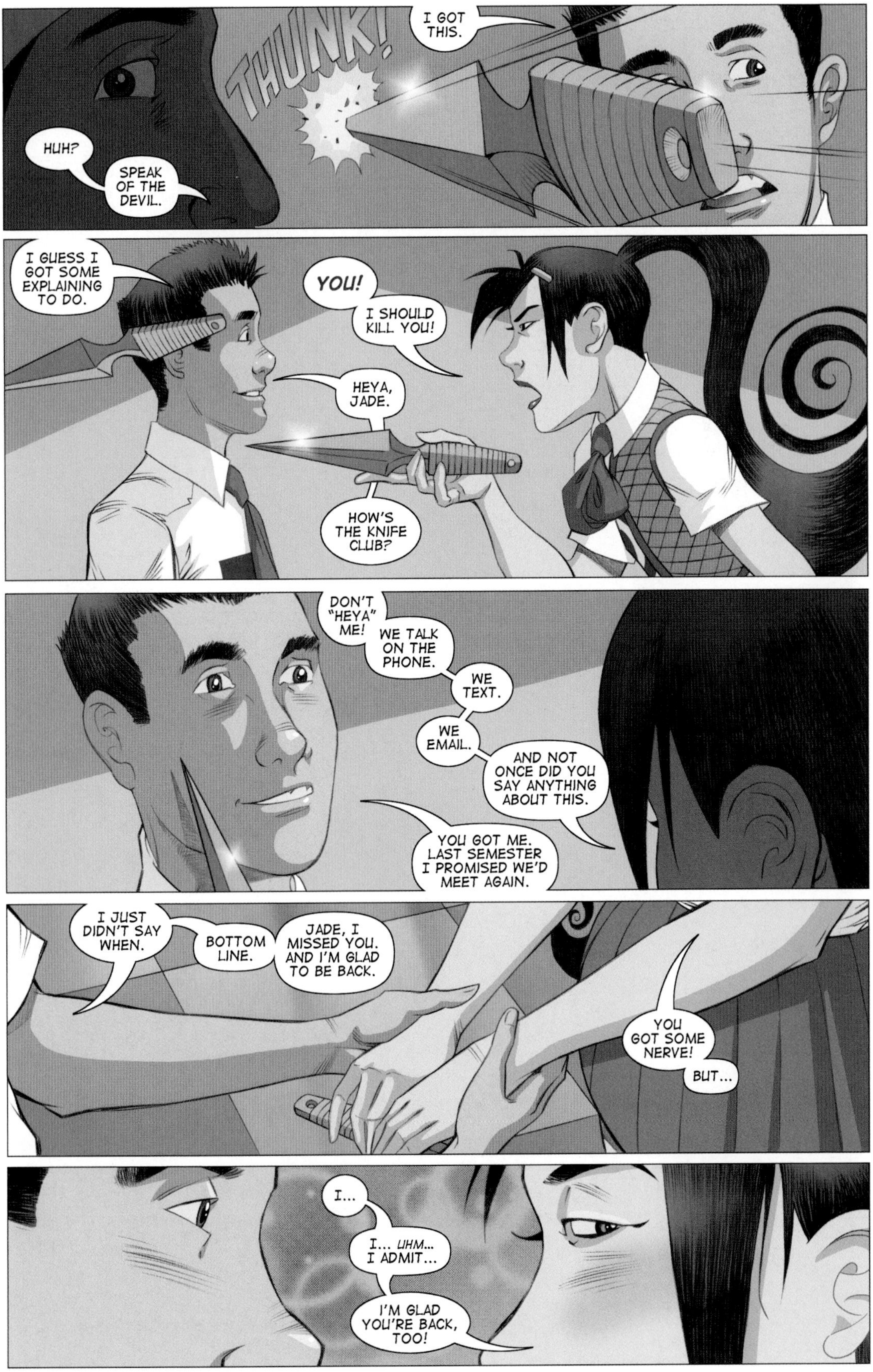
THUNK!
I GOT THIS.
HUH?
SPEAK OF THE DEVIL.
I GUESS I GOT SOME EXPLAINING TO DO.
YOU!
I SHOULD KILL YOU!
HEYA, JADE.
HOW'S THE KNIFE CLUB?
DON'T "HEYA" ME!
WE TALK ON THE PHONE.
WE TEXT.
WE EMAIL.
AND NOT ONCE DID YOU SAY ANYTHING ABOUT THIS.
YOU GOT ME. LAST SEMESTER I PROMISED WE'D MEET AGAIN.
I JUST DIDN'T SAY WHEN.
BOTTOM LINE.
JADE, I MISSED YOU. AND I'M GLAD TO BE BACK.
YOU GOT SOME NERVE!
BUT...
I...
I... UHM... I ADMIT...
I'M GLAD YOU'RE BACK, TOO!

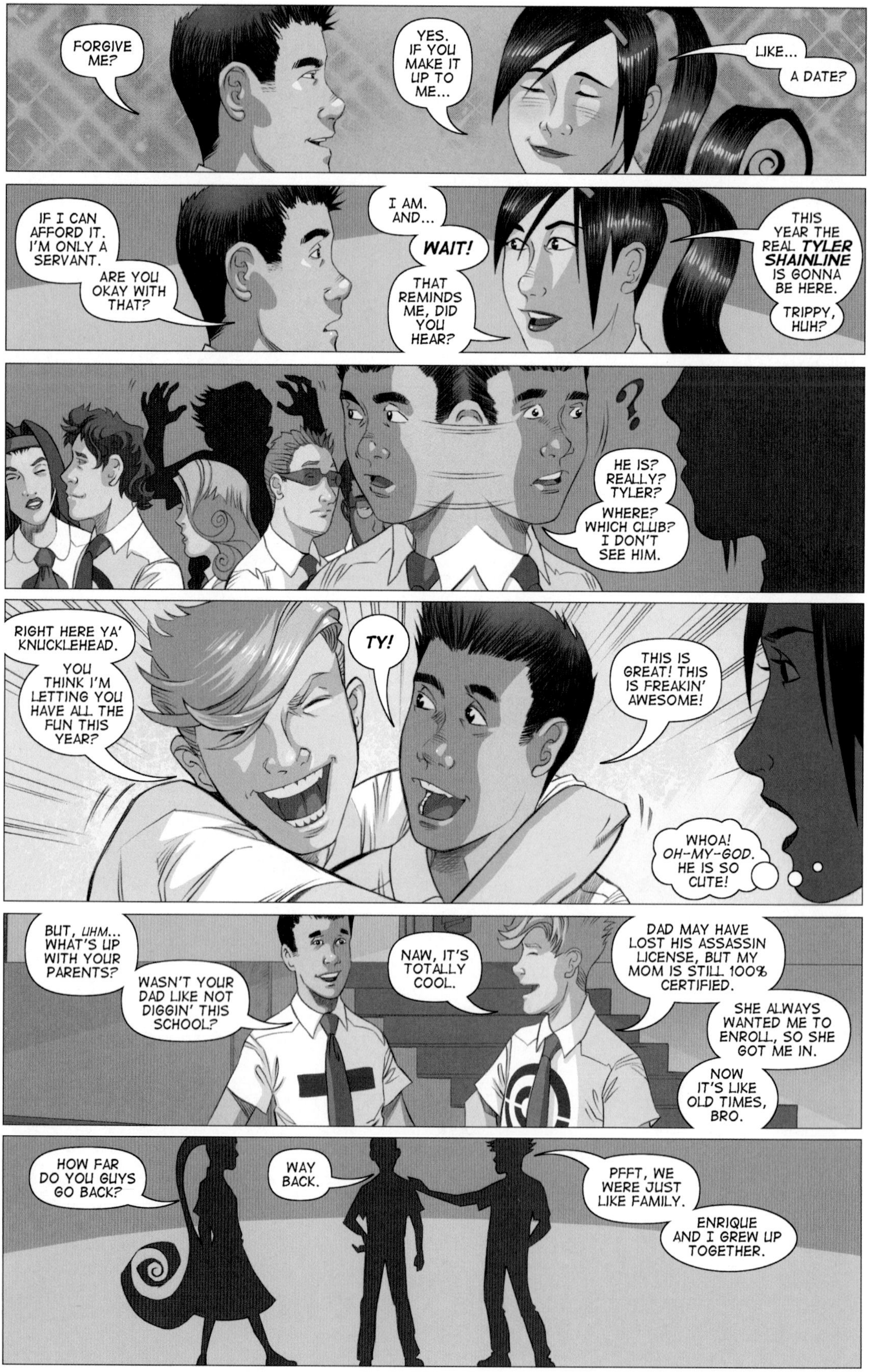
FORGIVE ME?
YES. IF YOU MAKE IT UP TO ME...
LIKE... A DATE?
IF I CAN AFFORD IT. I'M ONLY A SERVANT.
ARE YOU OKAY WITH THAT?
I AM. AND...
WAIT!
THAT REMINDS ME, DID YOU HEAR?
THIS YEAR THE REAL TYLER SHAINLINE IS GONNA BE HERE.
TRIPPY, HUH?
?
HE IS? REALLY? TYLER?
WHERE? WHICH CLUB? I DON'T SEE HIM.
RIGHT HERE YA' KNUCKLEHEAD.
YOU THINK I'M LETTING YOU HAVE ALL THE FUN THIS YEAR?
TY!
THIS IS GREAT! THIS IS FREAKIN' AWESOME!
WHOA! OH-MY-GOD. HE IS SO CUTE!
BUT, UHM... WHAT'S UP WITH YOUR PARENTS?
WASN'T YOUR DAD LIKE NOT DIGGIN' THIS SCHOOL?
NAW, IT'S TOTALLY COOL.
DAD MAY HAVE LOST HIS ASSASSIN LICENSE, BUT MY MOM IS STILL 100% CERTIFIED.
SHE ALWAYS WANTED ME TO ENROLL, SO SHE GOT ME IN.
NOW IT'S LIKE OLD TIMES, BRO.
HOW FAR DO YOU GUYS GO BACK?
WAY BACK.
PFFT, WE WERE JUST LIKE FAMILY.
ENRIQUE AND I GREW UP TOGETHER.

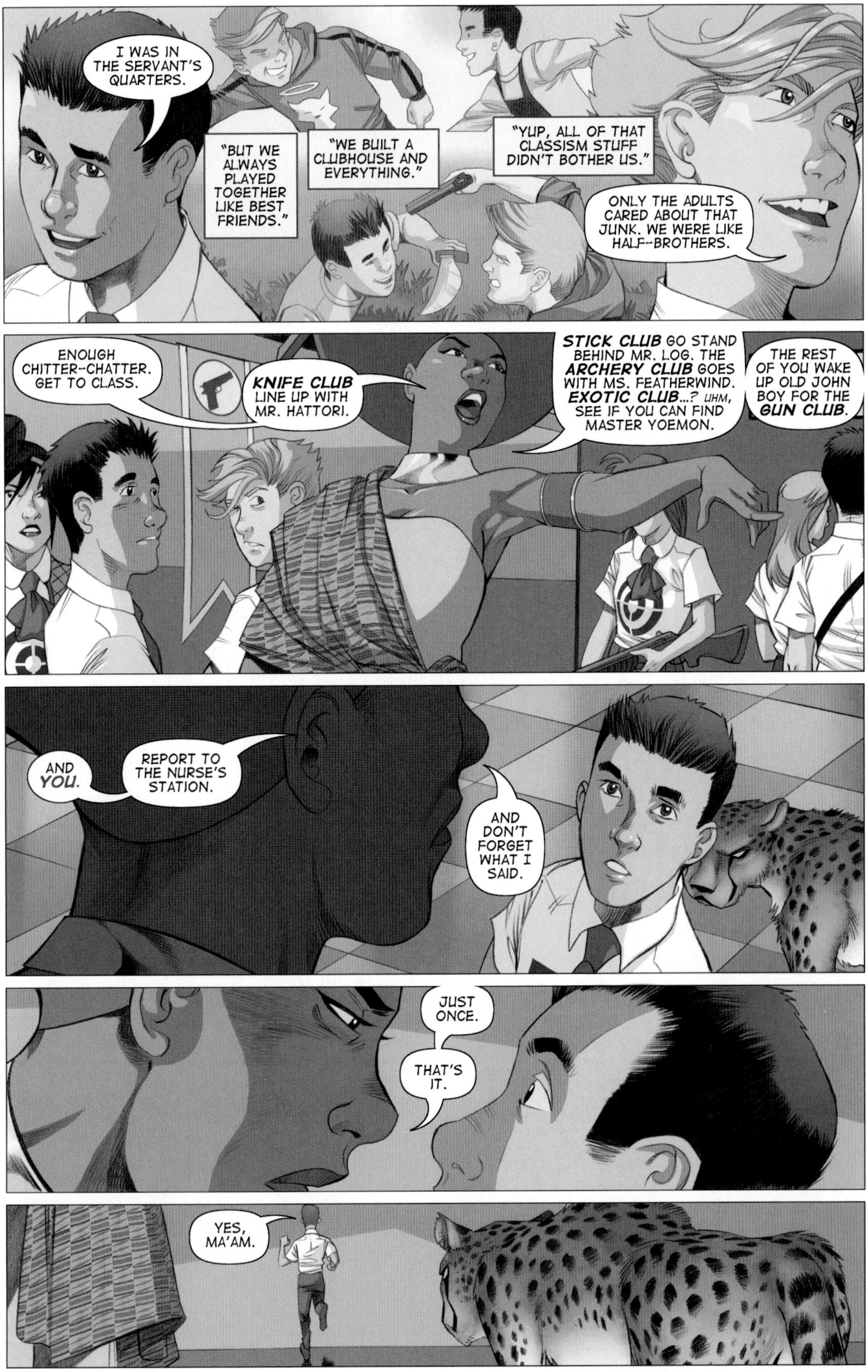
I WAS IN THE SERVANT'S QUARTERS.
"BUT WE ALWAYS PLAYED TOGETHER LIKE BEST FRIENDS."
"WE BUILT A CLUBHOUSE AND EVERYTHING."
"YUP, ALL OF THAT CLASSISM STUFF DIDN'T BOTHER US."
ONLY THE ADULTS CARED ABOUT THAT JUNK. WE WERE LIKE HALF--BROTHERS.
ENOUGH CHITTER--CHATTER. GET TO CLASS.
KNIFE CLUB LINE UP WITH MR. HATTORI.
STICK CLUB GO STAND BEHIND MR. LOG. THE ARCHERY CLUB GOES WITH MS. FEATHERWIND. EXOTIC CLUB...? UHM, SEE IF YOU CAN FIND MASTER YOEMON.
THE REST OF YOU WAKE UP OLD JOHN BOY FOR THE GUN CLUB.
AND YOU.
REPORT TO THE NURSE'S STATION.
AND DON'T FORGET WHAT I SAID.
JUST ONCE.
THAT'S IT.
YES, MA'AM.

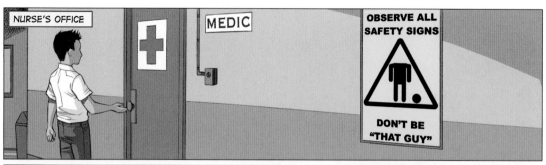

NURSE'S OFFICE

MEDIC

OBSERVE ALL
SAFETY SIGNS

DON'T BE
"THAT GUY"

HELLO.

HUH!?

OH, IT'S *YOU!*
ENRIQUE. YOU
STARTLED ME.

??
STARTLED *YOU?*

NEVER
MIND.

I'M GLAD
YOU'RE HERE. WE
CAN'T WASTE ANY
TIME.

JUST
LET ME GET
ORGANIZED.

AS A MEDICAL
ASSISTANT THERE ARE
A FEW RULES YOU
MUST OBSERVE.

FIRST OFF,
YOU CAN'T GET
INVOLVED IN ANY CLUB
CHALLENGES OR ANY
ACTUAL FIGHTING.

SECOND,
YOU...

UHM... SORRY
TO INTERRUPT,
BUT ACTUALLY
THE FIRST THING
SHOULD BE...

WHY
AM I HERE
AT ALL?

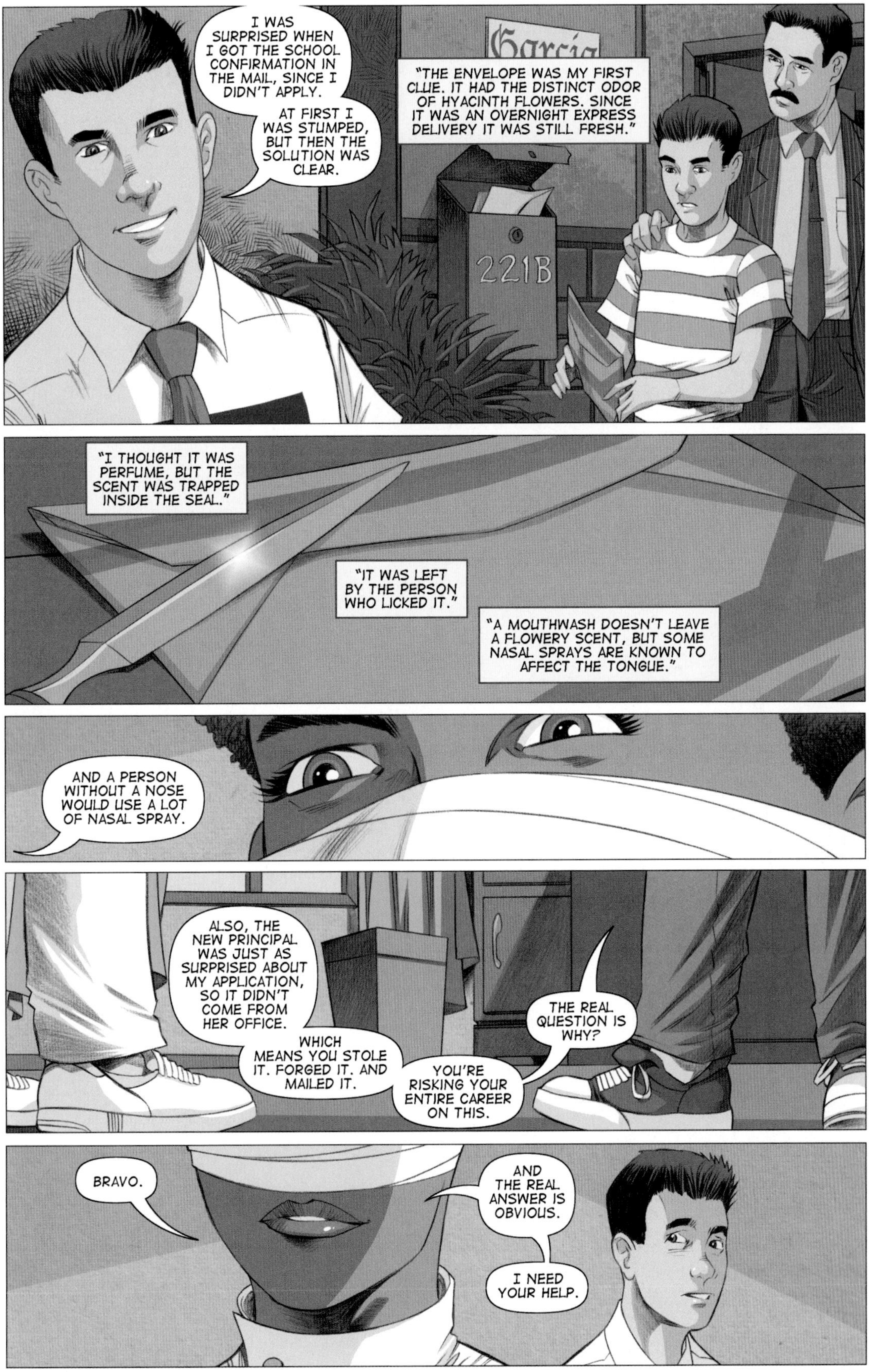
I WAS SURPRISED WHEN I GOT THE SCHOOL CONFIRMATION IN THE MAIL, SINCE I DIDN'T APPLY.
AT FIRST I WAS STUMPED, BUT THEN THE SOLUTION WAS CLEAR.
Garcia
"THE ENVELOPE WAS MY FIRST CLUE. IT HAD THE DISTINCT ODOR OF HYACINTH FLOWERS. SINCE IT WAS AN OVERNIGHT EXPRESS DELIVERY IT WAS STILL FRESH."
221B
"I THOUGHT IT WAS PERFUME, BUT THE SCENT WAS TRAPPED INSIDE THE SEAL."
"IT WAS LEFT BY THE PERSON WHO LICKED IT."
"A MOUTHWASH DOESN'T LEAVE A FLOWERY SCENT, BUT SOME NASAL SPRAYS ARE KNOWN TO AFFECT THE TONGUE."
AND A PERSON WITHOUT A NOSE WOULD USE A LOT OF NASAL SPRAY.
ALSO, THE NEW PRINCIPAL WAS JUST AS SURPRISED ABOUT MY APPLICATION, SO IT DIDN'T COME FROM HER OFFICE.
WHICH MEANS YOU STOLE IT. FORGED IT. AND MAILED IT.
YOU'RE RISKING YOUR ENTIRE CAREER ON THIS.
THE REAL QUESTION IS WHY?
BRAVO.
AND THE REAL ANSWER IS OBVIOUS.
I NEED YOUR HELP.

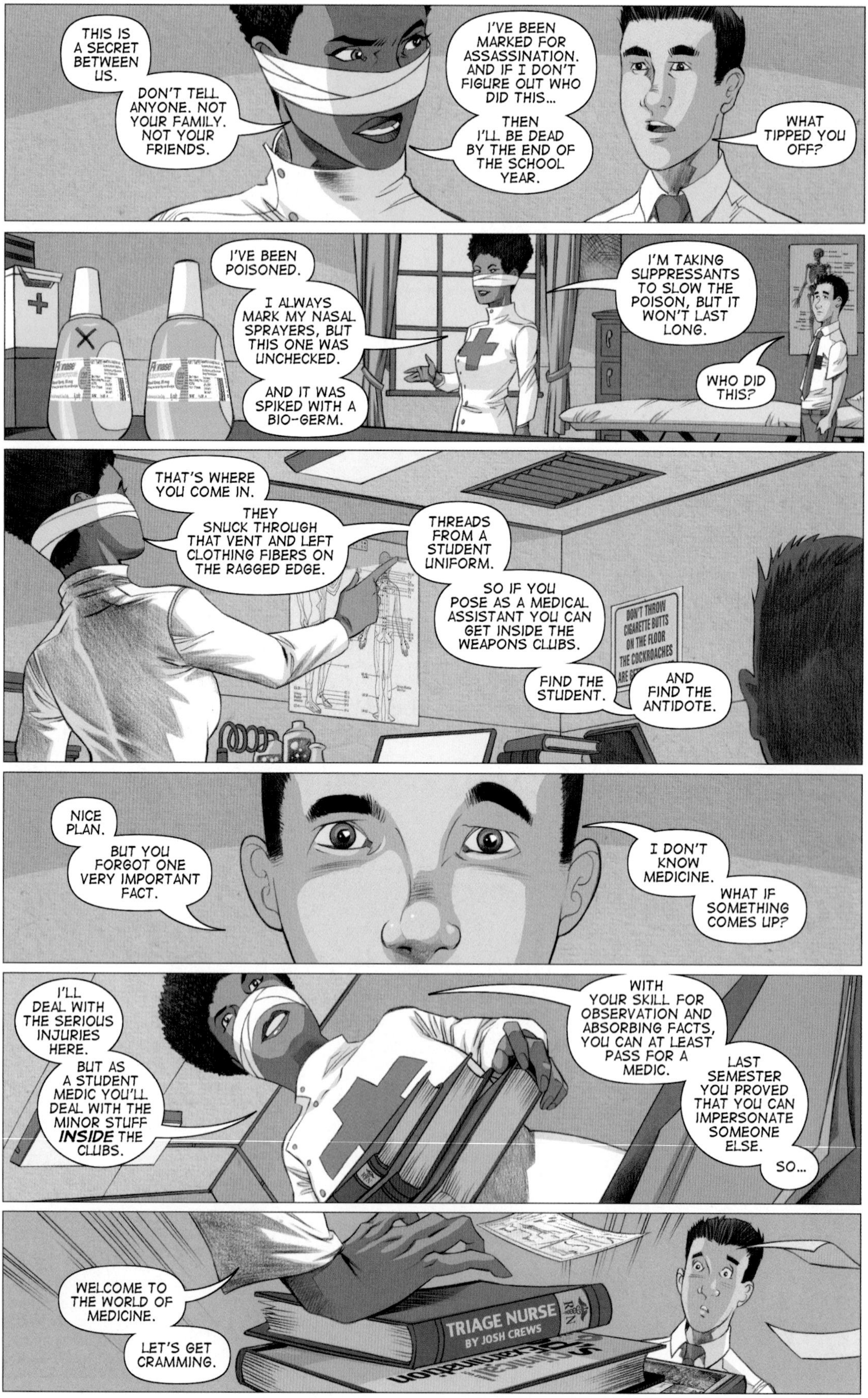
THIS IS A SECRET BETWEEN US.
DON'T TELL ANYONE. NOT YOUR FAMILY. NOT YOUR FRIENDS.
I'VE BEEN MARKED FOR ASSASSINATION. AND IF I DON'T FIGURE OUT WHO DID THIS...
THEN I'LL BE DEAD BY THE END OF THE SCHOOL YEAR.
WHAT TIPPED YOU OFF?
I'VE BEEN POISONED.
I ALWAYS MARK MY NASAL SPRAYERS, BUT THIS ONE WAS UNCHECKED.
AND IT WAS SPIKED WITH A BIO-GERM.
I'M TAKING SUPPRESSANTS TO SLOW THE POISON, BUT IT WON'T LAST LONG.
WHO DID THIS?
THAT'S WHERE YOU COME IN.
THEY SNUCK THROUGH THAT VENT AND LEFT CLOTHING FIBERS ON THE RAGGED EDGE.
THREADS FROM A STUDENT UNIFORM.
SO IF YOU POSE AS A MEDICAL ASSISTANT YOU CAN GET INSIDE THE WEAPONS CLUBS.
DON'T THROW CIGARETTE BUTTS ON THE FLOOR THE COCKROACHES
FIND THE STUDENT.
AND FIND THE ANTIDOTE.
NICE PLAN.
BUT YOU FORGOT ONE VERY IMPORTANT FACT.
I DON'T KNOW MEDICINE.
WHAT IF SOMETHING COMES UP?
I'LL DEAL WITH THE SERIOUS INJURIES HERE.
BUT AS A STUDENT MEDIC YOU'LL DEAL WITH THE MINOR STUFF *INSIDE* THE CLUBS.
WITH YOUR SKILL FOR OBSERVATION AND ABSORBING FACTS, YOU CAN AT LEAST PASS FOR A MEDIC.
LAST SEMESTER YOU PROVED THAT YOU CAN IMPERSONATE SOMEONE ELSE.
SO...
WELCOME TO THE WORLD OF MEDICINE.
LET'S GET CRAMMING.
TRIAGE NURSE
BY JOSH CREWS

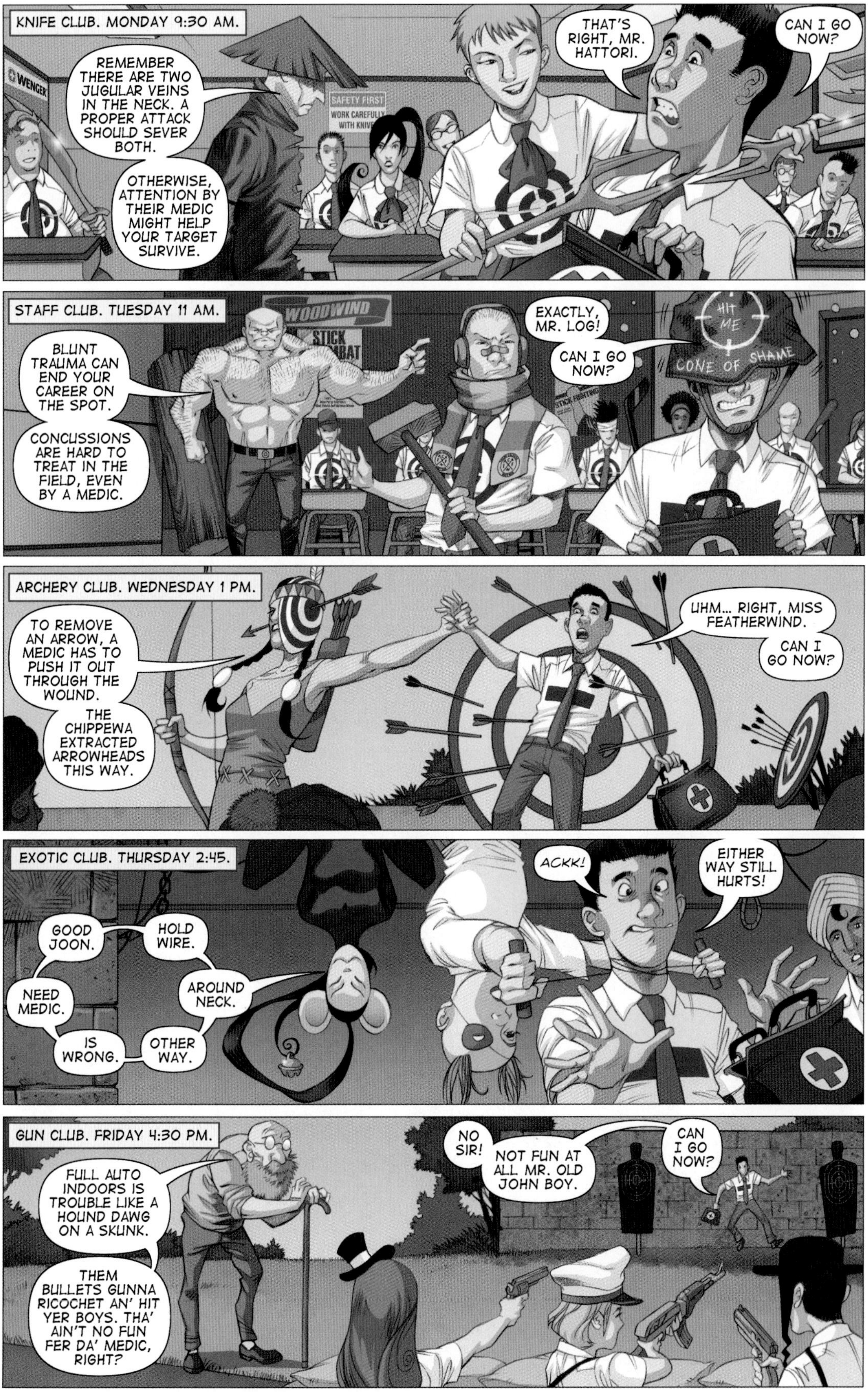

KNIFE CLUB. MONDAY 9:30 AM.
REMEMBER THERE ARE TWO JUGULAR VEINS IN THE NECK. A PROPER ATTACK SHOULD SEVER BOTH.
OTHERWISE, ATTENTION BY THEIR MEDIC MIGHT HELP YOUR TARGET SURVIVE.
THAT'S RIGHT, MR. HATTORI.
CAN I GO NOW?
SAFETY FIRST
WENGER
STAFF CLUB. TUESDAY 11 AM.
BLUNT TRAUMA CAN END YOUR CAREER ON THE SPOT.
CONCUSSIONS ARE HARD TO TREAT IN THE FIELD, EVEN BY A MEDIC.
EXACTLY, MR. LOG!
CAN I GO NOW?
WOODWIND
HIT ME
CONE OF SHAME
ARCHERY CLUB. WEDNESDAY 1 PM.
TO REMOVE AN ARROW, A MEDIC HAS TO PUSH IT OUT THROUGH THE WOUND.
THE CHIPPEWA EXTRACTED ARROWHEADS THIS WAY.
UHM... RIGHT, MISS FEATHERWIND.
CAN I GO NOW?
EXOTIC CLUB. THURSDAY 2:45.
HOLD WIRE.
AROUND NECK.
GOOD JOON.
NEED MEDIC.
IS WRONG.
OTHER WAY.
ACKK!
EITHER WAY STILL HURTS!
GUN CLUB. FRIDAY 4:30 PM.
FULL AUTO INDOORS IS TROUBLE LIKE A HOUND DAWG ON A SKUNK.
THEM BULLETS GUNNA RICOCHET AN' HIT YER BOYS. THA' AIN'T NO FUN FER DA' MEDIC, RIGHT?
NO SIR!
NOT FUN AT ALL MR. OLD JOHN BOY.
CAN I GO NOW?

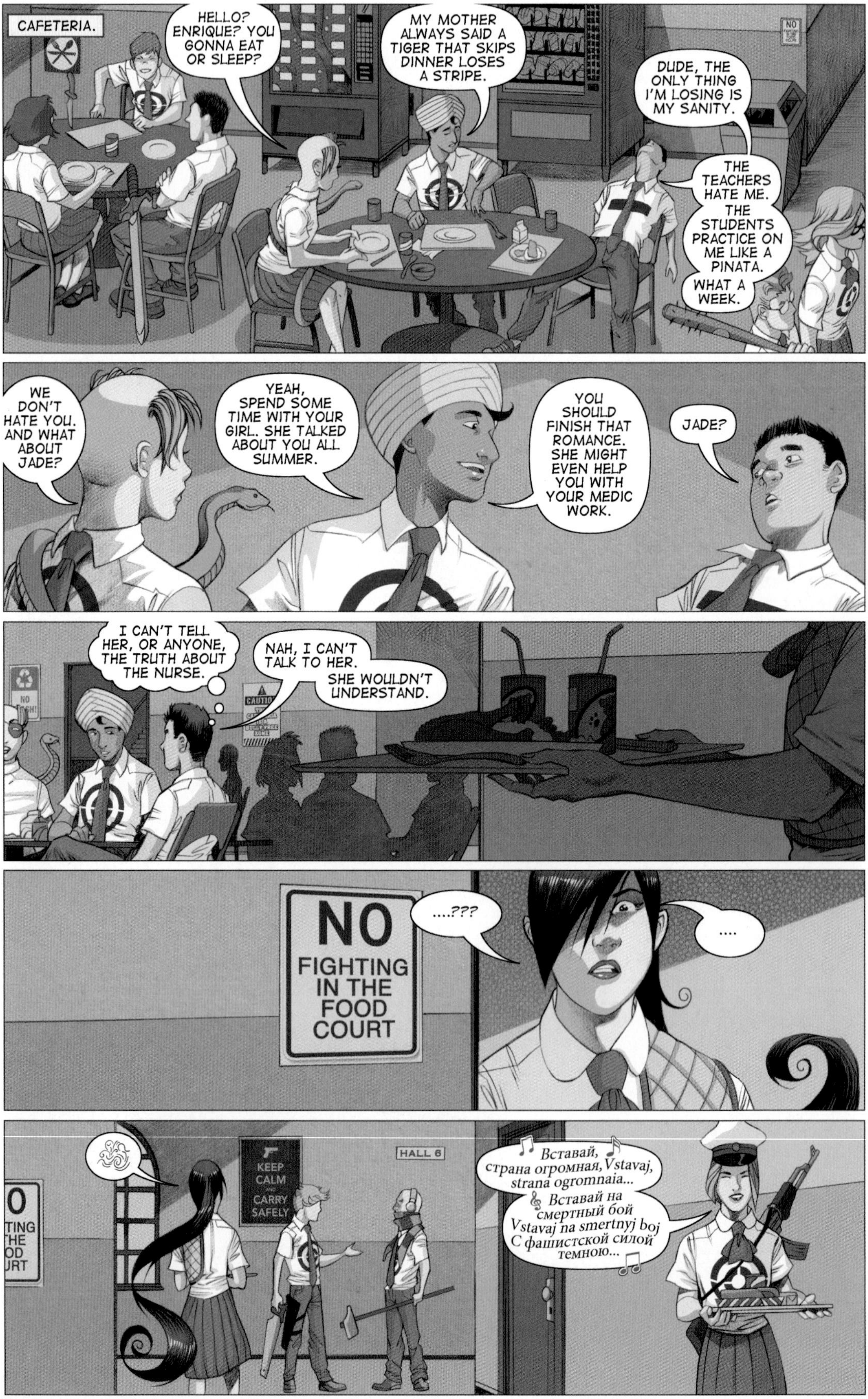
CAFETERIA.
HELLO? ENRIQUE? YOU GONNA EAT OR SLEEP?
MY MOTHER ALWAYS SAID A TIGER THAT SKIPS DINNER LOSES A STRIPE.
NO
DUDE, THE ONLY THING I'M LOSING IS MY SANITY.
THE TEACHERS HATE ME.
THE STUDENTS PRACTICE ON ME LIKE A PINATA.
WHAT A WEEK.
WE DON'T HATE YOU. AND WHAT ABOUT JADE?
YEAH, SPEND SOME TIME WITH YOUR GIRL. SHE TALKED ABOUT YOU ALL SUMMER.
YOU SHOULD FINISH THAT ROMANCE. SHE MIGHT EVEN HELP YOU WITH YOUR MEDIC WORK.
JADE?
I CAN'T TELL HER, OR ANYONE, THE TRUTH ABOUT THE NURSE.
NAH, I CAN'T TALK TO HER.
SHE WOULDN'T UNDERSTAND.
CAUTION
NO FIGHTING IN THE FOOD COURT
....???
....
KEEP CALM AND CARRY SAFELY
HALL 6
Вставай, страна огромная, Vstavaj, strana ogromnaia...
Вставай на смертный бой Vstavaj na smertnyj boj С фашистской силой темною...

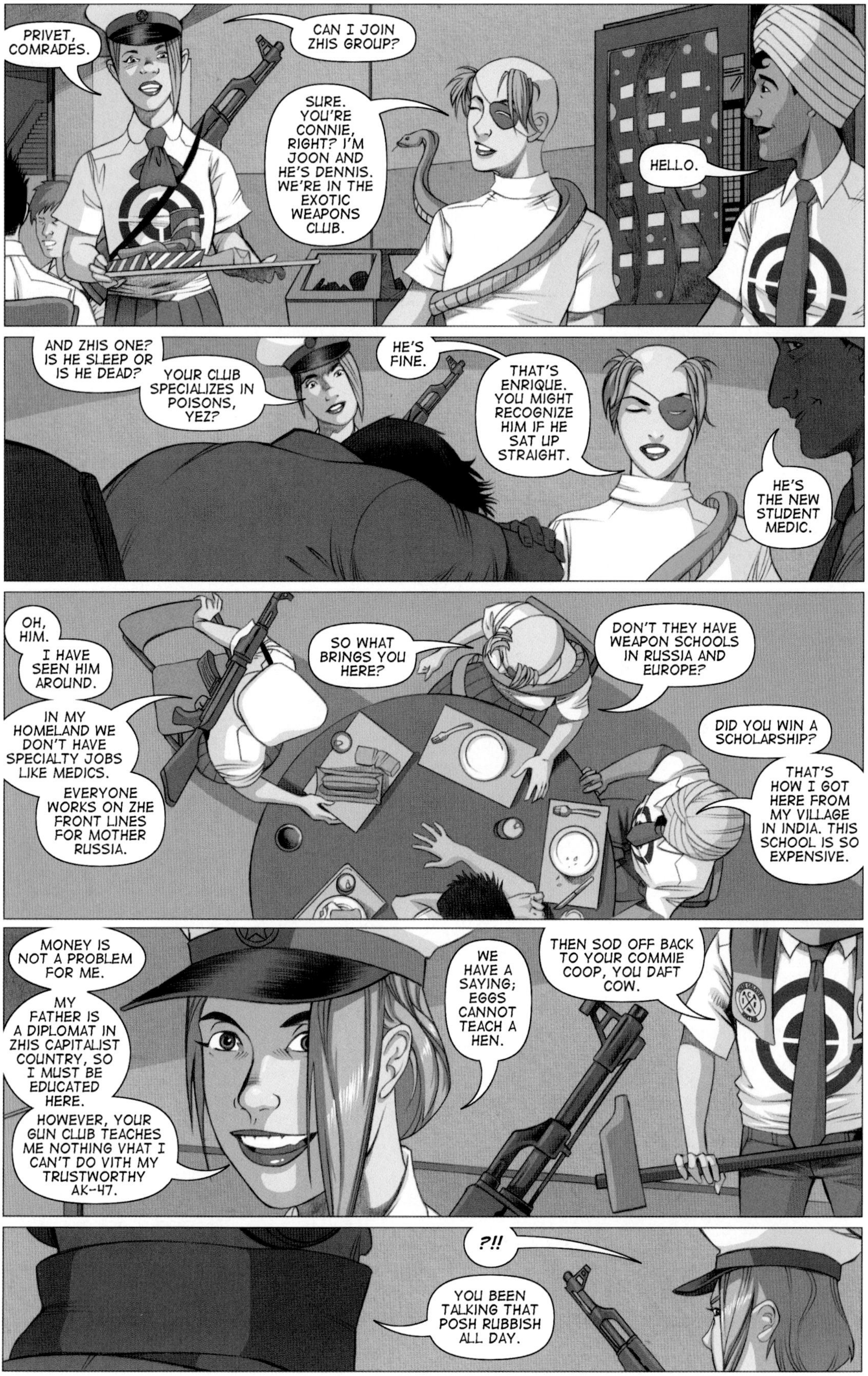
PRIVET, COMRADES.
CAN I JOIN ZHIS GROUP?
SURE. YOU'RE CONNIE, RIGHT? I'M JOON AND HE'S DENNIS. WE'RE IN THE EXOTIC WEAPONS CLUB.
HELLO.
AND ZHIS ONE? IS HE SLEEP OR IS HE DEAD?
YOUR CLUB SPECIALIZES IN POISONS, YEZ?
HE'S FINE.
THAT'S ENRIQUE. YOU MIGHT RECOGNIZE HIM IF HE SAT UP STRAIGHT.
HE'S THE NEW STUDENT MEDIC.
OH, HIM.
I HAVE SEEN HIM AROUND.
IN MY HOMELAND WE DON'T HAVE SPECIALTY JOBS LIKE MEDICS.
EVERYONE WORKS ON ZHE FRONT LINES FOR MOTHER RUSSIA.
SO WHAT BRINGS YOU HERE?
DON'T THEY HAVE WEAPON SCHOOLS IN RUSSIA AND EUROPE?
DID YOU WIN A SCHOLARSHIP?
THAT'S HOW I GOT HERE FROM MY VILLAGE IN INDIA. THIS SCHOOL IS SO EXPENSIVE.
MONEY IS NOT A PROBLEM FOR ME.
MY FATHER IS A DIPLOMAT IN ZHIS CAPITALIST COUNTRY, SO I MUST BE EDUCATED HERE.
HOWEVER, YOUR GUN CLUB TEACHES ME NOTHING VHAT I CAN'T DO VITH MY TRUSTWORTHY AK-47.
WE HAVE A SAYING; EGGS CANNOT TEACH A HEN.
THEN SOD OFF BACK TO YOUR COMMIE COOP, YOU DAFT COW.
?!!
YOU BEEN TALKING THAT POSH RUBBISH ALL DAY.

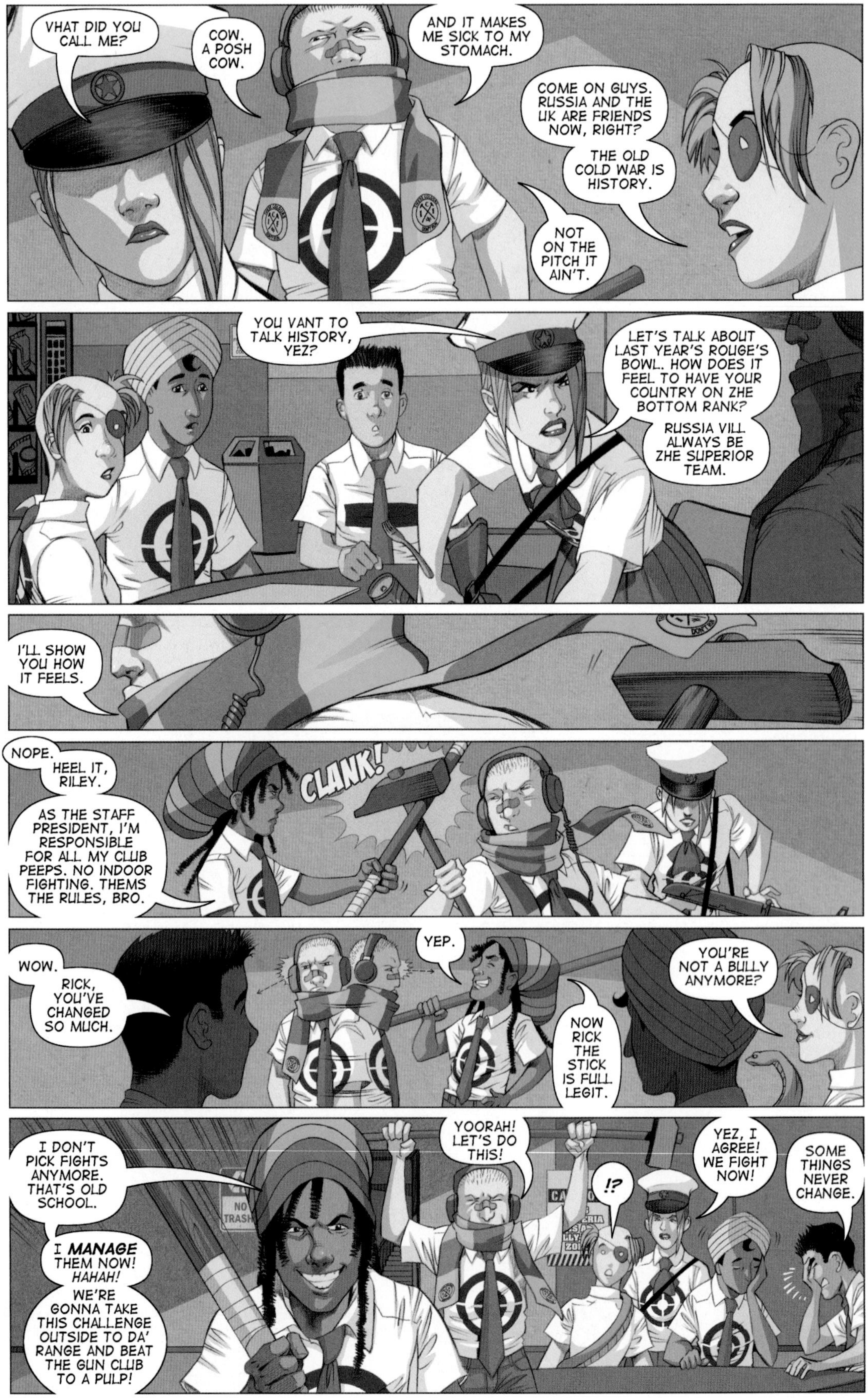
VHAT DID YOU CALL ME?
COW. A POSH COW.
AND IT MAKES ME SICK TO MY STOMACH.
COME ON GUYS. RUSSIA AND THE UK ARE FRIENDS NOW, RIGHT?
THE OLD COLD WAR IS HISTORY.
NOT ON THE PITCH IT AIN'T.
YOU VANT TO TALK HISTORY, YEZ?
LET'S TALK ABOUT LAST YEAR'S ROUGE'S BOWL. HOW DOES IT FEEL TO HAVE YOUR COUNTRY ON ZHE BOTTOM RANK?
RUSSIA VILL ALWAYS BE ZHE SUPERIOR TEAM.
I'LL SHOW YOU HOW IT FEELS.
NOPE.
HEEL IT, RILEY.
CLANK!
AS THE STAFF PRESIDENT, I'M RESPONSIBLE FOR ALL MY CLUB PEEPS. NO INDOOR FIGHTING. THEMS THE RULES, BRO.
WOW.
RICK, YOU'VE CHANGED SO MUCH.
YEP.
NOW RICK THE STICK IS FULL LEGIT.
YOU'RE NOT A BULLY ANYMORE?
I DON'T PICK FIGHTS ANYMORE. THAT'S OLD SCHOOL.
I ***MANAGE*** THEM NOW! *HAHAH!*
WE'RE GONNA TAKE THIS CHALLENGE OUTSIDE TO DA' RANGE AND BEAT THE GUN CLUB TO A PULP!
YOORAH! LET'S DO THIS!
!?
YEZ, I AGREE! WE FIGHT NOW!
SOME THINGS NEVER CHANGE.
NO TRASH

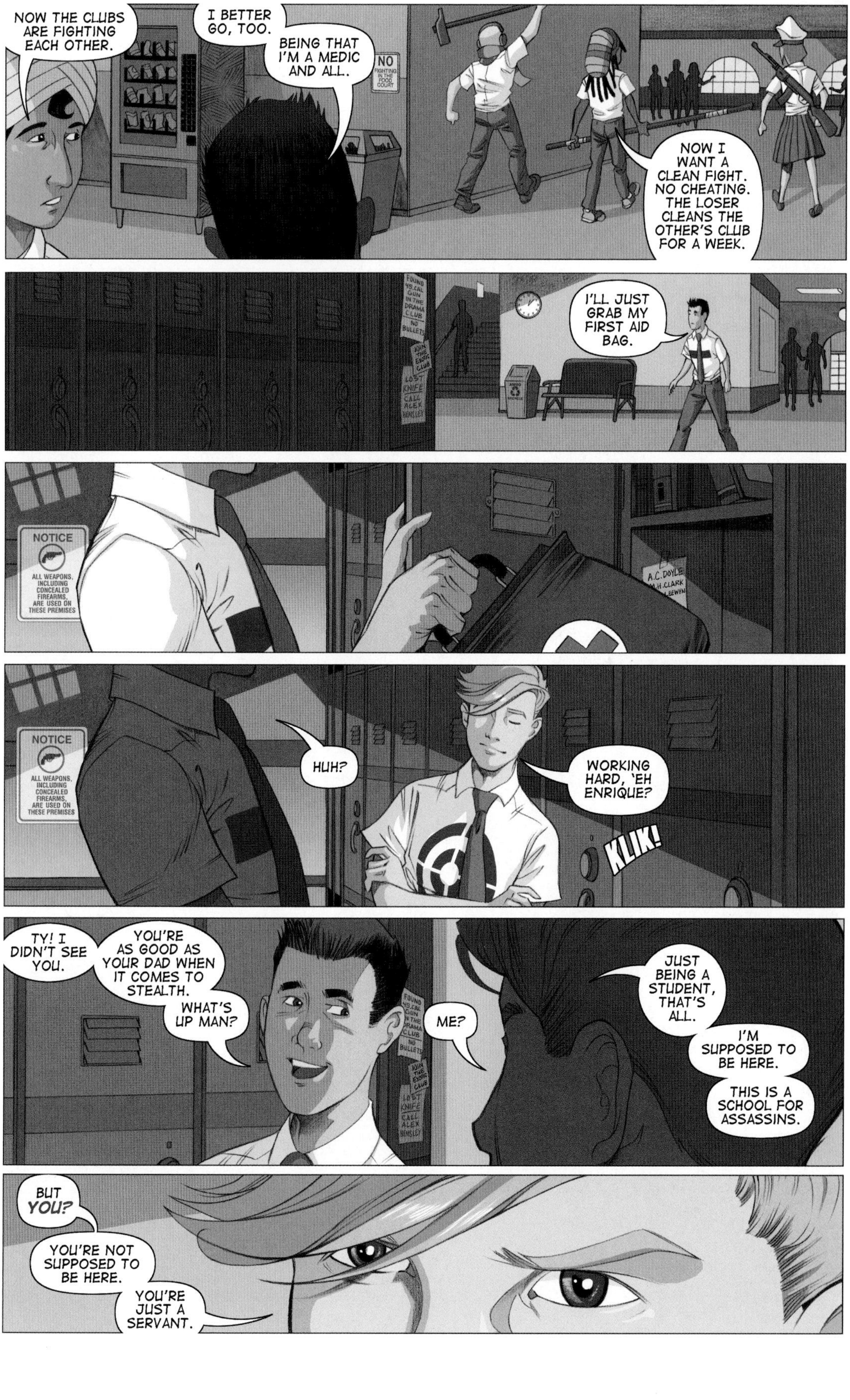
NOW THE CLUBS ARE FIGHTING EACH OTHER.
I BETTER GO, TOO.
BEING THAT I'M A MEDIC AND ALL.
NO FIGHTING IN THE FOOD COURT
NOW I WANT A CLEAN FIGHT. NO CHEATING. THE LOSER CLEANS THE OTHER'S CLUB FOR A WEEK.
FOUND 45 CAL GUN IN THE DRAMA CLUB NO BULLETS
JOIN THE EXOTIC CLUB
LOST KNIFE CALL ALEX BENSLEY
I'LL JUST GRAB MY FIRST AID BAG.
NOTICE
ALL WEAPONS, INCLUDING CONCEALED FIREARMS, ARE USED ON THESE PREMISES
A.C. DOYLE
M.H. CLARK
NOTICE
ALL WEAPONS, INCLUDING CONCEALED FIREARMS, ARE USED ON THESE PREMISES
HUH?
WORKING HARD, 'EH ENRIQUE?
KLIK!
TY! I DIDN'T SEE YOU.
YOU'RE AS GOOD AS YOUR DAD WHEN IT COMES TO STEALTH.
WHAT'S UP MAN?
ME?
JUST BEING A STUDENT, THAT'S ALL.
I'M SUPPOSED TO BE HERE.
THIS IS A SCHOOL FOR ASSASSINS.
BUT YOU?
YOU'RE NOT SUPPOSED TO BE HERE.
YOU'RE JUST A SERVANT.

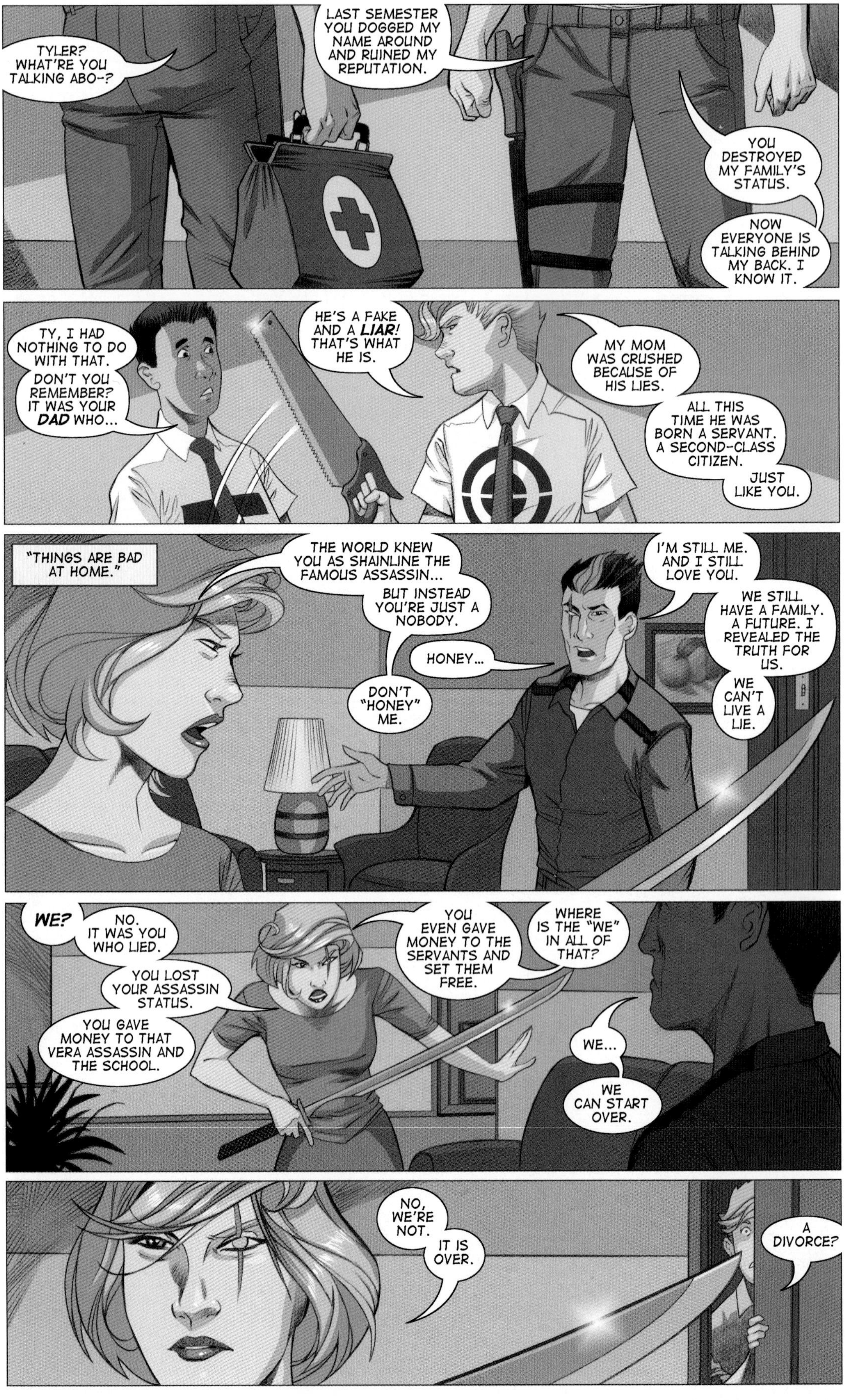
TYLER? WHAT'RE YOU TALKING ABO-?
LAST SEMESTER YOU DOGGED MY NAME AROUND AND RUINED MY REPUTATION.
YOU DESTROYED MY FAMILY'S STATUS.
NOW EVERYONE IS TALKING BEHIND MY BACK. I KNOW IT.
TY, I HAD NOTHING TO DO WITH THAT.
DON'T YOU REMEMBER? IT WAS YOUR DAD WHO...
HE'S A FAKE AND A LIAR! THAT'S WHAT HE IS.
MY MOM WAS CRUSHED BECAUSE OF HIS LIES.
ALL THIS TIME HE WAS BORN A SERVANT. A SECOND-CLASS CITIZEN.
JUST LIKE YOU.
"THINGS ARE BAD AT HOME."
THE WORLD KNEW YOU AS SHAINLINE THE FAMOUS ASSASSIN...
BUT INSTEAD YOU'RE JUST A NOBODY.
HONEY...
DON'T "HONEY" ME.
I'M STILL ME. AND I STILL LOVE YOU.
WE STILL HAVE A FAMILY. A FUTURE. I REVEALED THE TRUTH FOR US.
WE CAN'T LIVE A LIE.
WE?
NO. IT WAS YOU WHO LIED.
YOU LOST YOUR ASSASSIN STATUS.
YOU GAVE MONEY TO THAT VERA ASSASSIN AND THE SCHOOL.
YOU EVEN GAVE MONEY TO THE SERVANTS AND SET THEM FREE.
WHERE IS THE "WE" IN ALL OF THAT?
WE...
WE CAN START OVER.
NO, WE'RE NOT.
IT IS OVER.
A DIVORCE?

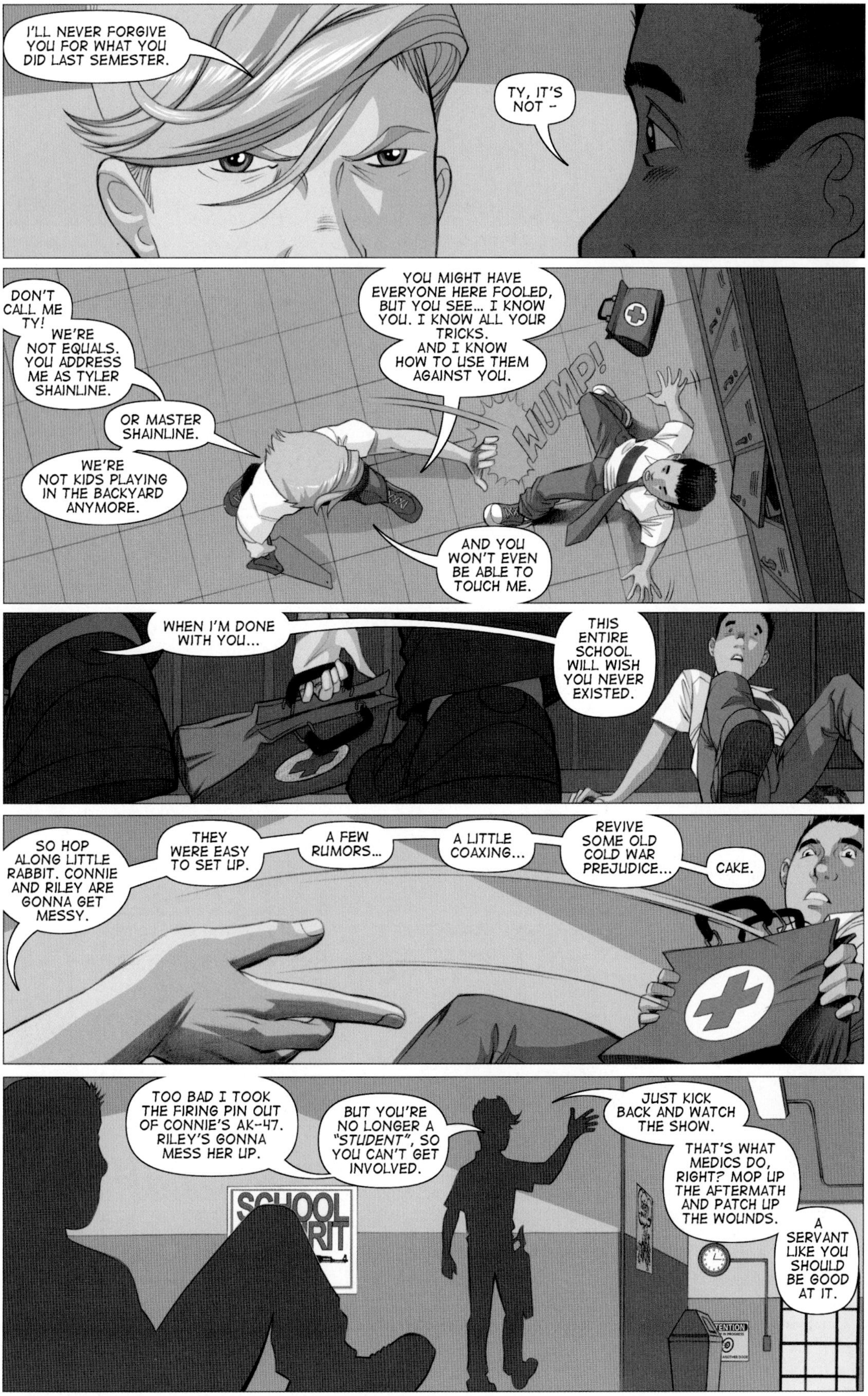
I'LL NEVER FORGIVE YOU FOR WHAT YOU DID LAST SEMESTER.
TY, IT'S NOT -
DON'T CALL ME TY!
WE'RE NOT EQUALS. YOU ADDRESS ME AS TYLER SHAINLINE.
OR MASTER SHAINLINE.
WE'RE NOT KIDS PLAYING IN THE BACKYARD ANYMORE.
YOU MIGHT HAVE EVERYONE HERE FOOLED, BUT YOU SEE... I KNOW YOU. I KNOW ALL YOUR TRICKS.
AND I KNOW HOW TO USE THEM AGAINST YOU.
WUMP!
AND YOU WON'T EVEN BE ABLE TO TOUCH ME.
WHEN I'M DONE WITH YOU...
THIS ENTIRE SCHOOL WILL WISH YOU NEVER EXISTED.
SO HOP ALONG LITTLE RABBIT. CONNIE AND RILEY ARE GONNA GET MESSY.
THEY WERE EASY TO SET UP.
A FEW RUMORS...
A LITTLE COAXING...
REVIVE SOME OLD COLD WAR PREJUDICE...
CAKE.
TOO BAD I TOOK THE FIRING PIN OUT OF CONNIE'S AK-47. RILEY'S GONNA MESS HER UP.
BUT YOU'RE NO LONGER A "STUDENT", SO YOU CAN'T GET INVOLVED.
JUST KICK BACK AND WATCH THE SHOW.
THAT'S WHAT MEDICS DO, RIGHT? MOP UP THE AFTERMATH AND PATCH UP THE WOUNDS.
A SERVANT LIKE YOU SHOULD BE GOOD AT IT.
SCHOOL

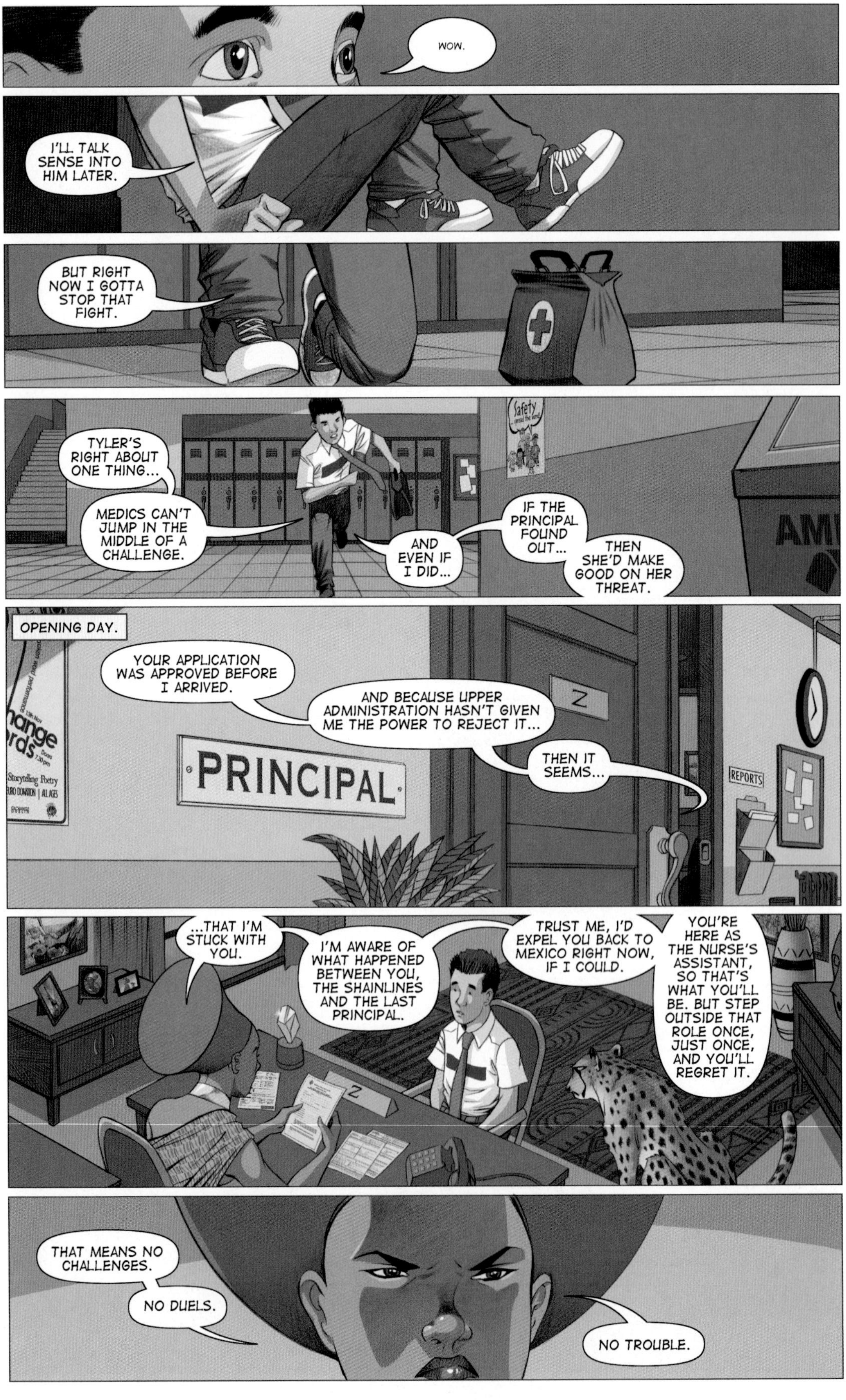
WOW.
I'LL TALK SENSE INTO HIM LATER.
BUT RIGHT NOW I GOTTA STOP THAT FIGHT.
TYLER'S RIGHT ABOUT ONE THING...
MEDICS CAN'T JUMP IN THE MIDDLE OF A CHALLENGE.
AND EVEN IF I DID...
IF THE PRINCIPAL FOUND OUT...
THEN SHE'D MAKE GOOD ON HER THREAT.
Safety
OPENING DAY.
YOUR APPLICATION WAS APPROVED BEFORE I ARRIVED.
AND BECAUSE UPPER ADMINISTRATION HASN'T GIVEN ME THE POWER TO REJECT IT...
PRINCIPAL
Z
THEN IT SEEMS...
REPORTS
...THAT I'M STUCK WITH YOU.
I'M AWARE OF WHAT HAPPENED BETWEEN YOU, THE SHAINLINES AND THE LAST PRINCIPAL.
TRUST ME, I'D EXPEL YOU BACK TO MEXICO RIGHT NOW, IF I COULD.
YOU'RE HERE AS THE NURSE'S ASSISTANT, SO THAT'S WHAT YOU'LL BE. BUT STEP OUTSIDE THAT ROLE ONCE, JUST ONCE, AND YOU'LL REGRET IT.
THAT MEANS NO CHALLENGES.
NO DUELS.
NO TROUBLE.

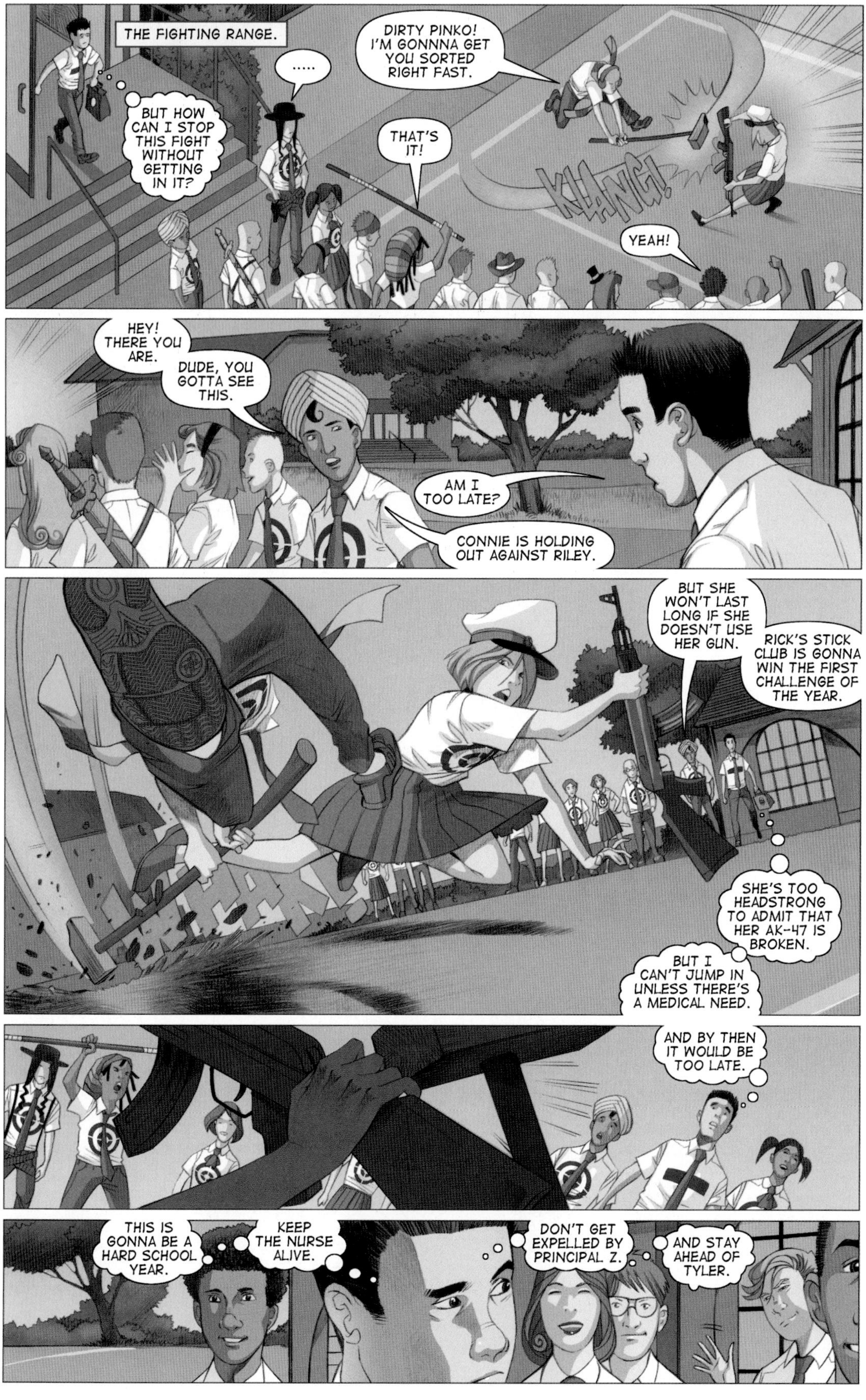
THE FIGHTING RANGE.
.....
BUT HOW CAN I STOP THIS FIGHT WITHOUT GETTING IN IT?
DIRTY PINKO! I'M GONNA GET YOU SORTED RIGHT FAST.
THAT'S IT!
KLANG!
YEAH!
HEY! THERE YOU ARE.
DUDE, YOU GOTTA SEE THIS.
AM I TOO LATE?
CONNIE IS HOLDING OUT AGAINST RILEY.
BUT SHE WON'T LAST LONG IF SHE DOESN'T USE HER GUN.
RICK'S STICK CLUB IS GONNA WIN THE FIRST CHALLENGE OF THE YEAR.
SHE'S TOO HEADSTRONG TO ADMIT THAT HER AK-47 IS BROKEN.
BUT I CAN'T JUMP IN UNLESS THERE'S A MEDICAL NEED.
AND BY THEN IT WOULD BE TOO LATE.
THIS IS GONNA BE A HARD SCHOOL YEAR.
KEEP THE NURSE ALIVE.
DON'T GET EXPELLED BY PRINCIPAL Z.
AND STAY AHEAD OF TYLER.

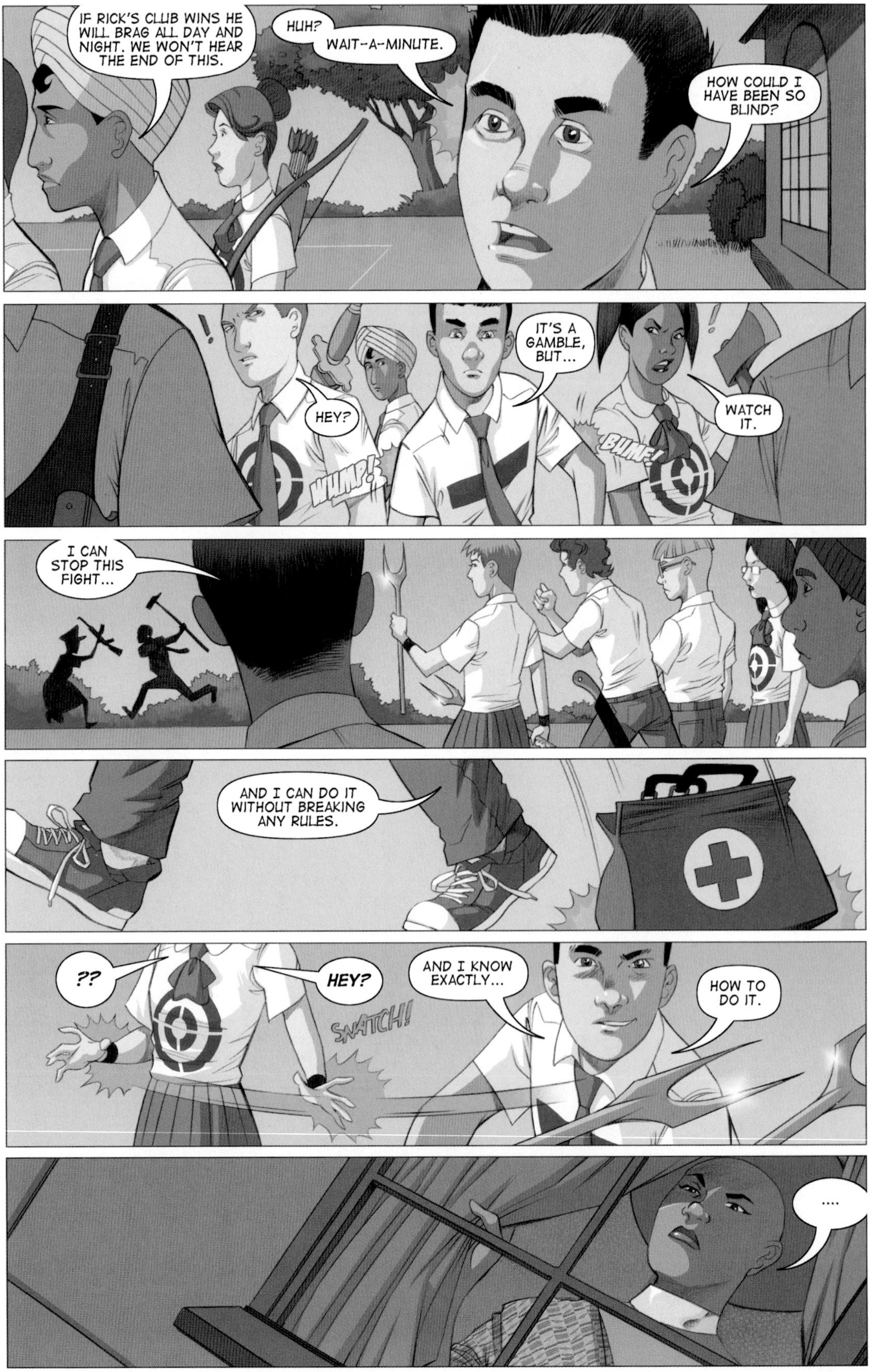
IF RICK'S CLUB WINS HE WILL BRAG ALL DAY AND NIGHT. WE WON'T HEAR THE END OF THIS.
HUH?
WAIT-A-MINUTE.
HOW COULD I HAVE BEEN SO BLIND?
!
HEY?
WUMP!
IT'S A GAMBLE, BUT...
!
BUMF!
WATCH IT.
I CAN STOP THIS FIGHT...
AND I CAN DO IT WITHOUT BREAKING ANY RULES.
??
HEY?
SNATCH!
AND I KNOW EXACTLY...
HOW TO DO IT.
....

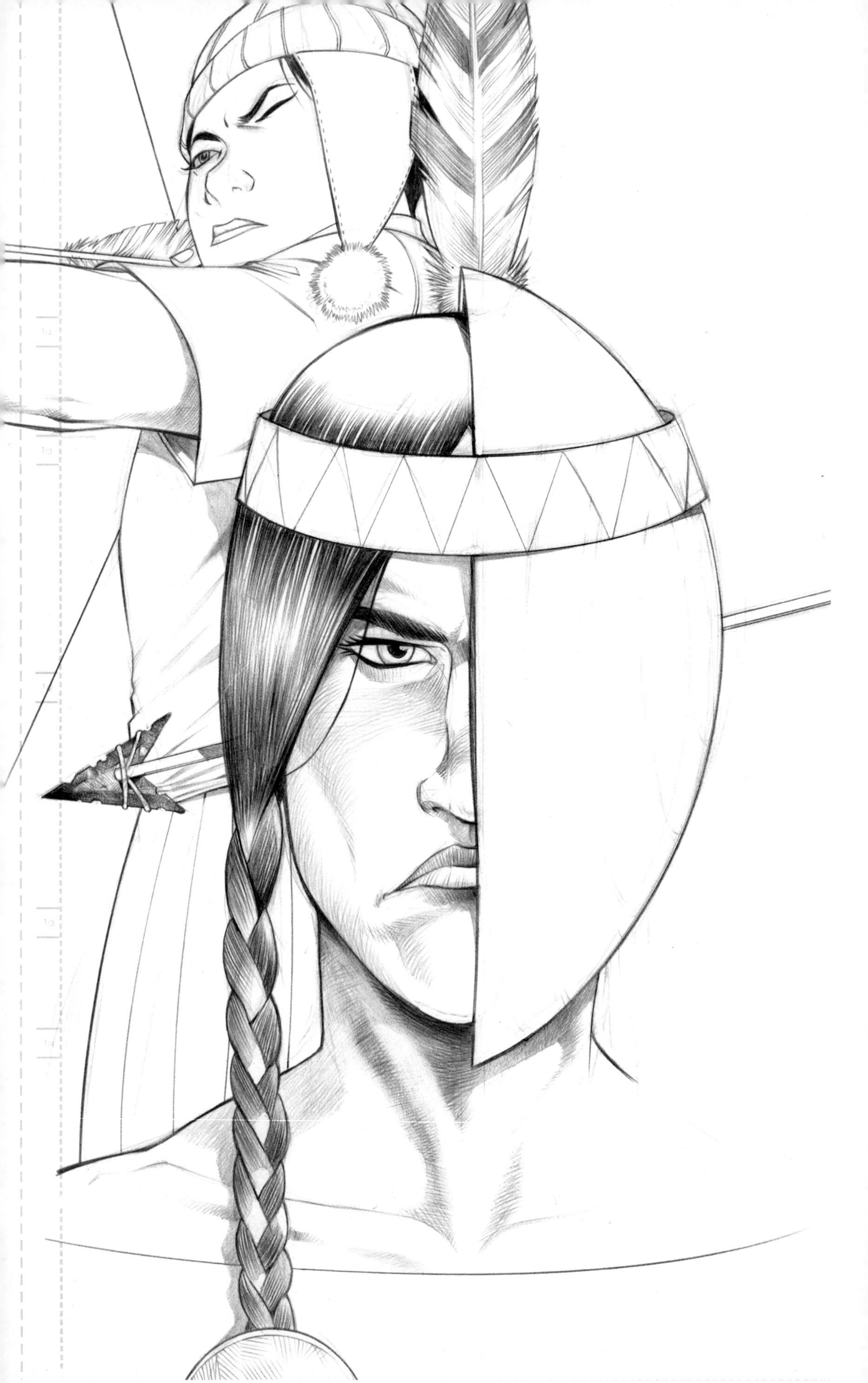

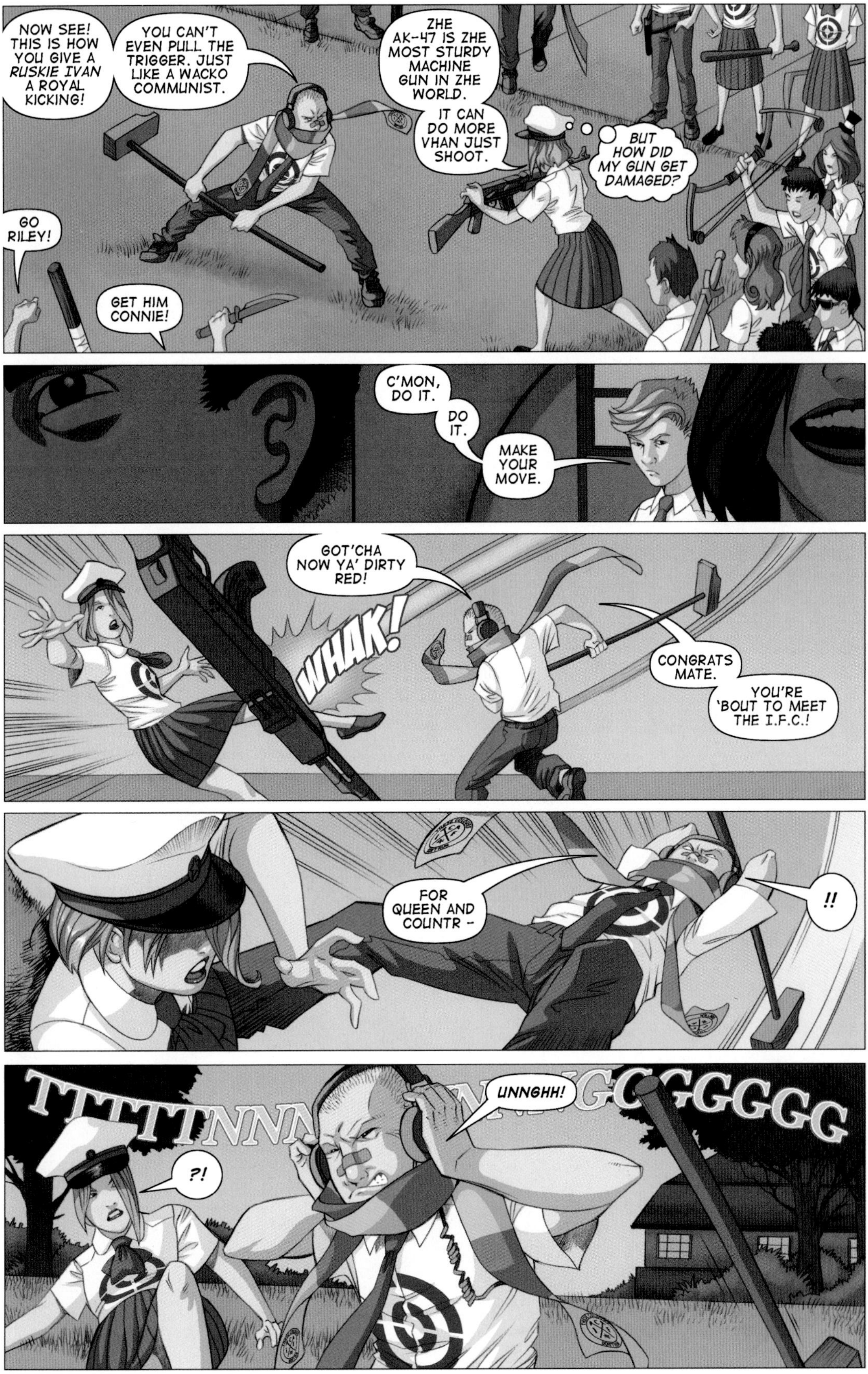
NOW SEE! THIS IS HOW YOU GIVE A RUSKIE IVAN A ROYAL KICKING!
YOU CAN'T EVEN PULL THE TRIGGER. JUST LIKE A WACKO COMMUNIST.
ZHE AK-47 IS ZHE MOST STURDY MACHINE GUN IN ZHE WORLD.
IT CAN DO MORE VHAN JUST SHOOT.
BUT HOW DID MY GUN GET DAMAGED?
GO RILEY!
GET HIM CONNIE!
C'MON, DO IT.
DO IT.
MAKE YOUR MOVE.
GOT'CHA NOW YA' DIRTY RED!
WHAK!
CONGRATS MATE.
YOU'RE 'BOUT TO MEET THE I.F.C.!
FOR QUEEN AND COUNTR –
!!
TTTTTNNNNNNNGGGGGGG
UNNGHH!
?!

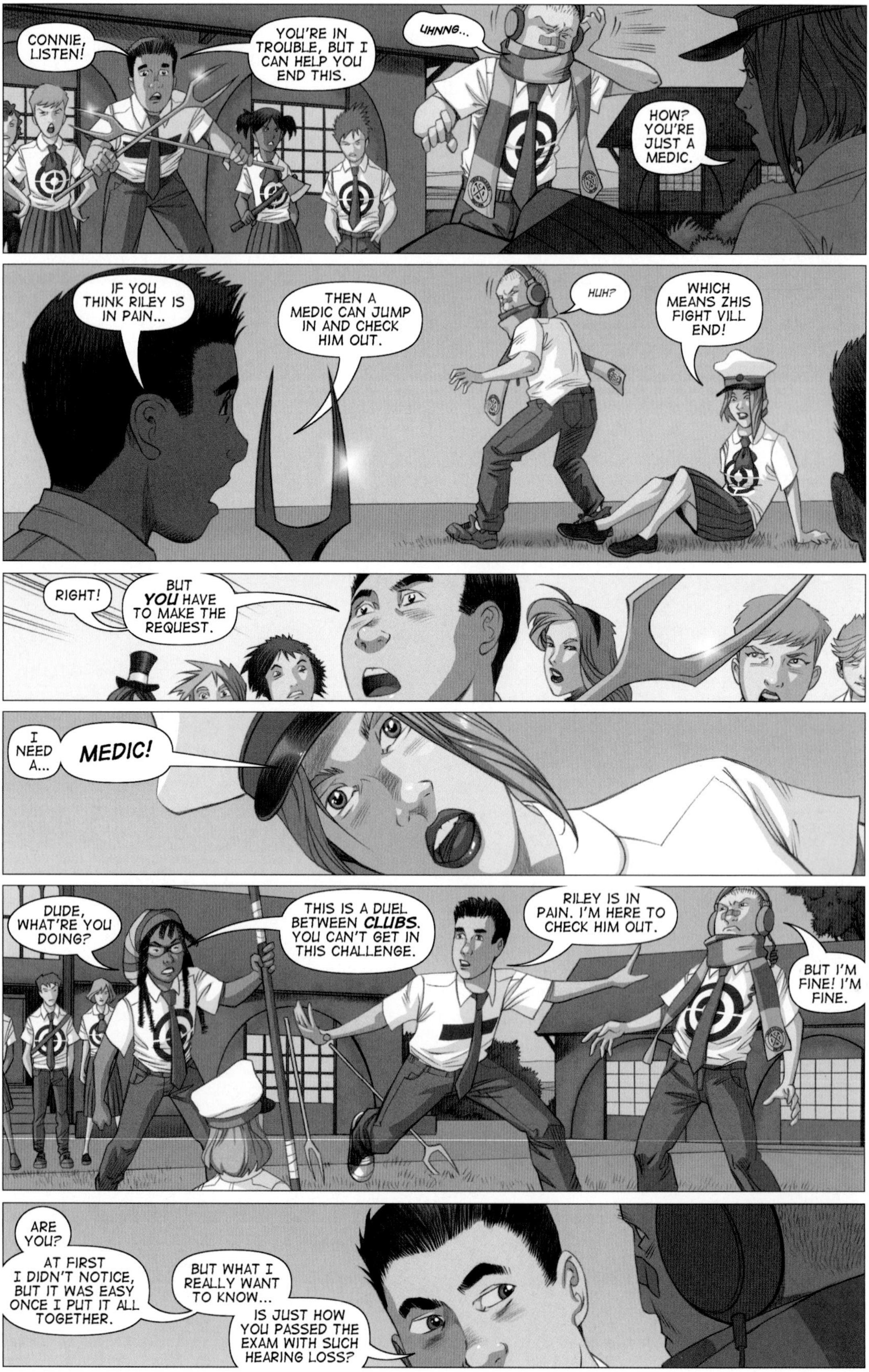
CONNIE, LISTEN!
YOU'RE IN TROUBLE, BUT I CAN HELP YOU END THIS.
UHNNG...
HOW? YOU'RE JUST A MEDIC.
IF YOU THINK RILEY IS IN PAIN...
THEN A MEDIC CAN JUMP IN AND CHECK HIM OUT.
HUH?
WHICH MEANS ZHIS FIGHT VILL END!
RIGHT!
BUT YOU HAVE TO MAKE THE REQUEST.
I NEED A...
MEDIC!
DUDE, WHAT'RE YOU DOING?
THIS IS A DUEL BETWEEN CLUBS. YOU CAN'T GET IN THIS CHALLENGE.
RILEY IS IN PAIN. I'M HERE TO CHECK HIM OUT.
BUT I'M FINE! I'M FINE.
ARE YOU?
AT FIRST I DIDN'T NOTICE, BUT IT WAS EASY ONCE I PUT IT ALL TOGETHER.
BUT WHAT I REALLY WANT TO KNOW...
IS JUST HOW YOU PASSED THE EXAM WITH SUCH HEARING LOSS?

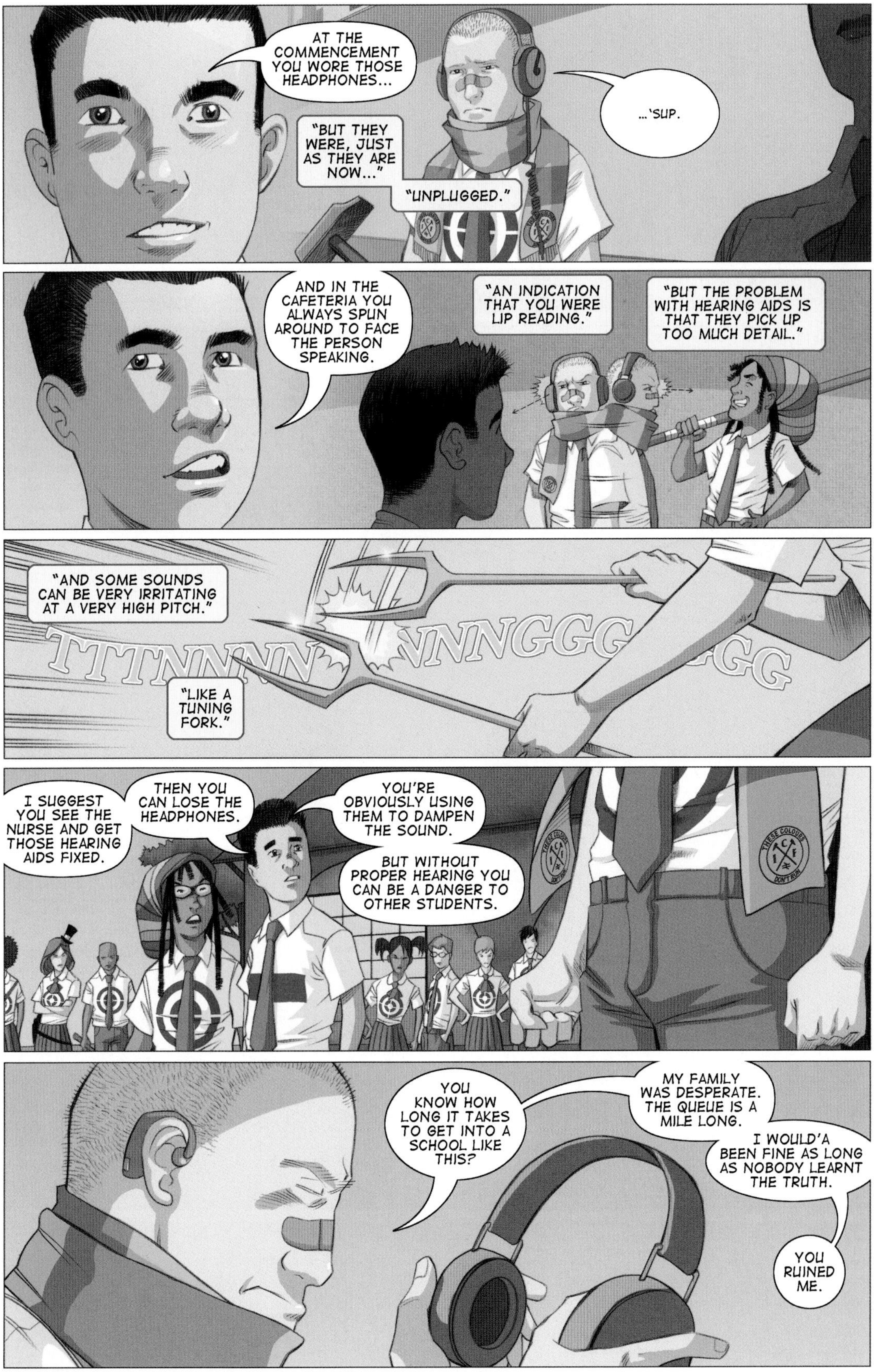
AT THE COMMENCEMENT YOU WORE THOSE HEADPHONES...
"BUT THEY WERE, JUST AS THEY ARE NOW..."
"UNPLUGGED."
...'SUP.
AND IN THE CAFETERIA YOU ALWAYS SPUN AROUND TO FACE THE PERSON SPEAKING.
"AN INDICATION THAT YOU WERE LIP READING."
"BUT THE PROBLEM WITH HEARING AIDS IS THAT THEY PICK UP TOO MUCH DETAIL."
"AND SOME SOUNDS CAN BE VERY IRRITATING AT A VERY HIGH PITCH."
TTTNNNNNNNNNGGGGGG
"LIKE A TUNING FORK."
I SUGGEST YOU SEE THE NURSE AND GET THOSE HEARING AIDS FIXED.
THEN YOU CAN LOSE THE HEADPHONES.
YOU'RE OBVIOUSLY USING THEM TO DAMPEN THE SOUND.
BUT WITHOUT PROPER HEARING YOU CAN BE A DANGER TO OTHER STUDENTS.
YOU KNOW HOW LONG IT TAKES TO GET INTO A SCHOOL LIKE THIS?
MY FAMILY WAS DESPERATE. THE QUEUE IS A MILE LONG.
I WOULD'A BEEN FINE AS LONG AS NOBODY LEARNT THE TRUTH.
YOU RUINED ME.

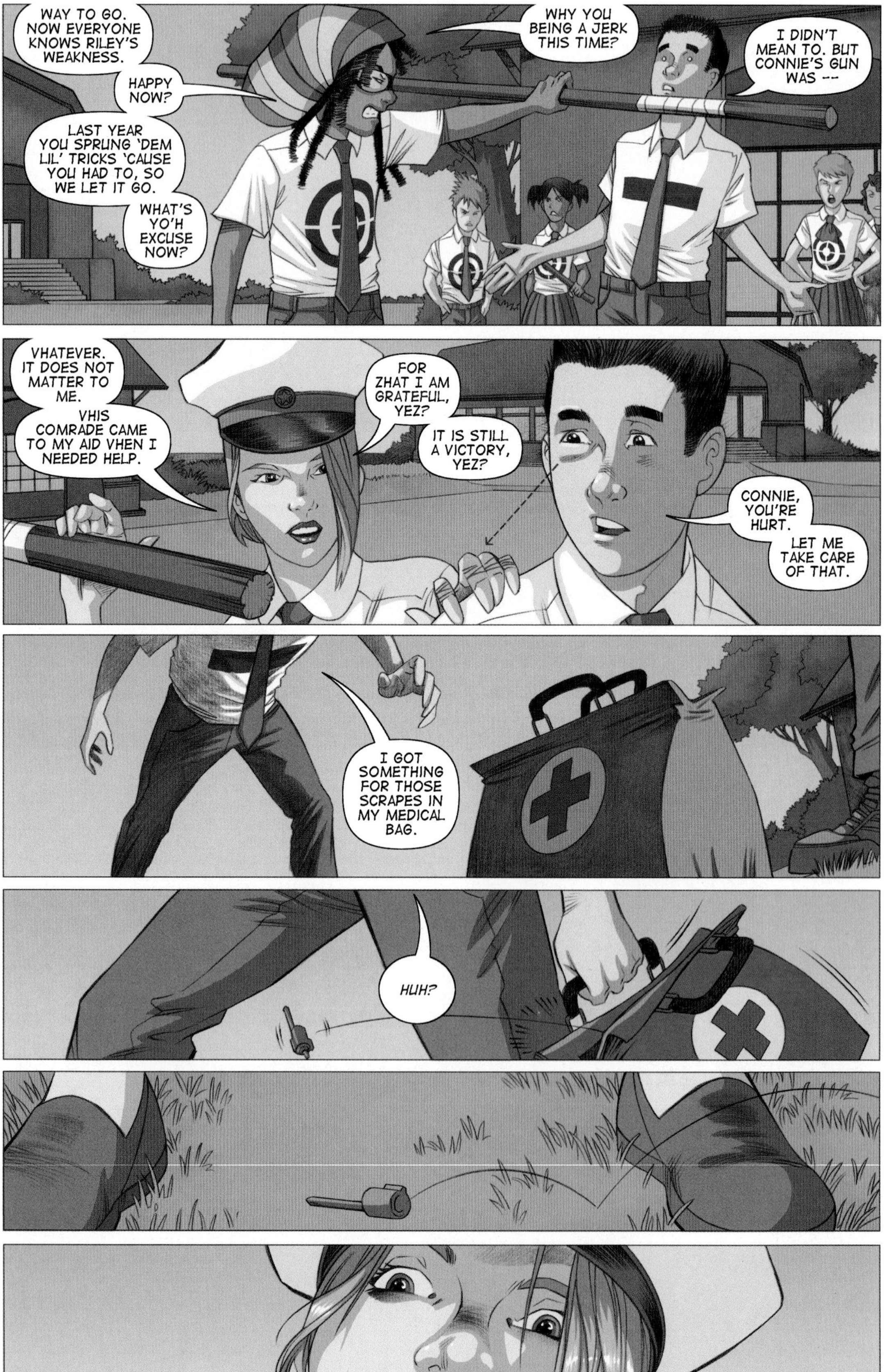
WAY TO GO. NOW EVERYONE KNOWS RILEY'S WEAKNESS.
HAPPY NOW?
LAST YEAR YOU SPRUNG 'DEM LIL' TRICKS 'CAUSE YOU HAD TO, SO WE LET IT GO.
WHAT'S YO'H EXCUSE NOW?
WHY YOU BEING A JERK THIS TIME?
I DIDN'T MEAN TO. BUT CONNIE'S GUN WAS --
VHATEVER. IT DOES NOT MATTER TO ME.
VHIS COMRADE CAME TO MY AID VHEN I NEEDED HELP.
FOR ZHAT I AM GRATEFUL, YEZ?
IT IS STILL A VICTORY, YEZ?
CONNIE, YOU'RE HURT.
LET ME TAKE CARE OF THAT.
I GOT SOMETHING FOR THOSE SCRAPES IN MY MEDICAL BAG.
HUH?

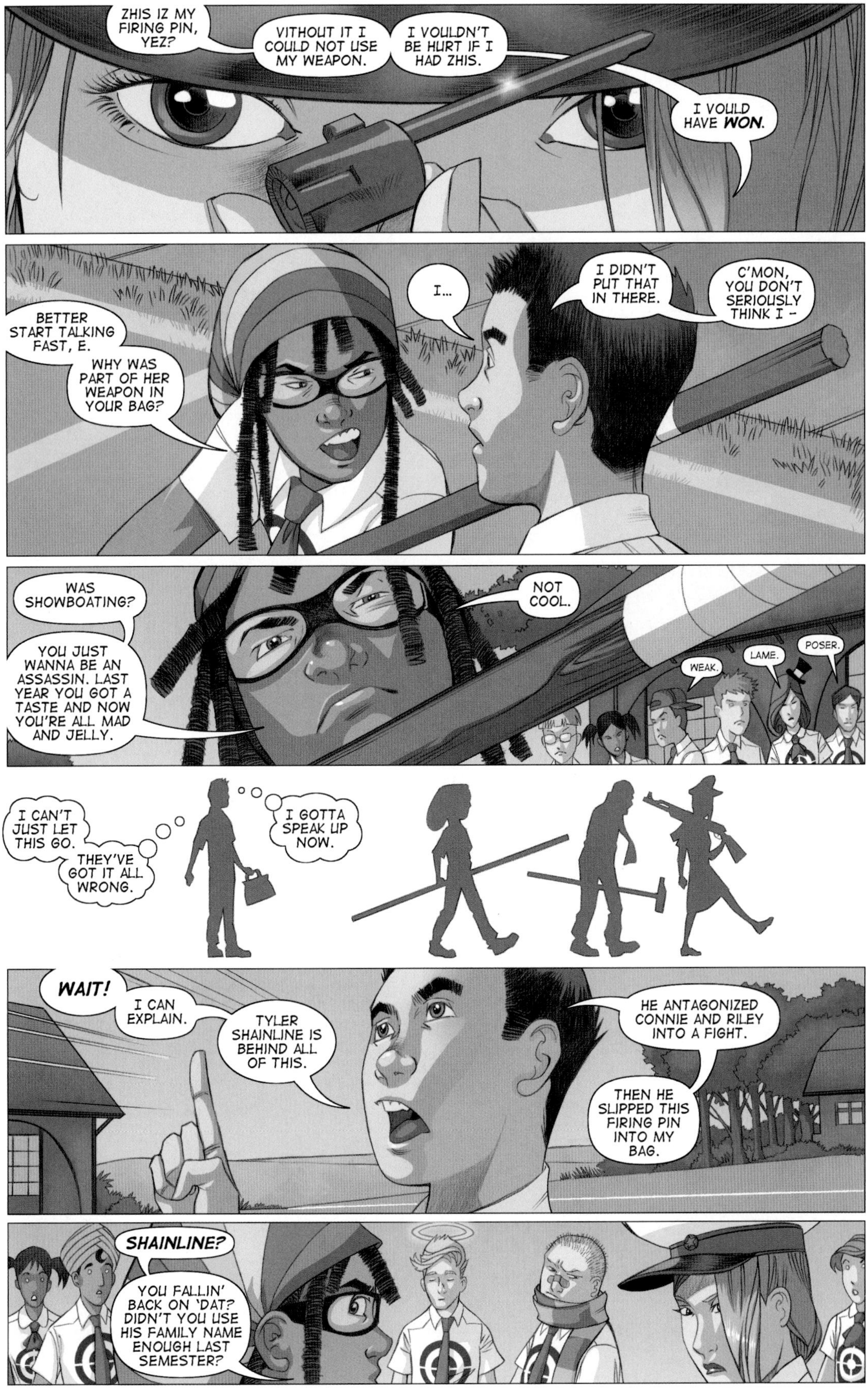
ZHIS IZ MY FIRING PIN, YEZ?
VITHOUT IT I COULD NOT USE MY WEAPON.
I VOULDN'T BE HURT IF I HAD ZHIS.
I VOULD HAVE **WON**.
BETTER START TALKING FAST, E.
WHY WAS PART OF HER WEAPON IN YOUR BAG?
I...
I DIDN'T PUT THAT IN THERE.
C'MON, YOU DON'T SERIOUSLY THINK I –
WAS SHOWBOATING?
YOU JUST WANNA BE AN ASSASSIN. LAST YEAR YOU GOT A TASTE AND NOW YOU'RE ALL MAD AND JELLY.
NOT COOL.
WEAK.
LAME.
POSER.
I CAN'T JUST LET THIS GO.
THEY'VE GOT IT ALL WRONG.
I GOTTA SPEAK UP NOW.
WAIT!
I CAN EXPLAIN.
TYLER SHAINLINE IS BEHIND ALL OF THIS.
HE ANTAGONIZED CONNIE AND RILEY INTO A FIGHT.
THEN HE SLIPPED THIS FIRING PIN INTO MY BAG.
SHAINLINE?
YOU FALLIN' BACK ON 'DAT? DIDN'T YOU USE HIS FAMILY NAME ENOUGH LAST SEMESTER?

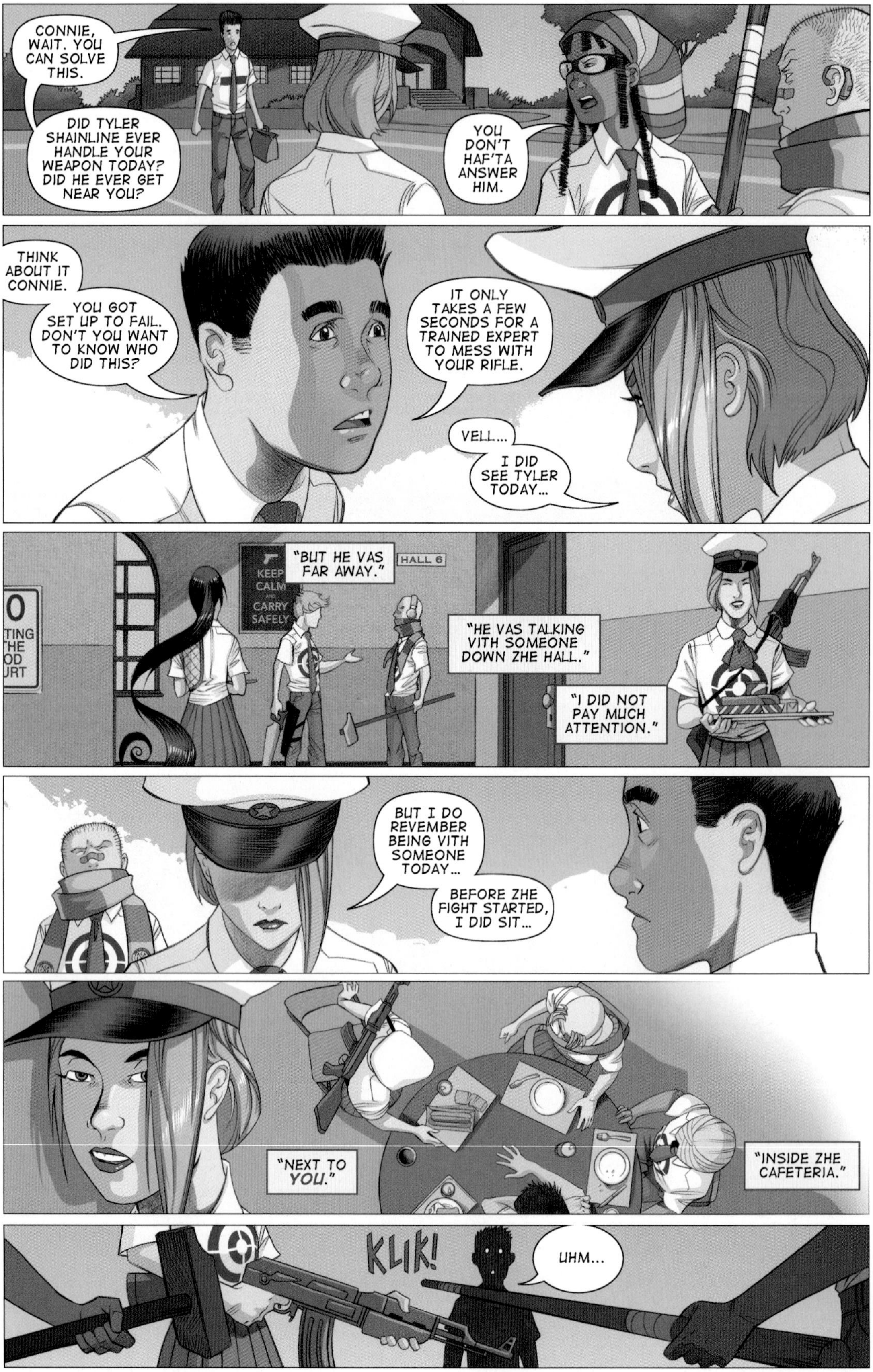
CONNIE, WAIT. YOU CAN SOLVE THIS.
DID TYLER SHAINLINE EVER HANDLE YOUR WEAPON TODAY? DID HE EVER GET NEAR YOU?
YOU DON'T HAF'TA ANSWER HIM.
THINK ABOUT IT CONNIE.
YOU GOT SET UP TO FAIL. DON'T YOU WANT TO KNOW WHO DID THIS?
IT ONLY TAKES A FEW SECONDS FOR A TRAINED EXPERT TO MESS WITH YOUR RIFLE.
VELL...
I DID SEE TYLER TODAY...
KEEP CALM AND CARRY SAFELY
"BUT HE VAS FAR AWAY."
HALL 6
"HE VAS TALKING VITH SOMEONE DOWN ZHE HALL."
"I DID NOT PAY MUCH ATTENTION."
BUT I DO REVEMBER BEING VITH SOMEONE TODAY...
BEFORE ZHE FIGHT STARTED, I DID SIT...
"NEXT TO *YOU*."
"INSIDE ZHE CAFETERIA."
KLIK!
UHM...

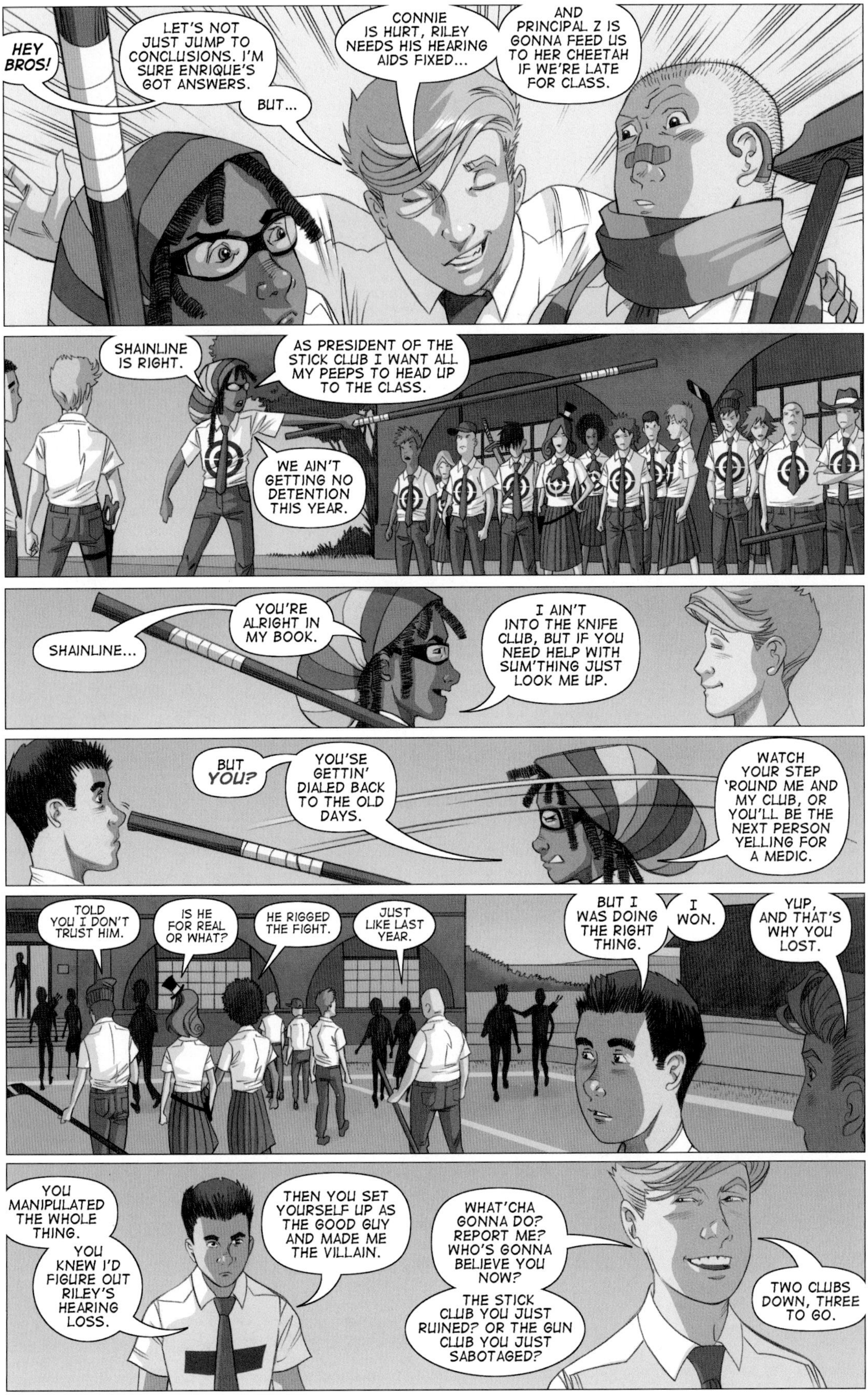
HEY BROS!
LET'S NOT JUST JUMP TO CONCLUSIONS. I'M SURE ENRIQUE'S GOT ANSWERS.
BUT...
CONNIE IS HURT, RILEY NEEDS HIS HEARING AIDS FIXED...
AND PRINCIPAL Z IS GONNA FEED US TO HER CHEETAH IF WE'RE LATE FOR CLASS.
SHAINLINE IS RIGHT.
AS PRESIDENT OF THE STICK CLUB I WANT ALL MY PEEPS TO HEAD UP TO THE CLASS.
WE AIN'T GETTING NO DETENTION THIS YEAR.
SHAINLINE...
YOU'RE ALRIGHT IN MY BOOK.
I AIN'T INTO THE KNIFE CLUB, BUT IF YOU NEED HELP WITH SUM'THING JUST LOOK ME UP.
BUT YOU?
YOU'SE GETTIN' DIALED BACK TO THE OLD DAYS.
WATCH YOUR STEP 'ROUND ME AND MY CLUB, OR YOU'LL BE THE NEXT PERSON YELLING FOR A MEDIC.
TOLD YOU I DON'T TRUST HIM.
IS HE FOR REAL OR WHAT?
HE RIGGED THE FIGHT.
JUST LIKE LAST YEAR.
BUT I WAS DOING THE RIGHT THING.
I WON.
YUP, AND THAT'S WHY YOU LOST.
YOU MANIPULATED THE WHOLE THING.
YOU KNEW I'D FIGURE OUT RILEY'S HEARING LOSS.
THEN YOU SET YOURSELF UP AS THE GOOD GUY AND MADE ME THE VILLAIN.
WHAT'CHA GONNA DO? REPORT ME? WHO'S GONNA BELIEVE YOU NOW?
THE STICK CLUB YOU JUST RUINED? OR THE GUN CLUB YOU JUST SABOTAGED?
TWO CLUBS DOWN, THREE TO GO.

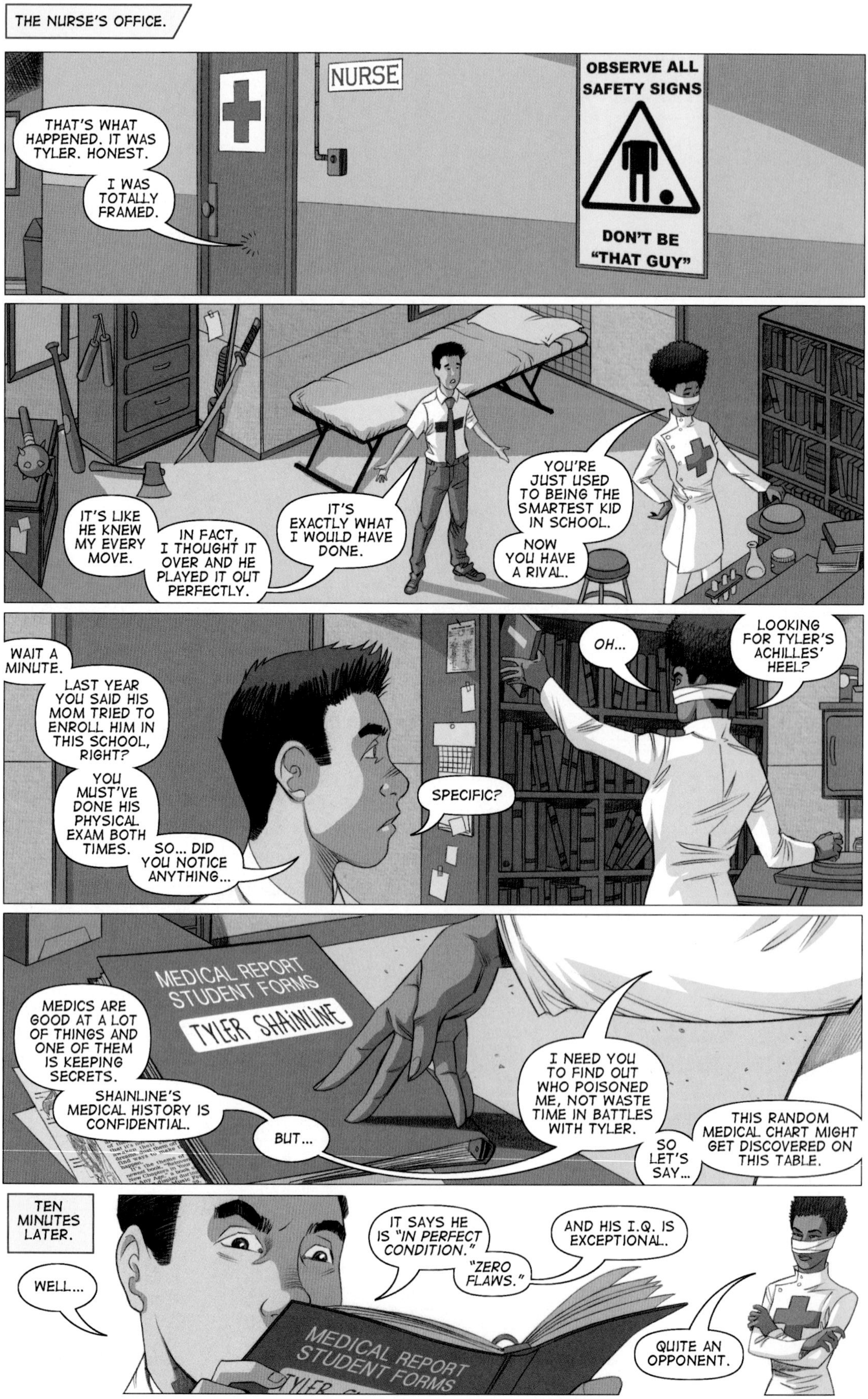
THE NURSE'S OFFICE.
NURSE
THAT'S WHAT HAPPENED. IT WAS TYLER. HONEST.
I WAS TOTALLY FRAMED.
OBSERVE ALL SAFETY SIGNS
DON'T BE "THAT GUY"
IT'S LIKE HE KNEW MY EVERY MOVE.
IN FACT, I THOUGHT IT OVER AND HE PLAYED IT OUT PERFECTLY.
IT'S EXACTLY WHAT I WOULD HAVE DONE.
YOU'RE JUST USED TO BEING THE SMARTEST KID IN SCHOOL.
NOW YOU HAVE A RIVAL.
WAIT A MINUTE.
LAST YEAR YOU SAID HIS MOM TRIED TO ENROLL HIM IN THIS SCHOOL, RIGHT?
YOU MUST'VE DONE HIS PHYSICAL EXAM BOTH TIMES.
SO... DID YOU NOTICE ANYTHING...
SPECIFIC?
OH...
LOOKING FOR TYLER'S ACHILLES' HEEL?
MEDICAL REPORT STUDENT FORMS
TYLER SHAINLINE
MEDICS ARE GOOD AT A LOT OF THINGS AND ONE OF THEM IS KEEPING SECRETS.
SHAINLINE'S MEDICAL HISTORY IS CONFIDENTIAL.
BUT...
I NEED YOU TO FIND OUT WHO POISONED ME, NOT WASTE TIME IN BATTLES WITH TYLER.
SO LET'S SAY...
THIS RANDOM MEDICAL CHART MIGHT GET DISCOVERED ON THIS TABLE.
TEN MINUTES LATER.
WELL...
IT SAYS HE IS *"IN PERFECT CONDITION."*
"ZERO FLAWS."
AND HIS I.Q. IS EXCEPTIONAL.
MEDICAL REPORT STUDENT FORMS
QUITE AN OPPONENT.

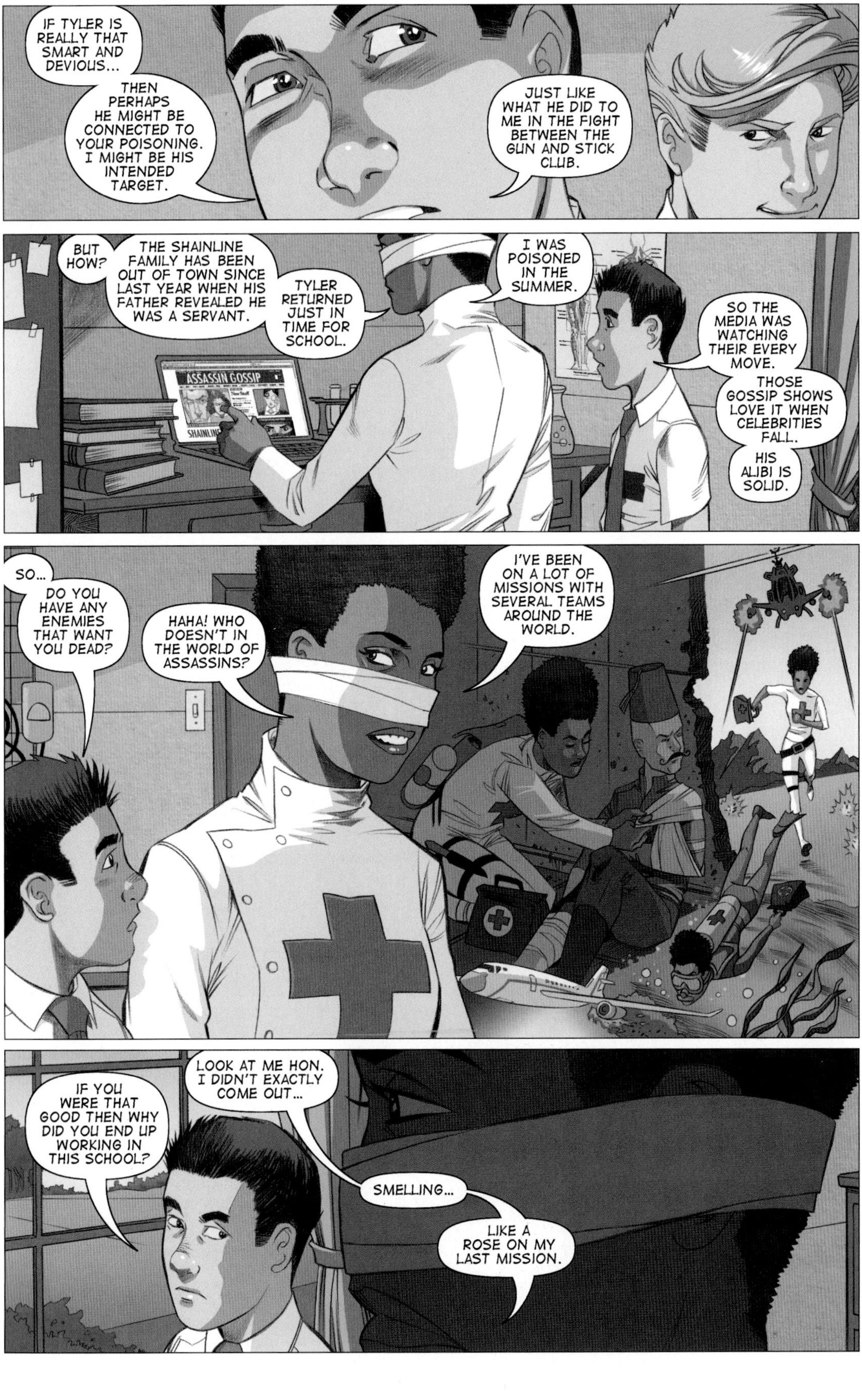

IF TYLER IS REALLY THAT SMART AND DEVIOUS...
THEN PERHAPS HE MIGHT BE CONNECTED TO YOUR POISONING. I MIGHT BE HIS INTENDED TARGET.
JUST LIKE WHAT HE DID TO ME IN THE FIGHT BETWEEN THE GUN AND STICK CLUB.
BUT HOW?
THE SHAINLINE FAMILY HAS BEEN OUT OF TOWN SINCE LAST YEAR WHEN HIS FATHER REVEALED HE WAS A SERVANT.
TYLER RETURNED JUST IN TIME FOR SCHOOL.
I WAS POISONED IN THE SUMMER.
SO THE MEDIA WAS WATCHING THEIR EVERY MOVE.
THOSE GOSSIP SHOWS LOVE IT WHEN CELEBRITIES FALL.
HIS ALIBI IS SOLID.
ASSASSIN GOSSIP
SO...
DO YOU HAVE ANY ENEMIES THAT WANT YOU DEAD?
HAHA! WHO DOESN'T IN THE WORLD OF ASSASSINS?
I'VE BEEN ON A LOT OF MISSIONS WITH SEVERAL TEAMS AROUND THE WORLD.
IF YOU WERE THAT GOOD THEN WHY DID YOU END UP WORKING IN THIS SCHOOL?
LOOK AT ME HON. I DIDN'T EXACTLY COME OUT...
SMELLING...
LIKE A ROSE ON MY LAST MISSION.

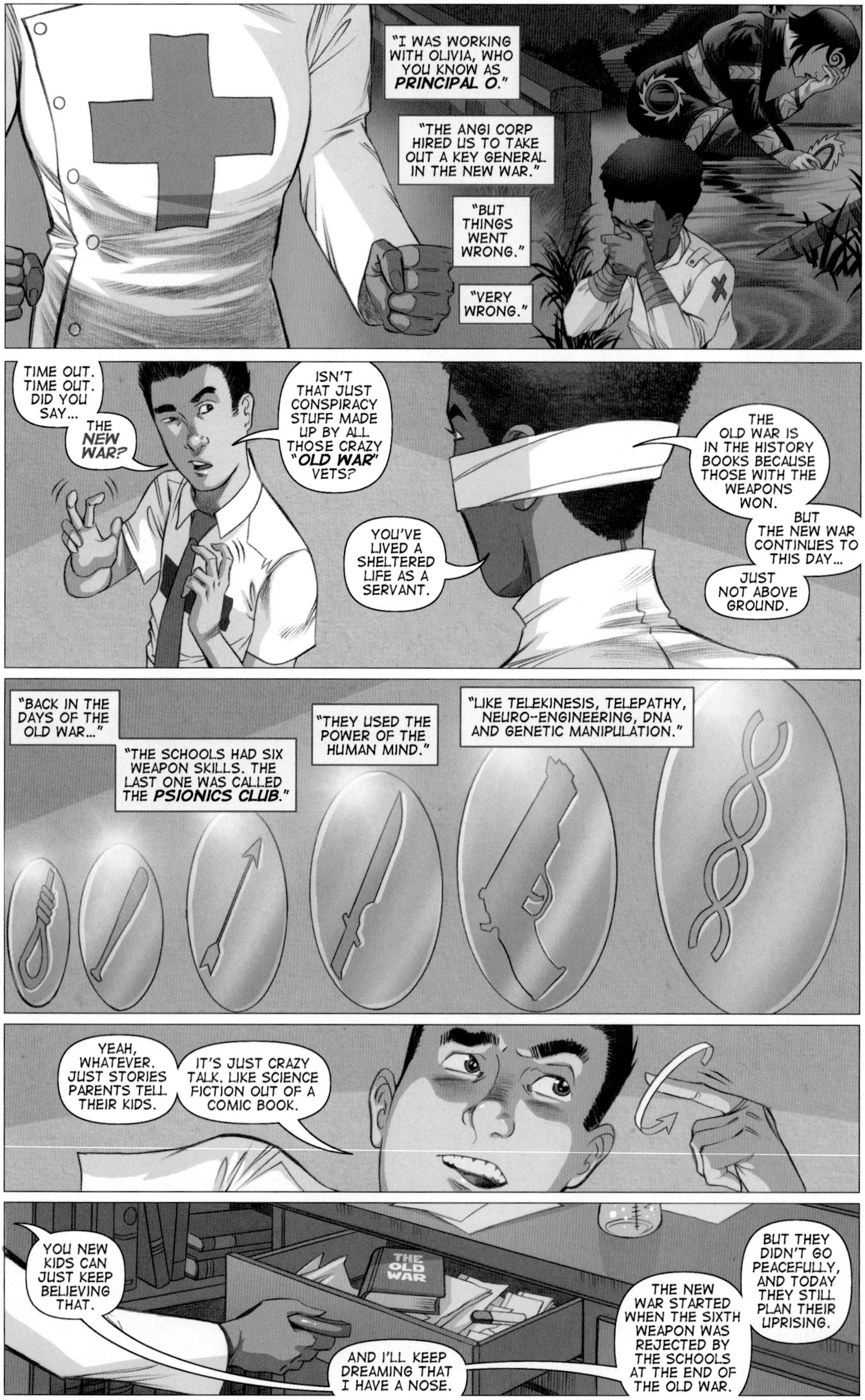
"I WAS WORKING WITH OLIVIA, WHO YOU KNOW AS PRINCIPAL O."
"THE ANGI CORP HIRED US TO TAKE OUT A KEY GENERAL IN THE NEW WAR."
"BUT THINGS WENT WRONG."
"VERY WRONG."
TIME OUT. TIME OUT. DID YOU SAY... THE NEW WAR?
ISN'T THAT JUST CONSPIRACY STUFF MADE UP BY ALL THOSE CRAZY "OLD WAR" VETS?
YOU'VE LIVED A SHELTERED LIFE AS A SERVANT.
THE OLD WAR IS IN THE HISTORY BOOKS BECAUSE THOSE WITH THE WEAPONS WON.
BUT THE NEW WAR CONTINUES TO THIS DAY...
JUST NOT ABOVE GROUND.
"BACK IN THE DAYS OF THE OLD WAR..."
"THE SCHOOLS HAD SIX WEAPON SKILLS. THE LAST ONE WAS CALLED THE PSIONICS CLUB."
"THEY USED THE POWER OF THE HUMAN MIND."
"LIKE TELEKINESIS, TELEPATHY, NEURO-ENGINEERING, DNA AND GENETIC MANIPULATION."
YEAH, WHATEVER. JUST STORIES PARENTS TELL THEIR KIDS.
IT'S JUST CRAZY TALK. LIKE SCIENCE FICTION OUT OF A COMIC BOOK.
YOU NEW KIDS CAN JUST KEEP BELIEVING THAT.
AND I'LL KEEP DREAMING THAT I HAVE A NOSE.
THE OLD WAR
THE NEW WAR STARTED WHEN THE SIXTH WEAPON WAS REJECTED BY THE SCHOOLS AT THE END OF THE OLD WAR.
BUT THEY DIDN'T GO PEACEFULLY, AND TODAY THEY STILL PLAN THEIR UPRISING.

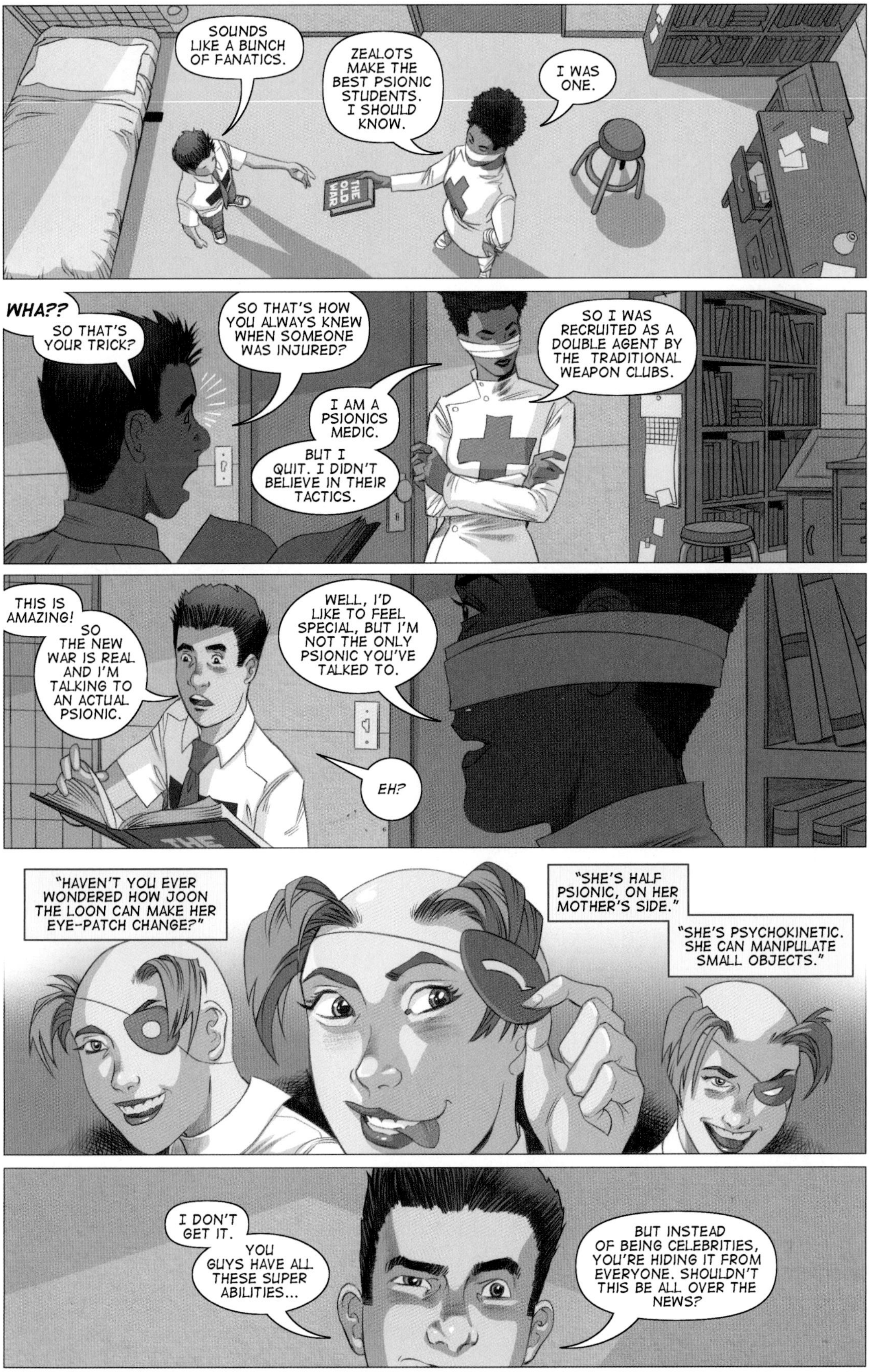
SOUNDS LIKE A BUNCH OF FANATICS.
ZEALOTS MAKE THE BEST PSIONIC STUDENTS. I SHOULD KNOW.
I WAS ONE.
THE OLD WAR
WHA??
SO THAT'S YOUR TRICK?
SO THAT'S HOW YOU ALWAYS KNEW WHEN SOMEONE WAS INJURED?
I AM A PSIONICS MEDIC.
BUT I QUIT. I DIDN'T BELIEVE IN THEIR TACTICS.
SO I WAS RECRUITED AS A DOUBLE AGENT BY THE TRADITIONAL WEAPON CLUBS.
THIS IS AMAZING!
SO THE NEW WAR IS REAL AND I'M TALKING TO AN ACTUAL PSIONIC.
WELL, I'D LIKE TO FEEL SPECIAL, BUT I'M NOT THE ONLY PSIONIC YOU'VE TALKED TO.
EH?
"HAVEN'T YOU EVER WONDERED HOW JOON THE LOON CAN MAKE HER EYE-PATCH CHANGE?"
"SHE'S HALF PSIONIC, ON HER MOTHER'S SIDE."
"SHE'S PSYCHOKINETIC. SHE CAN MANIPULATE SMALL OBJECTS."
I DON'T GET IT.
YOU GUYS HAVE ALL THESE SUPER ABILITIES...
BUT INSTEAD OF BEING CELEBRITIES, YOU'RE HIDING IT FROM EVERYONE. SHOULDN'T THIS BE ALL OVER THE NEWS?

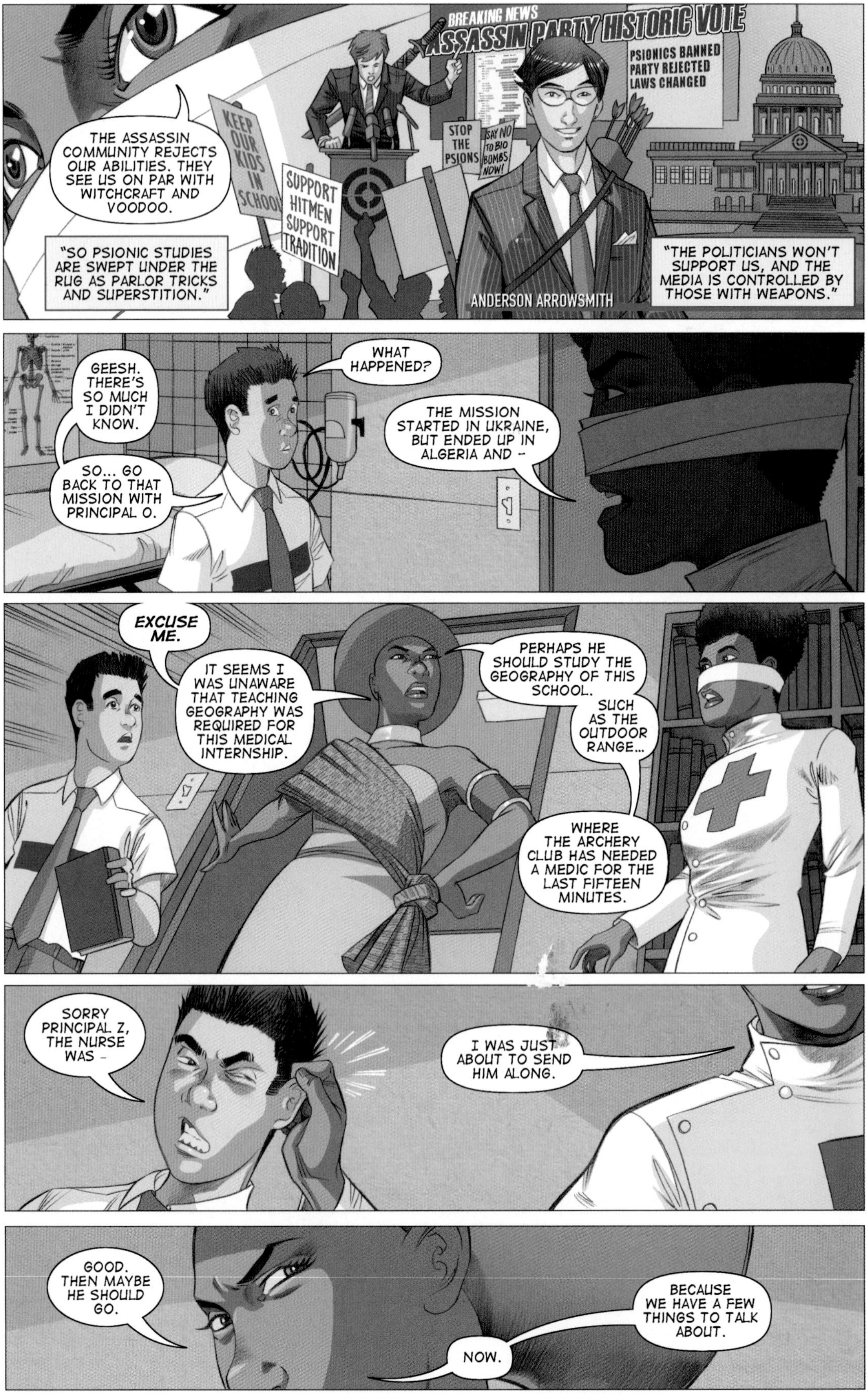
BREAKING NEWS
ASSASSIN PARTY HISTORIC VOTE
PSIONICS BANNED
PARTY REJECTED
LAWS CHANGED
THE ASSASSIN COMMUNITY REJECTS OUR ABILITIES. THEY SEE US ON PAR WITH WITCHCRAFT AND VOODOO.
KEEP OUR KIDS IN SCHOOL
SUPPORT HITMEN SUPPORT TRADITION
STOP THE PSIONS
SAY NO TO BIO BOMBS NOW!
"SO PSIONIC STUDIES ARE SWEPT UNDER THE RUG AS PARLOR TRICKS AND SUPERSTITION."
ANDERSON ARROWSMITH
"THE POLITICIANS WON'T SUPPORT US, AND THE MEDIA IS CONTROLLED BY THOSE WITH WEAPONS."
GEESH. THERE'S SO MUCH I DIDN'T KNOW.
SO... GO BACK TO THAT MISSION WITH PRINCIPAL O.
WHAT HAPPENED?
THE MISSION STARTED IN UKRAINE, BUT ENDED UP IN ALGERIA AND -
EXCUSE ME.
IT SEEMS I WAS UNAWARE THAT TEACHING GEOGRAPHY WAS REQUIRED FOR THIS MEDICAL INTERNSHIP.
PERHAPS HE SHOULD STUDY THE GEOGRAPHY OF THIS SCHOOL.
SUCH AS THE OUTDOOR RANGE...
WHERE THE ARCHERY CLUB HAS NEEDED A MEDIC FOR THE LAST FIFTEEN MINUTES.
SORRY PRINCIPAL Z, THE NURSE WAS -
I WAS JUST ABOUT TO SEND HIM ALONG.
GOOD. THEN MAYBE HE SHOULD GO.
BECAUSE WE HAVE A FEW THINGS TO TALK ABOUT.
NOW.

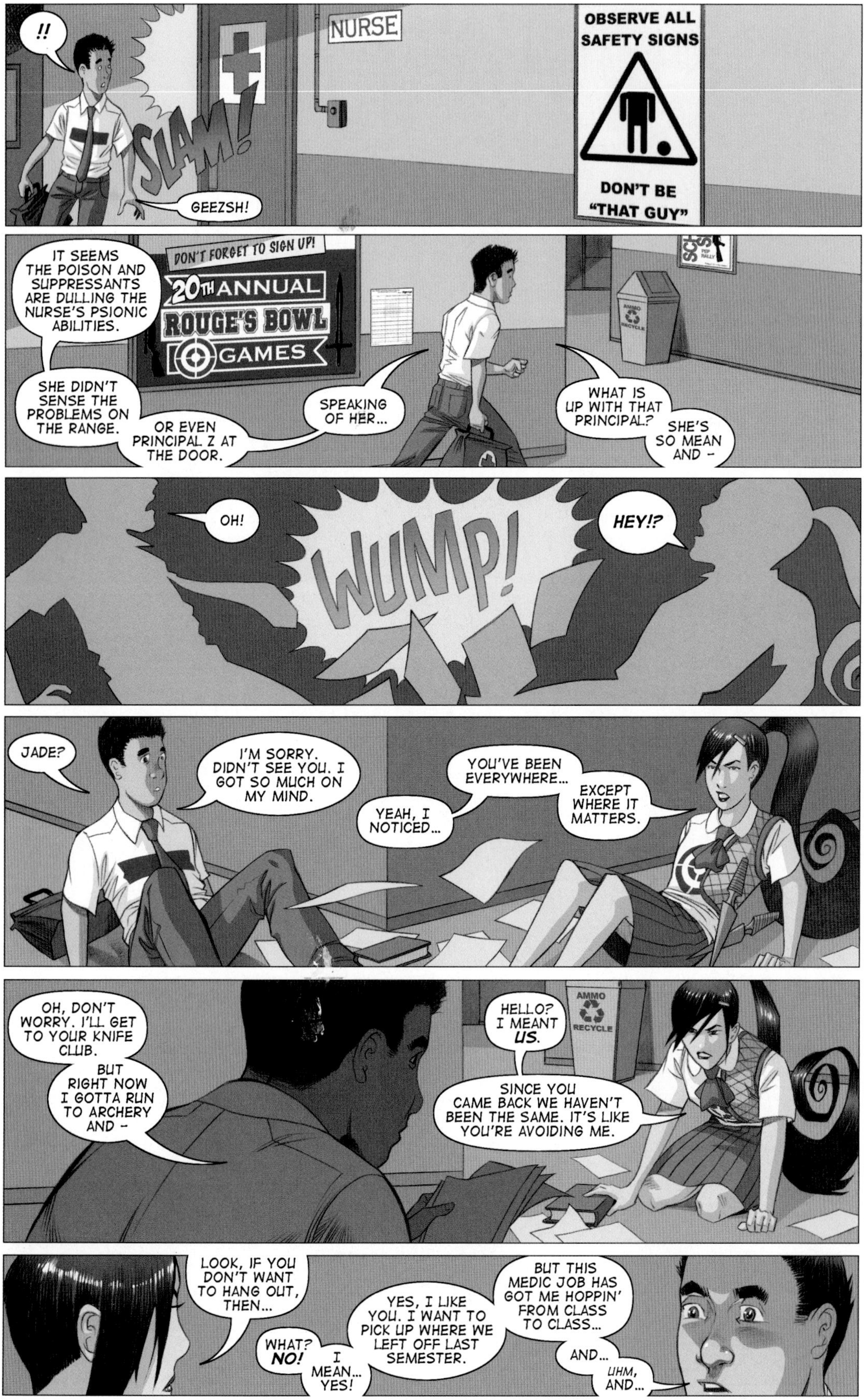
!!
NURSE
OBSERVE ALL SAFETY SIGNS
DON'T BE "THAT GUY"
SLAM!
GEEZSH!
IT SEEMS THE POISON AND SUPPRESSANTS ARE DULLING THE NURSE'S PSIONIC ABILITIES.
DON'T FORGET TO SIGN UP!
20TH ANNUAL ROUGE'S BOWL GAMES
SHE DIDN'T SENSE THE PROBLEMS ON THE RANGE.
OR EVEN PRINCIPAL Z AT THE DOOR.
SPEAKING OF HER...
AMMO RECYCLE
WHAT IS UP WITH THAT PRINCIPAL?
SHE'S SO MEAN AND -
OH!
WUMP!
HEY!?
JADE?
I'M SORRY. DIDN'T SEE YOU. I GOT SO MUCH ON MY MIND.
YOU'VE BEEN EVERYWHERE...
YEAH, I NOTICED...
EXCEPT WHERE IT MATTERS.
OH, DON'T WORRY. I'LL GET TO YOUR KNIFE CLUB.
BUT RIGHT NOW I GOTTA RUN TO ARCHERY AND -
HELLO? I MEANT US.
AMMO RECYCLE
SINCE YOU CAME BACK WE HAVEN'T BEEN THE SAME. IT'S LIKE YOU'RE AVOIDING ME.
LOOK, IF YOU DON'T WANT TO HANG OUT, THEN...
WHAT? NO!
I MEAN... YES!
YES, I LIKE YOU. I WANT TO PICK UP WHERE WE LEFT OFF LAST SEMESTER.
BUT THIS MEDIC JOB HAS GOT ME HOPPIN' FROM CLASS TO CLASS...
AND...
UHM, AND...

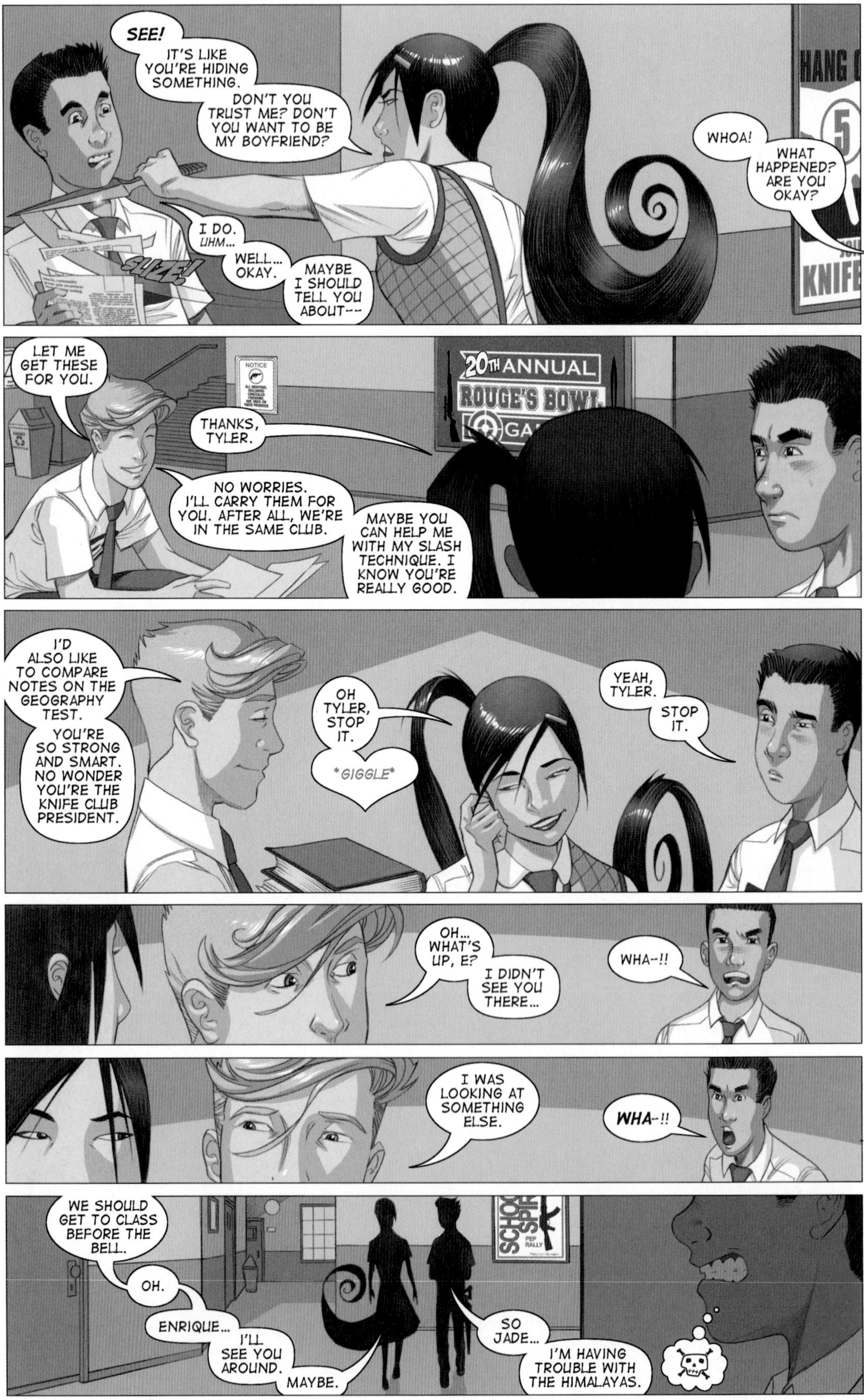
HANG O
5
KNIFE
SEE!
IT'S LIKE YOU'RE HIDING SOMETHING.
DON'T YOU TRUST ME? DON'T YOU WANT TO BE MY BOYFRIEND?
I DO. UHM...
WELL... OKAY.
SLIZE!
MAYBE I SHOULD TELL YOU ABOUT--
WHOA!
WHAT HAPPENED? ARE YOU OKAY?
20TH ANNUAL
ROUGE'S BOWL
LET ME GET THESE FOR YOU.
THANKS, TYLER.
NO WORRIES. I'LL CARRY THEM FOR YOU. AFTER ALL, WE'RE IN THE SAME CLUB.
MAYBE YOU CAN HELP ME WITH MY SLASH TECHNIQUE. I KNOW YOU'RE REALLY GOOD.
I'D ALSO LIKE TO COMPARE NOTES ON THE GEOGRAPHY TEST.
YOU'RE SO STRONG AND SMART. NO WONDER YOU'RE THE KNIFE CLUB PRESIDENT.
OH TYLER, STOP IT.
GIGGLE
YEAH, TYLER.
STOP IT.
OH... WHAT'S UP, E?
I DIDN'T SEE YOU THERE...
WHA-!!
I WAS LOOKING AT SOMETHING ELSE.
WHA-!!
WE SHOULD GET TO CLASS BEFORE THE BELL.
OH.
ENRIQUE...
I'LL SEE YOU AROUND.
MAYBE.
SO JADE...
I'M HAVING TROUBLE WITH THE HIMALAYAS.
PEP RALLY

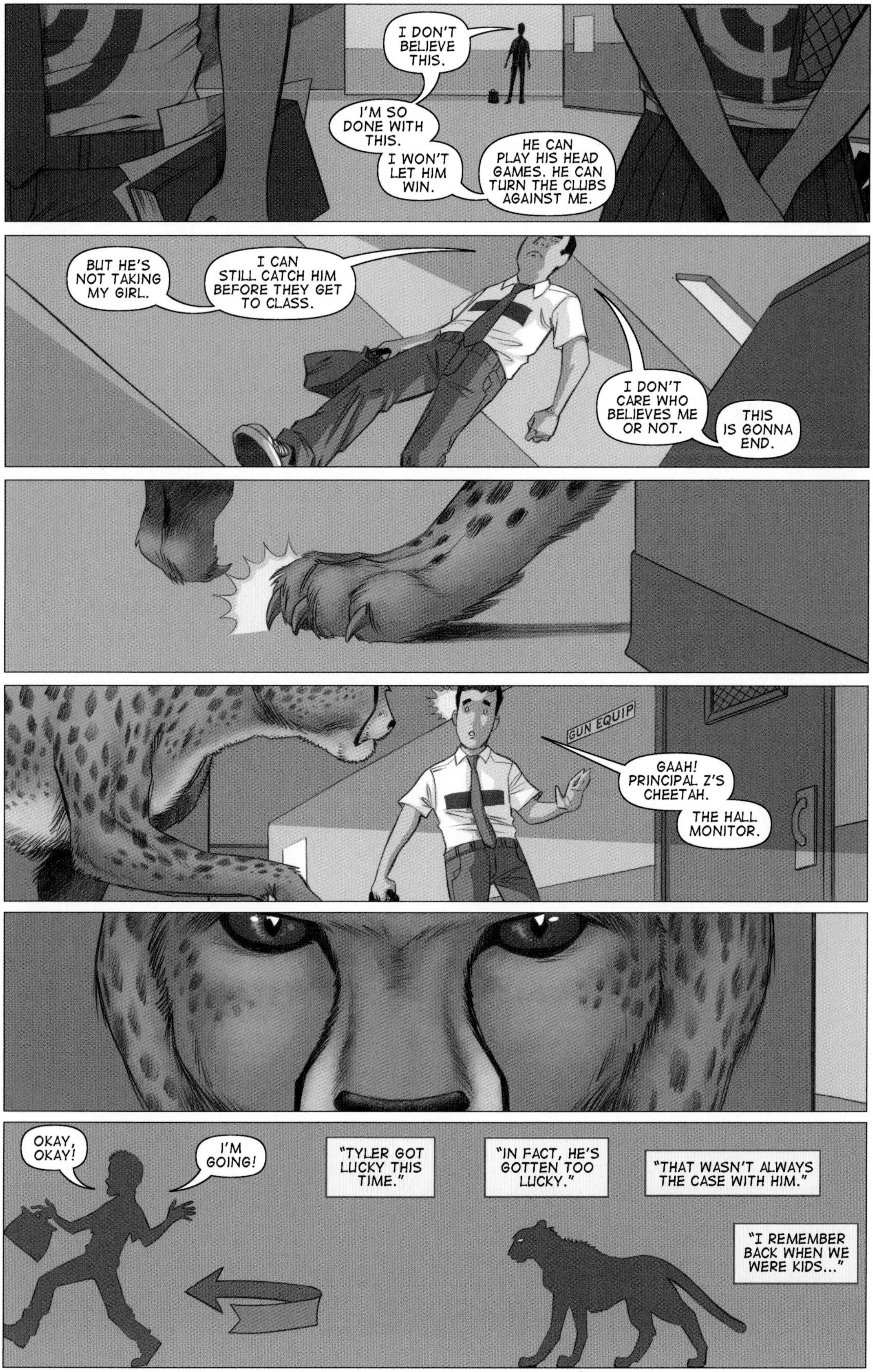
I DON'T BELIEVE THIS.
I'M SO DONE WITH THIS.
I WON'T LET HIM WIN.
HE CAN PLAY HIS HEAD GAMES. HE CAN TURN THE CLUBS AGAINST ME.
BUT HE'S NOT TAKING MY GIRL.
I CAN STILL CATCH HIM BEFORE THEY GET TO CLASS.
I DON'T CARE WHO BELIEVES ME OR NOT.
THIS IS GONNA END.
GUN EQUIP
GAAH! PRINCIPAL Z'S CHEETAH.
THE HALL MONITOR.
OKAY, OKAY!
I'M GOING!
"TYLER GOT LUCKY THIS TIME."
"IN FACT, HE'S GOTTEN TOO LUCKY."
"THAT WASN'T ALWAYS THE CASE WITH HIM."
"I REMEMBER BACK WHEN WE WERE KIDS..."

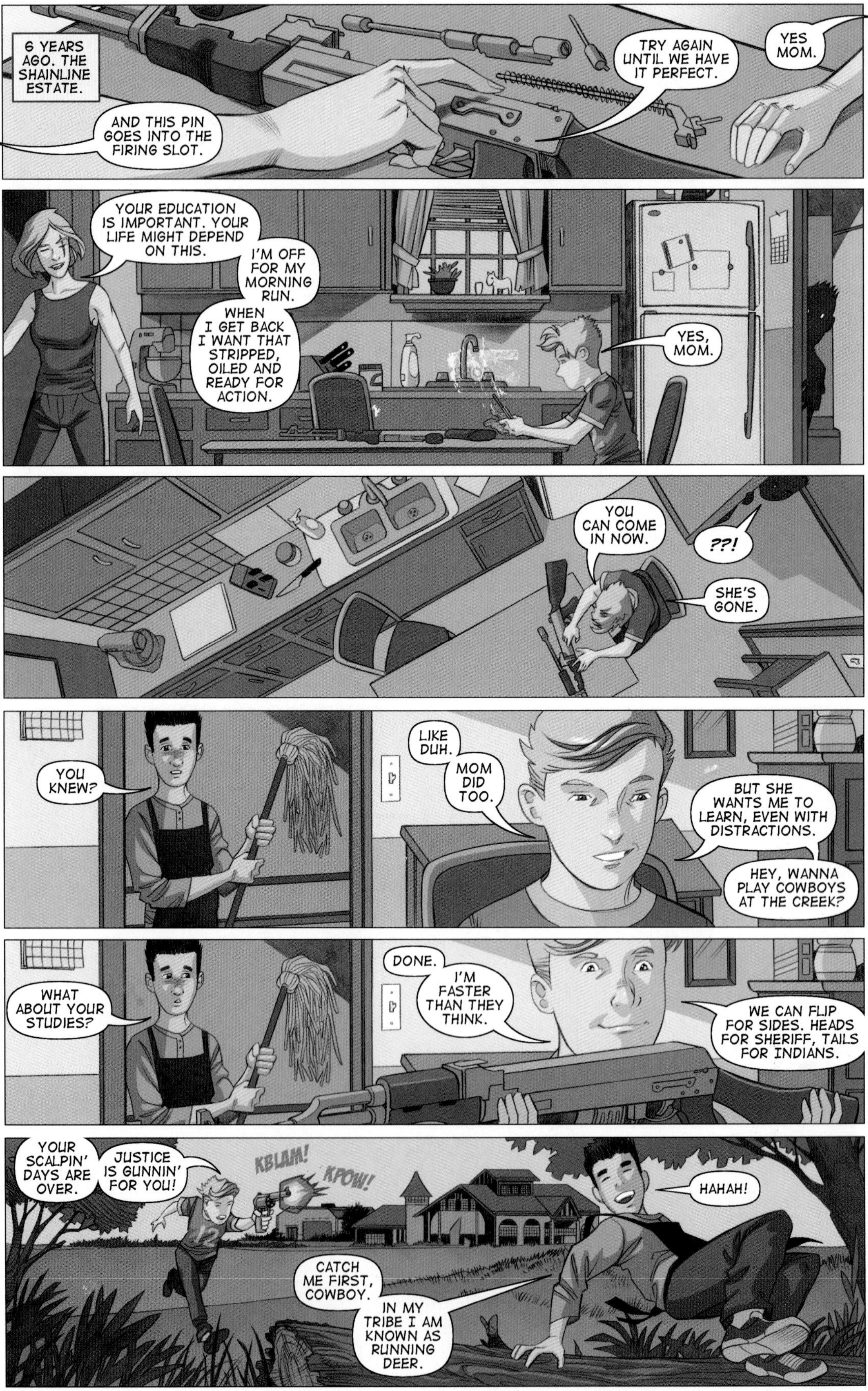
6 YEARS AGO. THE SHAINLINE ESTATE.
AND THIS PIN GOES INTO THE FIRING SLOT.
TRY AGAIN UNTIL WE HAVE IT PERFECT.
YES MOM.
YOUR EDUCATION IS IMPORTANT. YOUR LIFE MIGHT DEPEND ON THIS.
I'M OFF FOR MY MORNING RUN.
WHEN I GET BACK I WANT THAT STRIPPED, OILED AND READY FOR ACTION.
YES, MOM.
YOU CAN COME IN NOW.
??!
SHE'S GONE.
YOU KNEW?
LIKE DUH.
MOM DID TOO.
BUT SHE WANTS ME TO LEARN, EVEN WITH DISTRACTIONS.
HEY, WANNA PLAY COWBOYS AT THE CREEK?
WHAT ABOUT YOUR STUDIES?
DONE.
I'M FASTER THAN THEY THINK.
WE CAN FLIP FOR SIDES. HEADS FOR SHERIFF, TAILS FOR INDIANS.
YOUR SCALPIN' DAYS ARE OVER.
JUSTICE IS GUNNIN' FOR YOU!
KBLAM!
KPOW!
HAHAH!
CATCH ME FIRST, COWBOY.
IN MY TRIBE I AM KNOWN AS RUNNING DEER.

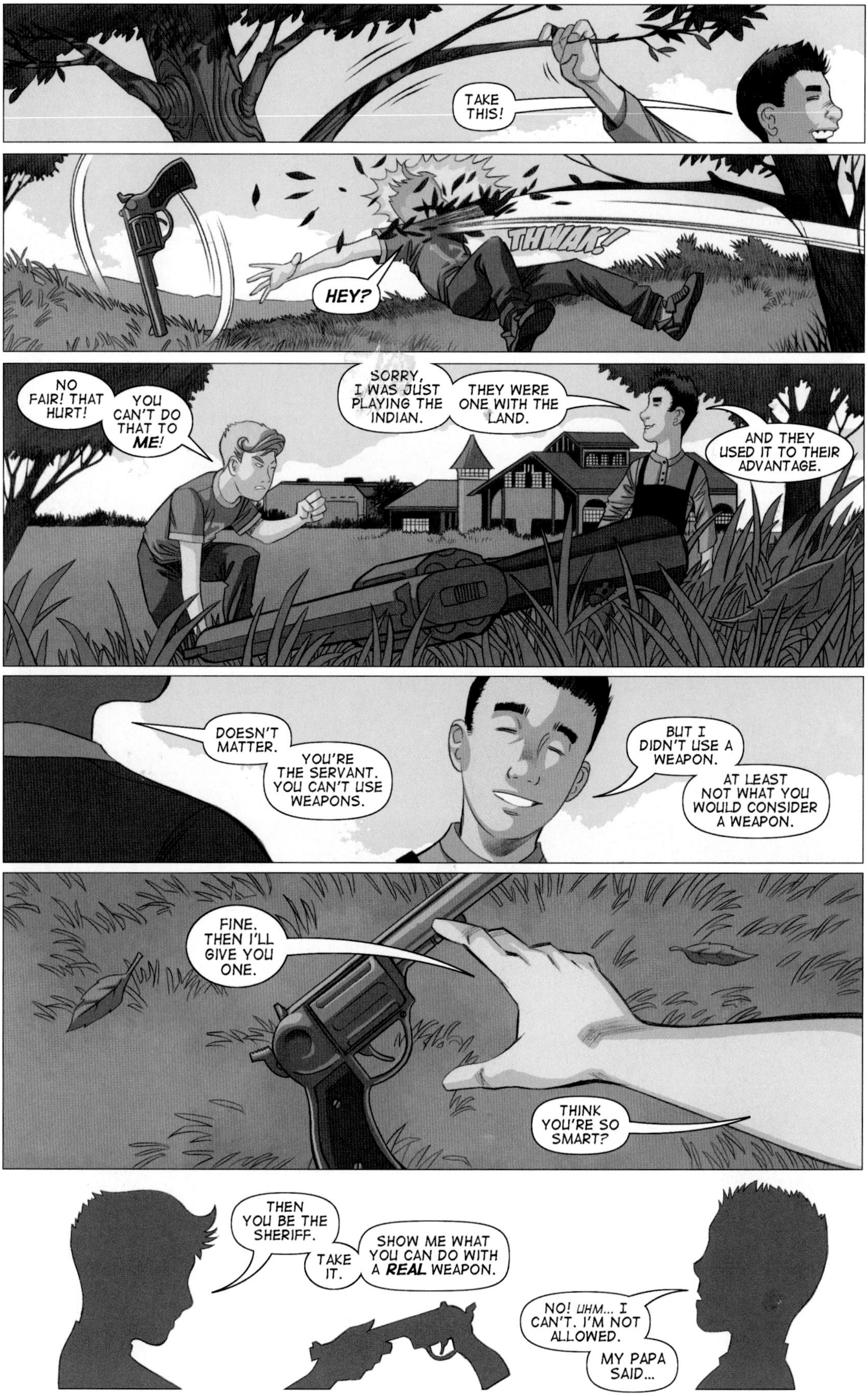
TAKE THIS!
HEY?
THWAK!
NO FAIR! THAT HURT!
YOU CAN'T DO THAT TO ME!
SORRY, I WAS JUST PLAYING THE INDIAN.
THEY WERE ONE WITH THE LAND.
AND THEY USED IT TO THEIR ADVANTAGE.
DOESN'T MATTER.
YOU'RE THE SERVANT. YOU CAN'T USE WEAPONS.
BUT I DIDN'T USE A WEAPON.
AT LEAST NOT WHAT YOU WOULD CONSIDER A WEAPON.
FINE. THEN I'LL GIVE YOU ONE.
THINK YOU'RE SO SMART?
THEN YOU BE THE SHERIFF.
TAKE IT.
SHOW ME WHAT YOU CAN DO WITH A REAL WEAPON.
NO! UHM... I CAN'T. I'M NOT ALLOWED.
MY PAPA SAID...

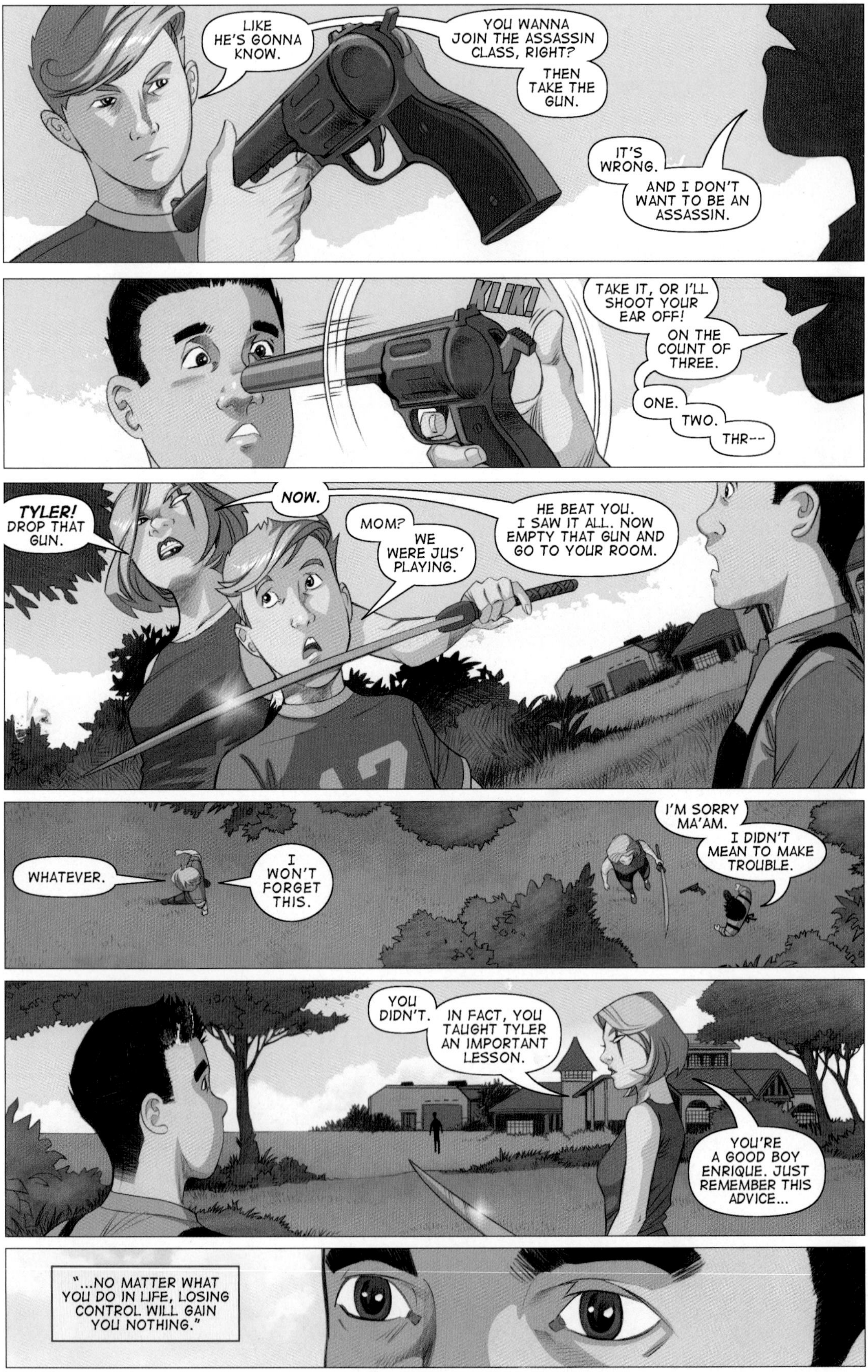
LIKE HE'S GONNA KNOW.
YOU WANNA JOIN THE ASSASSIN CLASS, RIGHT?
THEN TAKE THE GUN.
IT'S WRONG.
AND I DON'T WANT TO BE AN ASSASSIN.
KLIK!
TAKE IT, OR I'LL SHOOT YOUR EAR OFF!
ON THE COUNT OF THREE.
ONE.
TWO.
THR---
TYLER! DROP THAT GUN.
NOW.
MOM? WE WERE JUS' PLAYING.
HE BEAT YOU. I SAW IT ALL. NOW EMPTY THAT GUN AND GO TO YOUR ROOM.
WHATEVER.
I WON'T FORGET THIS.
I'M SORRY MA'AM.
I DIDN'T MEAN TO MAKE TROUBLE.
YOU DIDN'T.
IN FACT, YOU TAUGHT TYLER AN IMPORTANT LESSON.
YOU'RE A GOOD BOY ENRIQUE. JUST REMEMBER THIS ADVICE...
"...NO MATTER WHAT YOU DO IN LIFE, LOSING CONTROL WILL GAIN YOU NOTHING."

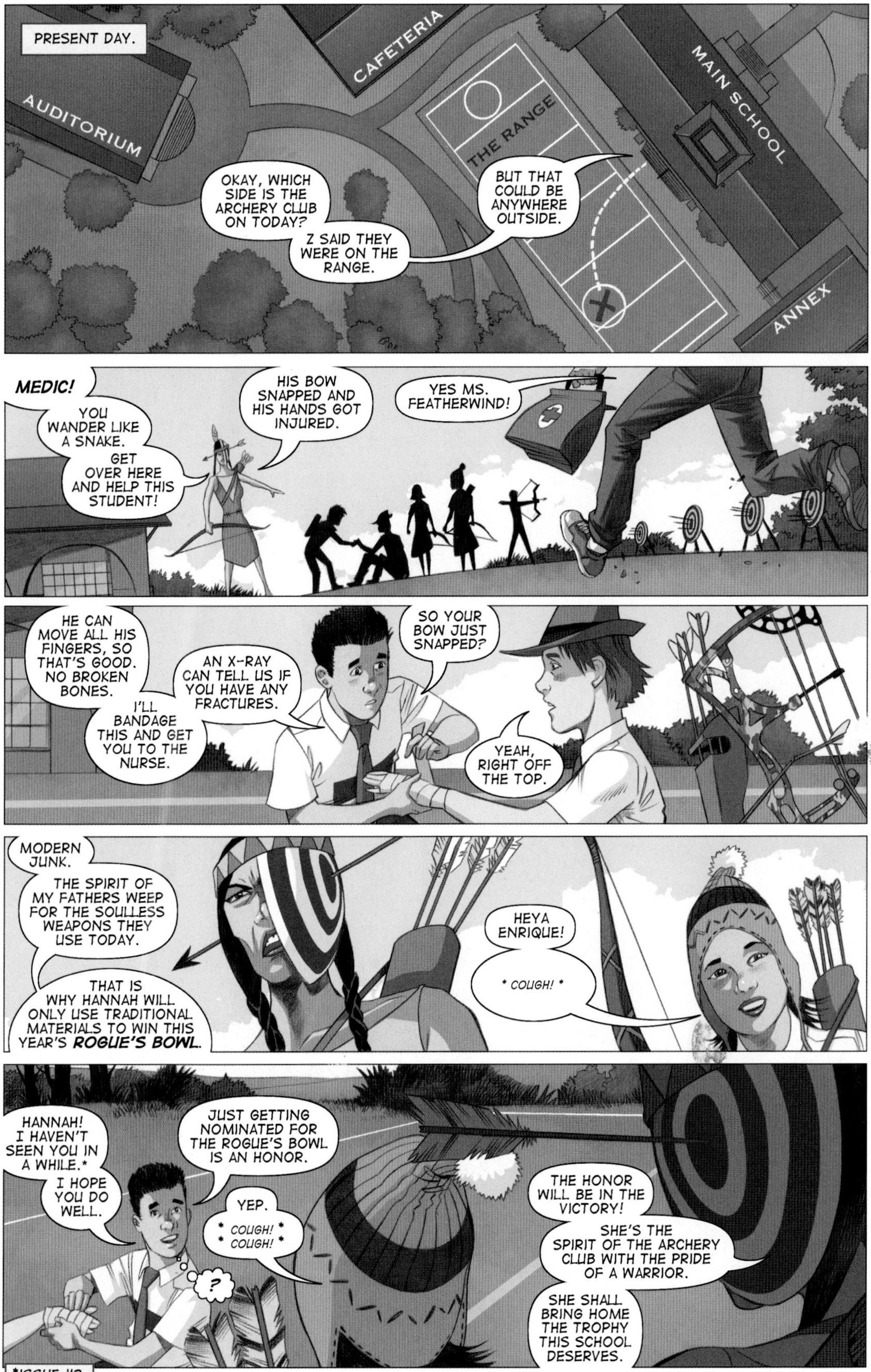
PRESENT DAY.
AUDITORIUM
CAFETERIA
THE RANGE
MAIN SCHOOL
ANNEX
OKAY, WHICH SIDE IS THE ARCHERY CLUB ON TODAY?
Z SAID THEY WERE ON THE RANGE.
BUT THAT COULD BE ANYWHERE OUTSIDE.
MEDIC!
YOU WANDER LIKE A SNAKE.
GET OVER HERE AND HELP THIS STUDENT!
HIS BOW SNAPPED AND HIS HANDS GOT INJURED.
YES MS. FEATHERWIND!
HE CAN MOVE ALL HIS FINGERS, SO THAT'S GOOD. NO BROKEN BONES.
I'LL BANDAGE THIS AND GET YOU TO THE NURSE.
AN X-RAY CAN TELL US IF YOU HAVE ANY FRACTURES.
SO YOUR BOW JUST SNAPPED?
YEAH, RIGHT OFF THE TOP.
MODERN JUNK.
THE SPIRIT OF MY FATHERS WEEP FOR THE SOULLESS WEAPONS THEY USE TODAY.
THAT IS WHY HANNAH WILL ONLY USE TRADITIONAL MATERIALS TO WIN THIS YEAR'S ROGUE'S BOWL.
HEYA ENRIQUE!
* COUGH! *
HANNAH! I HAVEN'T SEEN YOU IN A WHILE.*
I HOPE YOU DO WELL.
JUST GETTING NOMINATED FOR THE ROGUE'S BOWL IS AN HONOR.
?
YEP.
* COUGH! * * COUGH! *
THE HONOR WILL BE IN THE VICTORY!
SHE'S THE SPIRIT OF THE ARCHERY CLUB WITH THE PRIDE OF A WARRIOR.
SHE SHALL BRING HOME THE TROPHY THIS SCHOOL DESERVES.

*ISSUE #2.

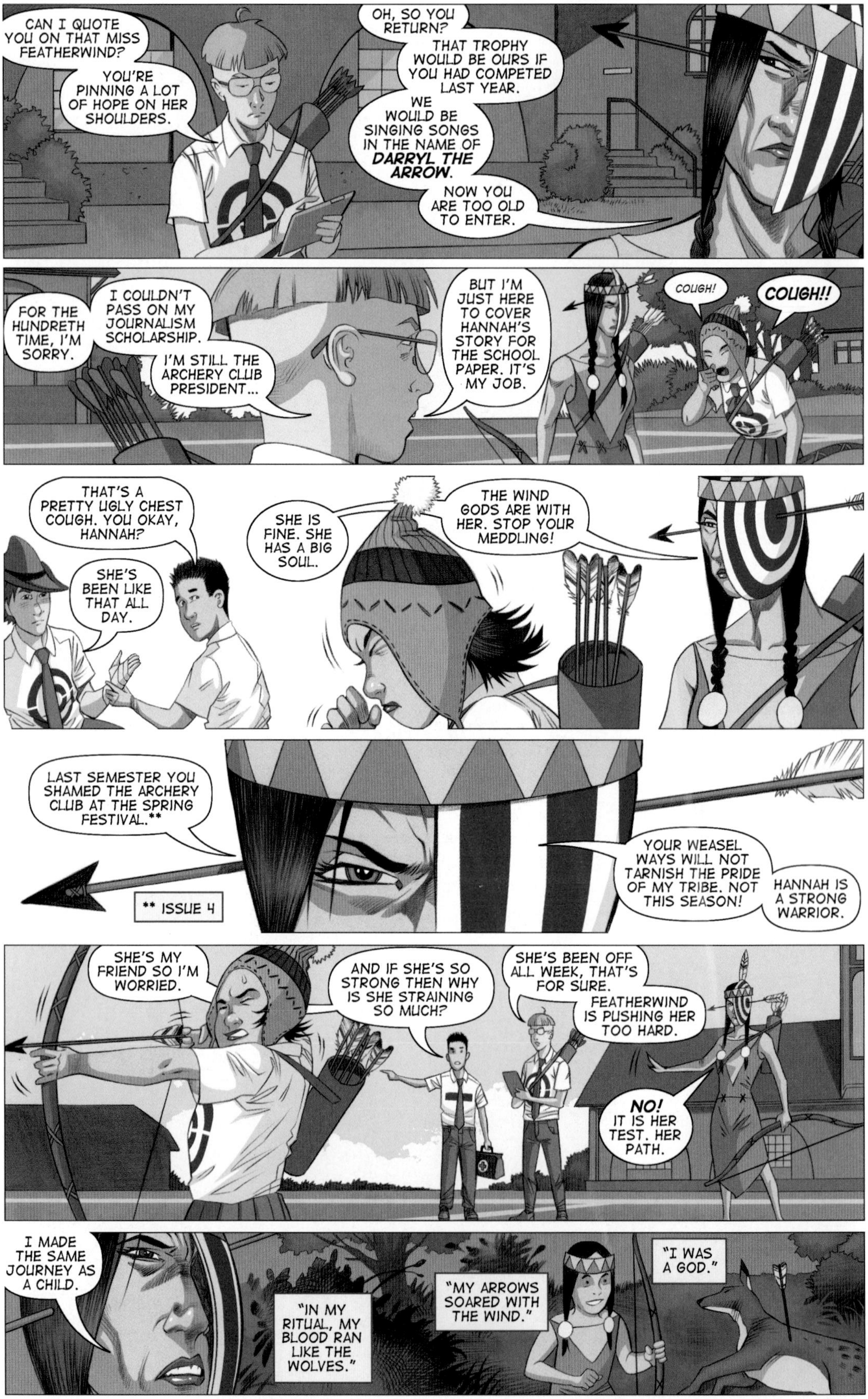
CAN I QUOTE YOU ON THAT MISS FEATHERWIND?
YOU'RE PINNING A LOT OF HOPE ON HER SHOULDERS.
OH, SO YOU RETURN?
THAT TROPHY WOULD BE OURS IF YOU HAD COMPETED LAST YEAR.
WE WOULD BE SINGING SONGS IN THE NAME OF DARRYL THE ARROW.
NOW YOU ARE TOO OLD TO ENTER.
FOR THE HUNDRETH TIME, I'M SORRY.
I COULDN'T PASS ON MY JOURNALISM SCHOLARSHIP.
I'M STILL THE ARCHERY CLUB PRESIDENT...
BUT I'M JUST HERE TO COVER HANNAH'S STORY FOR THE SCHOOL PAPER. IT'S MY JOB.
COUGH!
COUGH!!
THAT'S A PRETTY UGLY CHEST COUGH. YOU OKAY, HANNAH?
SHE'S BEEN LIKE THAT ALL DAY.
SHE IS FINE. SHE HAS A BIG SOUL.
THE WIND GODS ARE WITH HER. STOP YOUR MEDDLING!
LAST SEMESTER YOU SHAMED THE ARCHERY CLUB AT THE SPRING FESTIVAL.**
** ISSUE 4
YOUR WEASEL WAYS WILL NOT TARNISH THE PRIDE OF MY TRIBE. NOT THIS SEASON!
HANNAH IS A STRONG WARRIOR.
SHE'S MY FRIEND SO I'M WORRIED.
AND IF SHE'S SO STRONG THEN WHY IS SHE STRAINING SO MUCH?
SHE'S BEEN OFF ALL WEEK, THAT'S FOR SURE.
FEATHERWIND IS PUSHING HER TOO HARD.
NO! IT IS HER TEST. HER PATH.
I MADE THE SAME JOURNEY AS A CHILD.
"IN MY RITUAL, MY BLOOD RAN LIKE THE WOLVES."
"MY ARROWS SOARED WITH THE WIND."
"I WAS A GOD."

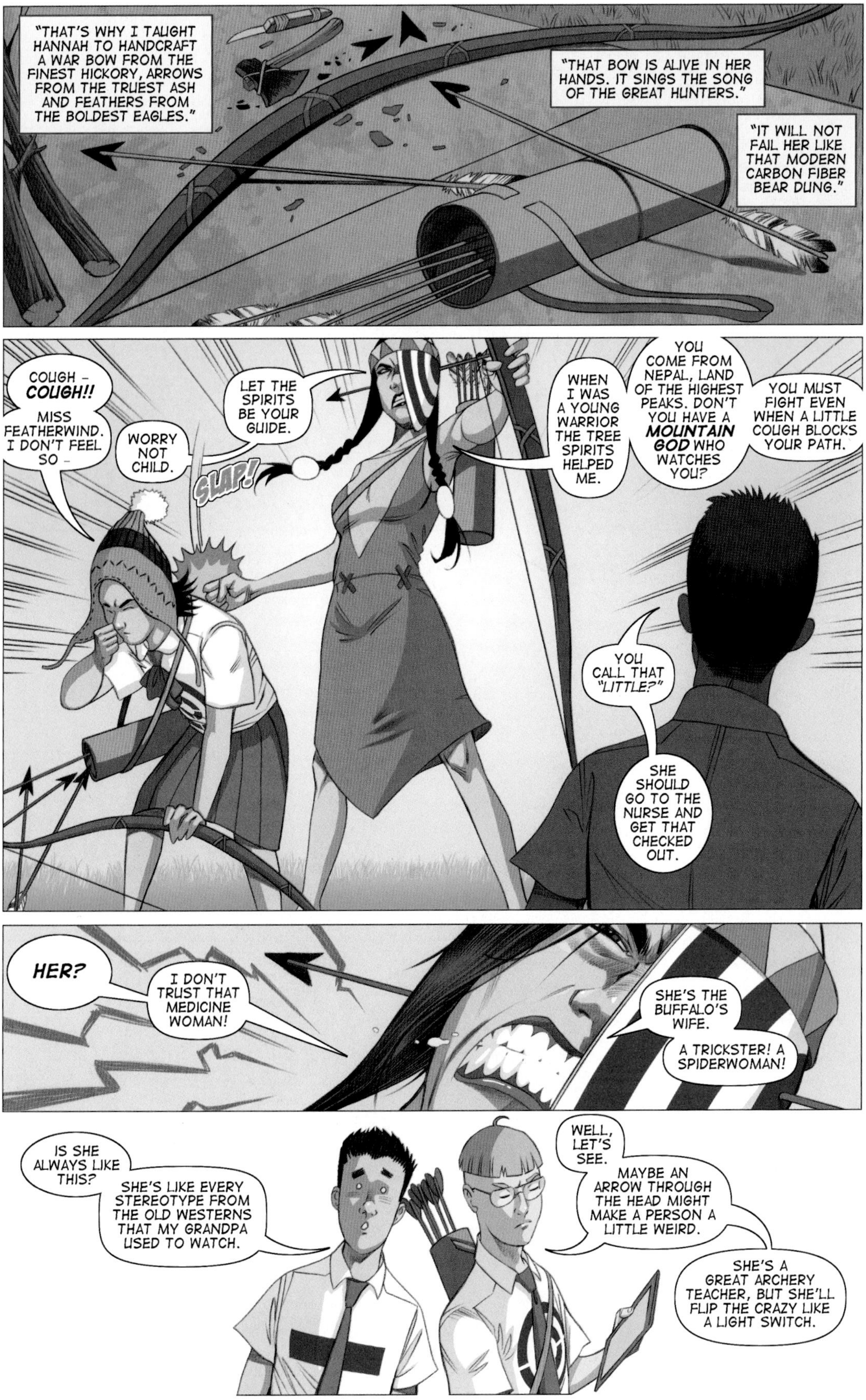
"THAT'S WHY I TAUGHT HANNAH TO HANDCRAFT A WAR BOW FROM THE FINEST HICKORY, ARROWS FROM THE TRUEST ASH AND FEATHERS FROM THE BOLDEST EAGLES."
"THAT BOW IS ALIVE IN HER HANDS. IT SINGS THE SONG OF THE GREAT HUNTERS."
"IT WILL NOT FAIL HER LIKE THAT MODERN CARBON FIBER BEAR DUNG."
COUGH – COUGH!!
MISS FEATHERWIND. I DON'T FEEL SO –
WORRY NOT CHILD.
LET THE SPIRITS BE YOUR GUIDE.
SLAP!
WHEN I WAS A YOUNG WARRIOR THE TREE SPIRITS HELPED ME.
YOU COME FROM NEPAL, LAND OF THE HIGHEST PEAKS. DON'T YOU HAVE A MOUNTAIN GOD WHO WATCHES YOU?
YOU MUST FIGHT EVEN WHEN A LITTLE COUGH BLOCKS YOUR PATH.
YOU CALL THAT "LITTLE?"
SHE SHOULD GO TO THE NURSE AND GET THAT CHECKED OUT.
HER?
I DON'T TRUST THAT MEDICINE WOMAN!
SHE'S THE BUFFALO'S WIFE.
A TRICKSTER! A SPIDERWOMAN!
IS SHE ALWAYS LIKE THIS?
SHE'S LIKE EVERY STEREOTYPE FROM THE OLD WESTERNS THAT MY GRANDPA USED TO WATCH.
WELL, LET'S SEE.
MAYBE AN ARROW THROUGH THE HEAD MIGHT MAKE A PERSON A LITTLE WEIRD.
SHE'S A GREAT ARCHERY TEACHER, BUT SHE'LL FLIP THE CRAZY LIKE A LIGHT SWITCH.

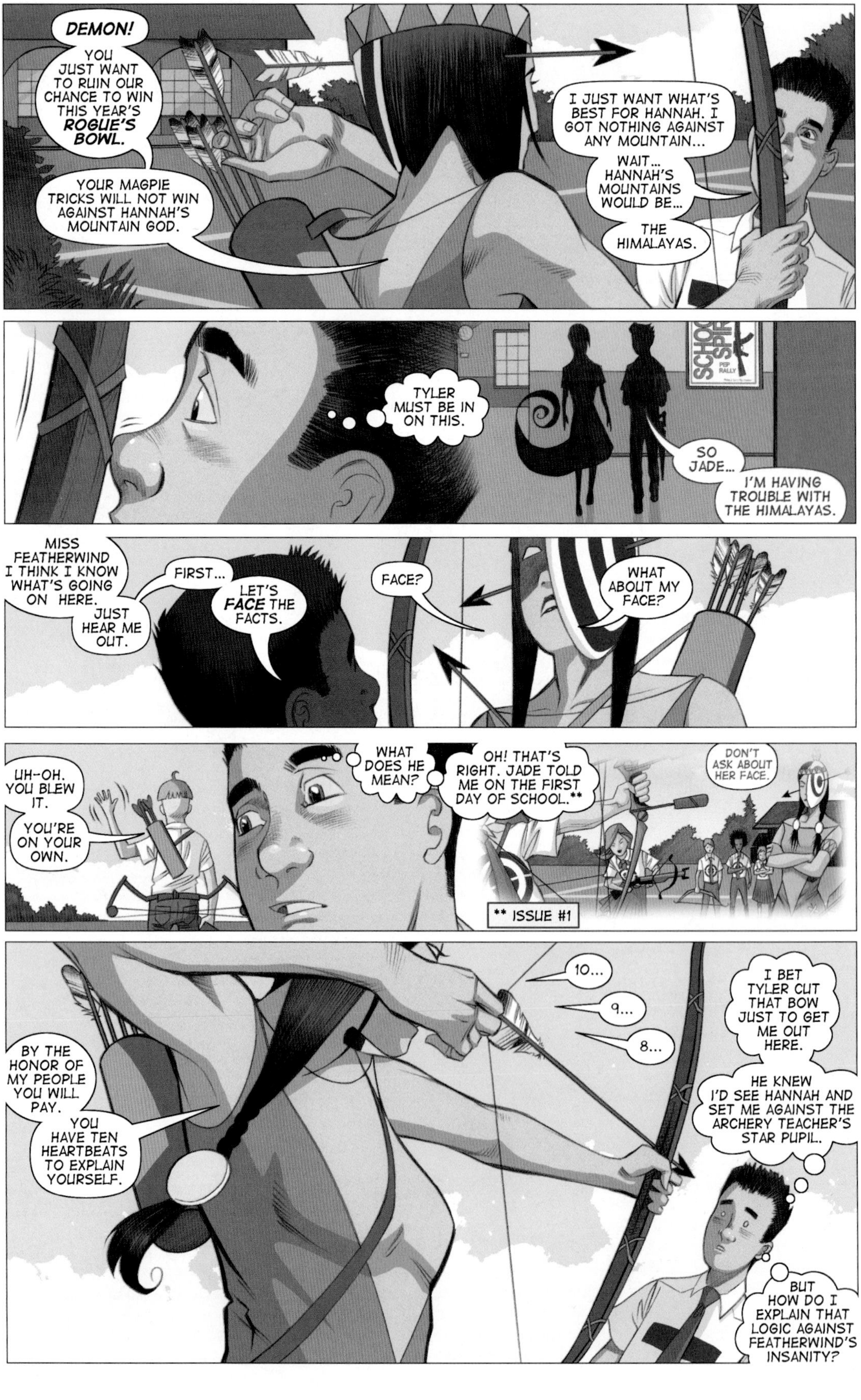
DEMON!
YOU JUST WANT TO RUIN OUR CHANCE TO WIN THIS YEAR'S ROGUE'S BOWL.
YOUR MAGPIE TRICKS WILL NOT WIN AGAINST HANNAH'S MOUNTAIN GOD.
I JUST WANT WHAT'S BEST FOR HANNAH. I GOT NOTHING AGAINST ANY MOUNTAIN...
WAIT... HANNAH'S MOUNTAINS WOULD BE...
THE HIMALAYAS.
TYLER MUST BE IN ON THIS.
SO JADE...
I'M HAVING TROUBLE WITH THE HIMALAYAS.
MISS FEATHERWIND I THINK I KNOW WHAT'S GOING ON HERE.
JUST HEAR ME OUT.
FIRST...
LET'S FACE THE FACTS.
FACE?
WHAT ABOUT MY FACE?
UH-OH. YOU BLEW IT.
YOU'RE ON YOUR OWN.
WHAT DOES HE MEAN?
OH! THAT'S RIGHT. JADE TOLD ME ON THE FIRST DAY OF SCHOOL.**
DON'T ASK ABOUT HER FACE.
** ISSUE #1
10...
9...
8...
BY THE HONOR OF MY PEOPLE YOU WILL PAY.
YOU HAVE TEN HEARTBEATS TO EXPLAIN YOURSELF.
I BET TYLER CUT THAT BOW JUST TO GET ME OUT HERE.
HE KNEW I'D SEE HANNAH AND SET ME AGAINST THE ARCHERY TEACHER'S STAR PUPIL.
BUT HOW DO I EXPLAIN THAT LOGIC AGAINST FEATHERWIND'S INSANITY?

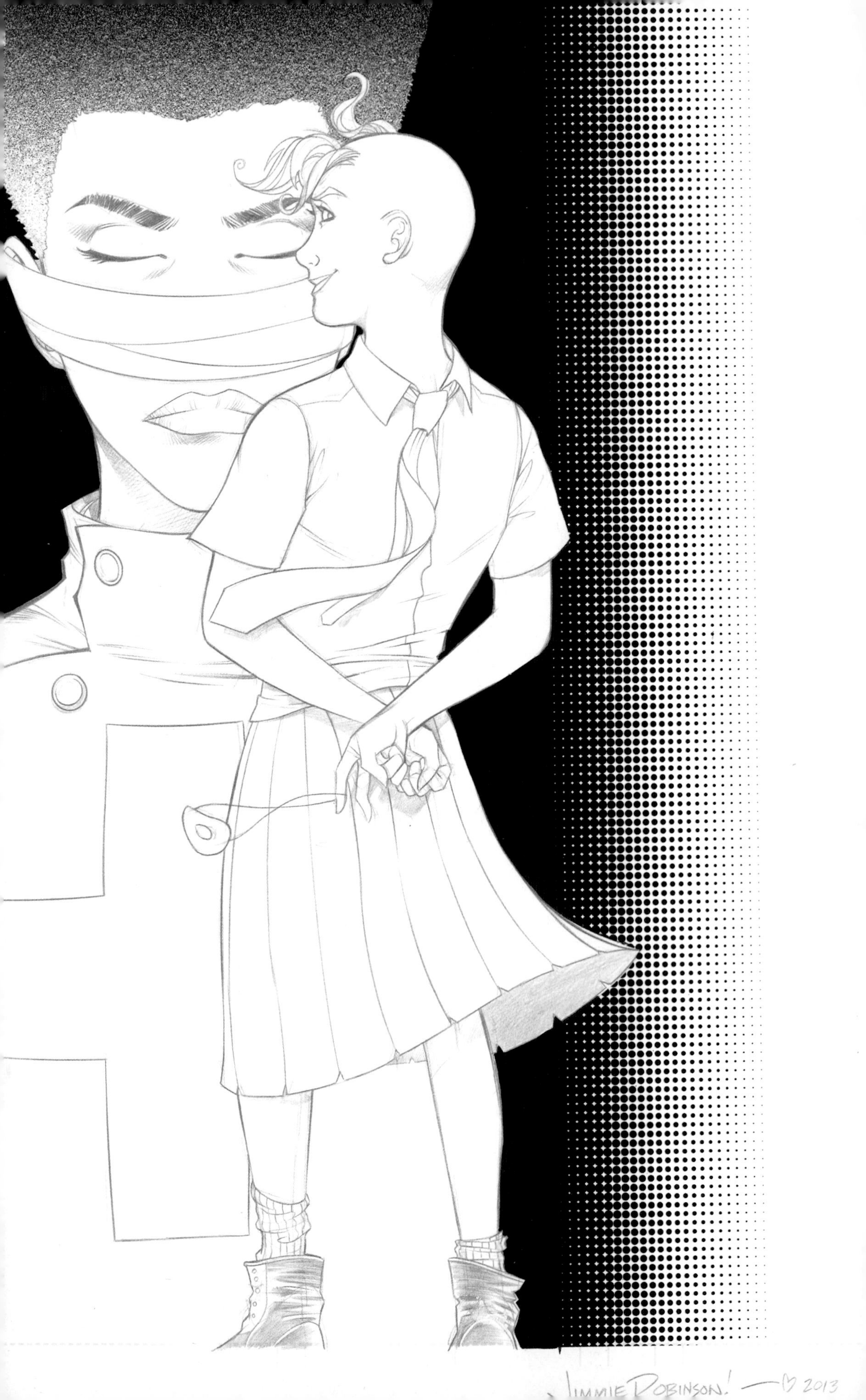
JIMMIE ROBINSON! 2013

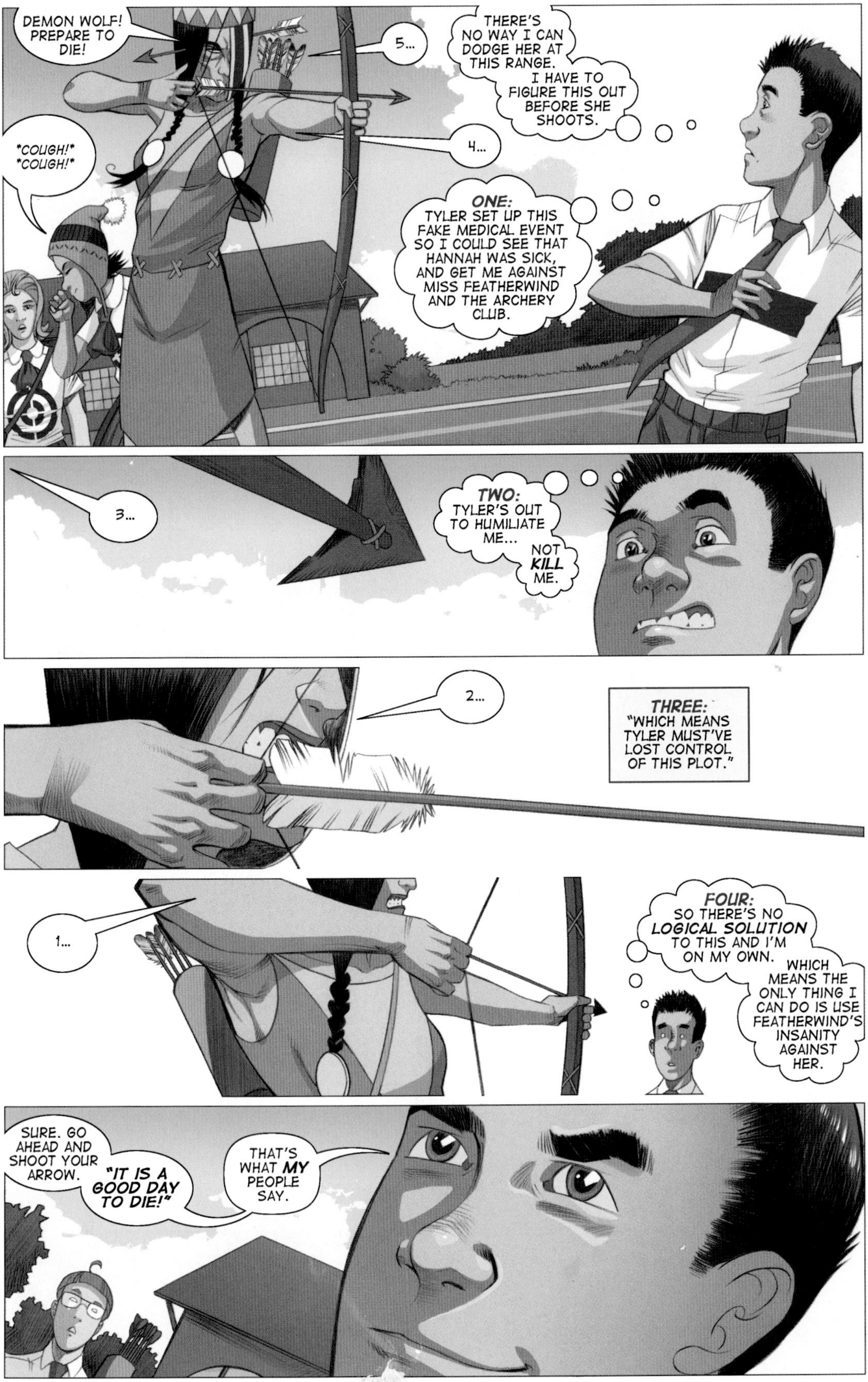
DEMON WOLF! PREPARE TO DIE!
5...
THERE'S NO WAY I CAN DODGE HER AT THIS RANGE.
I HAVE TO FIGURE THIS OUT BEFORE SHE SHOOTS.
COUGH! *COUGH!*
4...
ONE: TYLER SET UP THIS FAKE MEDICAL EVENT SO I COULD SEE THAT HANNAH WAS SICK, AND GET ME AGAINST MISS FEATHERWIND AND THE ARCHERY CLUB.
3...
TWO: TYLER'S OUT TO HUMILIATE ME...
NOT KILL ME.
2...
THREE: "WHICH MEANS TYLER MUST'VE LOST CONTROL OF THIS PLOT."
1...
FOUR: SO THERE'S NO LOGICAL SOLUTION TO THIS AND I'M ON MY OWN.
WHICH MEANS THE ONLY THING I CAN DO IS USE FEATHERWIND'S INSANITY AGAINST HER.
SURE. GO AHEAD AND SHOOT YOUR ARROW.
"IT IS A GOOD DAY TO DIE!"
THAT'S WHAT MY PEOPLE SAY.

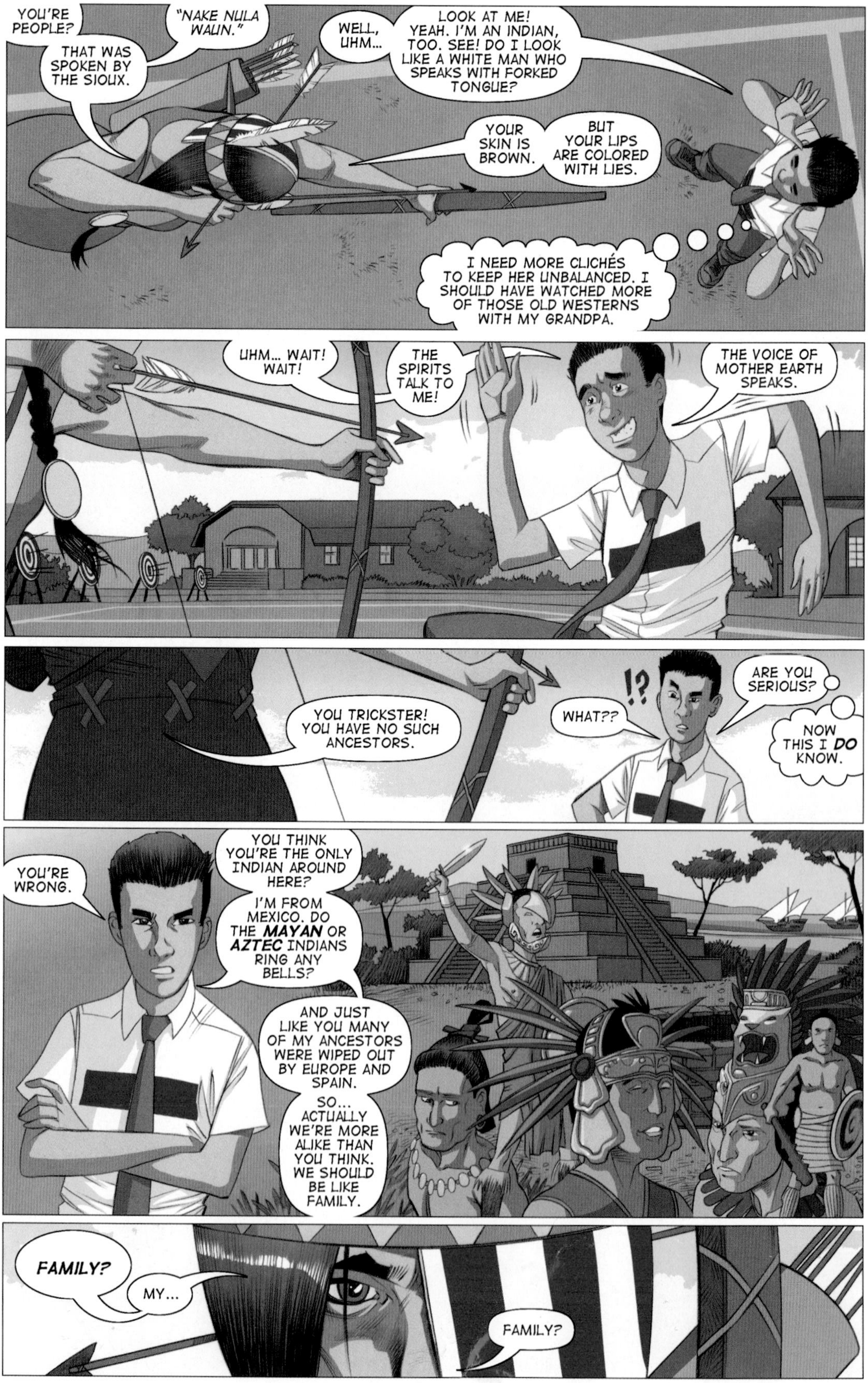
YOU'RE PEOPLE?
THAT WAS SPOKEN BY THE SIOUX.
"NAKE NULA WAUN."
WELL, UHM...
LOOK AT ME! YEAH. I'M AN INDIAN, TOO. SEE! DO I LOOK LIKE A WHITE MAN WHO SPEAKS WITH FORKED TONGUE?
YOUR SKIN IS BROWN.
BUT YOUR LIPS ARE COLORED WITH LIES.
I NEED MORE CLICHÉS TO KEEP HER UNBALANCED. I SHOULD HAVE WATCHED MORE OF THOSE OLD WESTERNS WITH MY GRANDPA.
UHM... WAIT! WAIT!
THE SPIRITS TALK TO ME!
THE VOICE OF MOTHER EARTH SPEAKS.
YOU TRICKSTER! YOU HAVE NO SUCH ANCESTORS.
!?
WHAT??
ARE YOU SERIOUS?
NOW THIS I *DO* KNOW.
YOU'RE WRONG.
YOU THINK YOU'RE THE ONLY INDIAN AROUND HERE?
I'M FROM MEXICO. DO THE ***MAYAN*** OR ***AZTEC*** INDIANS RING ANY BELLS?
AND JUST LIKE YOU MANY OF MY ANCESTORS WERE WIPED OUT BY EUROPE AND SPAIN.
SO... ACTUALLY WE'RE MORE ALIKE THAN YOU THINK. WE SHOULD BE LIKE FAMILY.
FAMILY?
MY...
FAMILY?

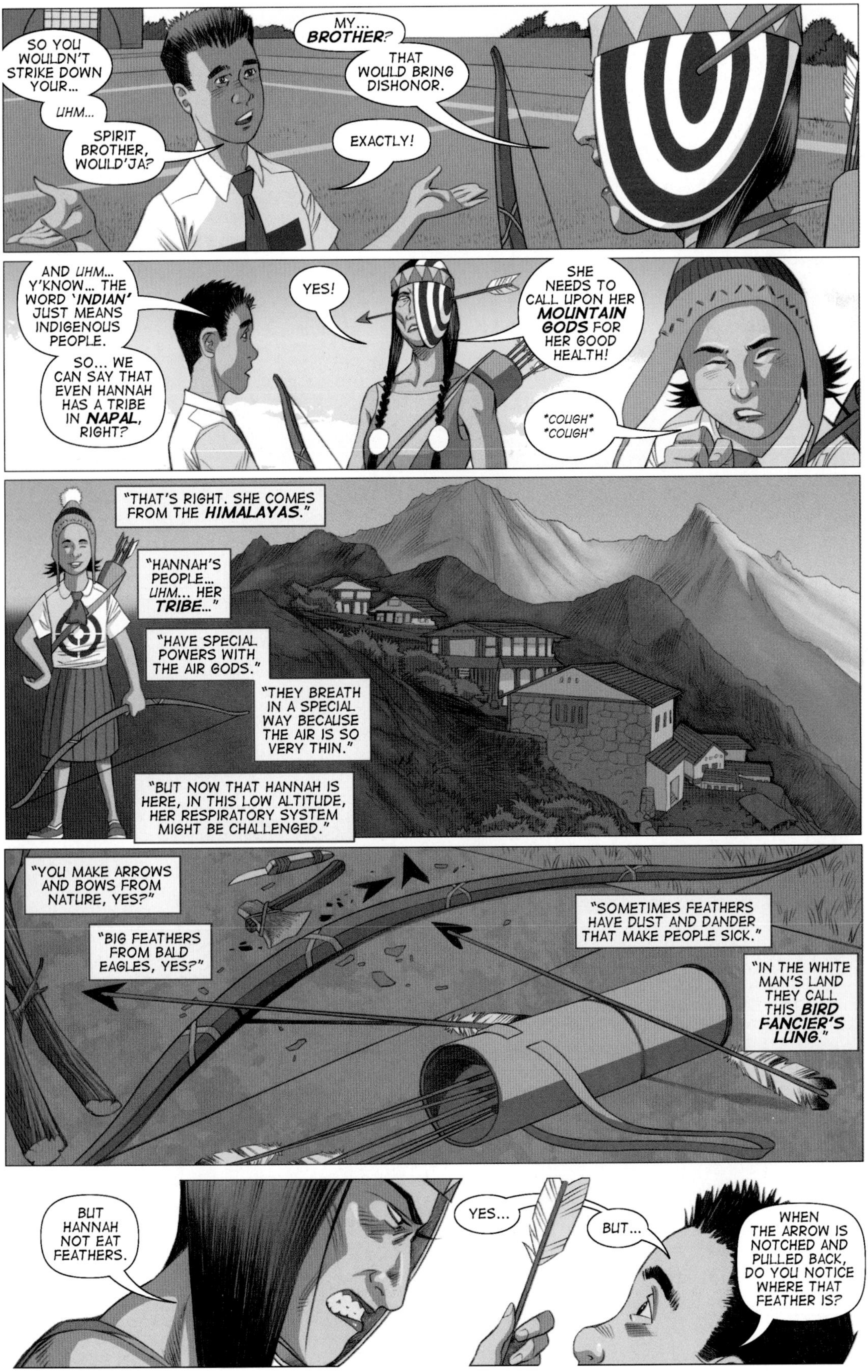
SO YOU WOULDN'T STRIKE DOWN YOUR...
UHM...
SPIRIT BROTHER, WOULD'JA?
MY... BROTHER?
THAT WOULD BRING DISHONOR.
EXACTLY!
AND UHM... Y'KNOW... THE WORD 'INDIAN' JUST MEANS INDIGENOUS PEOPLE.
SO... WE CAN SAY THAT EVEN HANNAH HAS A TRIBE IN NAPAL, RIGHT?
YES!
SHE NEEDS TO CALL UPON HER MOUNTAIN GODS FOR HER GOOD HEALTH!
COUGH *COUGH*
"THAT'S RIGHT. SHE COMES FROM THE HIMALAYAS."
"HANNAH'S PEOPLE... UHM... HER TRIBE..."
"HAVE SPECIAL POWERS WITH THE AIR GODS."
"THEY BREATH IN A SPECIAL WAY BECAUSE THE AIR IS SO VERY THIN."
"BUT NOW THAT HANNAH IS HERE, IN THIS LOW ALTITUDE, HER RESPIRATORY SYSTEM MIGHT BE CHALLENGED."
"YOU MAKE ARROWS AND BOWS FROM NATURE, YES?"
"BIG FEATHERS FROM BALD EAGLES, YES?"
"SOMETIMES FEATHERS HAVE DUST AND DANDER THAT MAKE PEOPLE SICK."
"IN THE WHITE MAN'S LAND THEY CALL THIS BIRD FANCIER'S LUNG."
BUT HANNAH NOT EAT FEATHERS.
YES...
BUT...
WHEN THE ARROW IS NOTCHED AND PULLED BACK, DO YOU NOTICE WHERE THAT FEATHER IS?

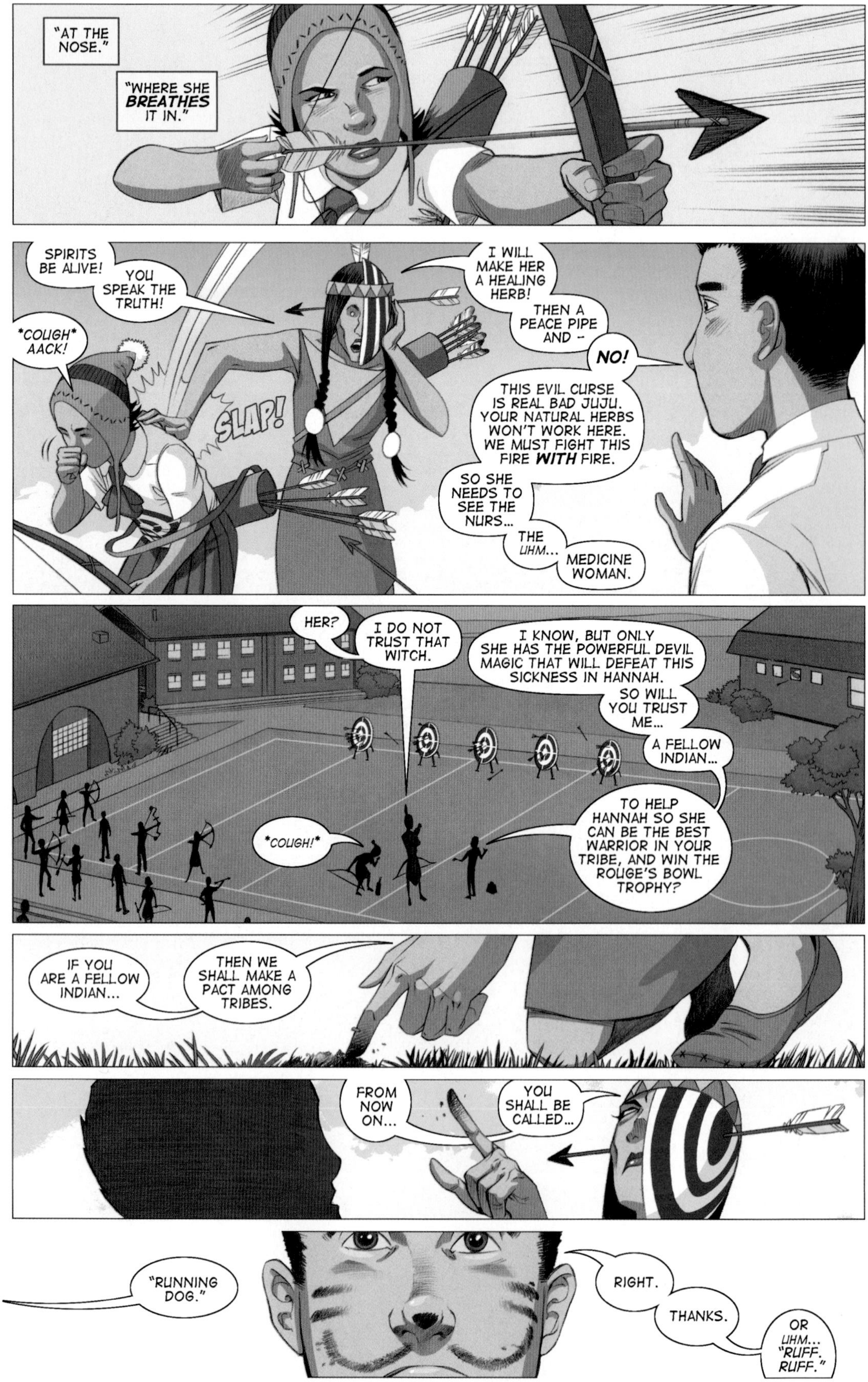
"AT THE NOSE."
"WHERE SHE BREATHES IT IN."
SPIRITS BE ALIVE!
YOU SPEAK THE TRUTH!
COUGH AACK!
I WILL MAKE HER A HEALING HERB!
THEN A PEACE PIPE AND –
NO!
SLAP!
THIS EVIL CURSE IS REAL BAD JUJU. YOUR NATURAL HERBS WON'T WORK HERE. WE MUST FIGHT THIS FIRE WITH FIRE.
SO SHE NEEDS TO SEE THE NURS...
THE UHM...
MEDICINE WOMAN.
HER?
I DO NOT TRUST THAT WITCH.
I KNOW, BUT ONLY SHE HAS THE POWERFUL DEVIL MAGIC THAT WILL DEFEAT THIS SICKNESS IN HANNAH.
SO WILL YOU TRUST ME...
A FELLOW INDIAN...
TO HELP HANNAH SO SHE CAN BE THE BEST WARRIOR IN YOUR TRIBE, AND WIN THE ROUGE'S BOWL TROPHY?
COUGH!
IF YOU ARE A FELLOW INDIAN...
THEN WE SHALL MAKE A PACT AMONG TRIBES.
FROM NOW ON...
YOU SHALL BE CALLED...
"RUNNING DOG."
RIGHT.
THANKS.
OR UHM... "RUFF. RUFF."

RIGHT.
SO...
UHM...
GUESS I'LL TAKE HANNAH TO SEE HER NOW.
COUGH! COUGH!
GO MY CHILDREN.
MAY YOUR FEET FIND THE POLLEN PATH, AND MAY YOUR HEART FIND THE BLESSING OF TSOHANOAI THE SUN BEARER.
....
NURSE'S OFFICE.
MEDIC
OBSERVE ALL SAFETY SIGNS
DON'T BE "THAT GUY"
I'M AMAZED YOU TALKED HER INTO IT.
I'VE BEEN HERE FOR YEARS AND I'VE NEVER HAD ONE OF HER ARCHERY STUDENTS INSIDE MY OFFICE.
WELL, I DID A LOT OF FAST TALKING, BUT IT WORKED.
THOUGH I FELT STUPID USING ALL THOSE CLICHE RACIAL STEREOTYPES.
HAS ANYONE TRIED TO REMOVE THAT ARROW OUT OF HER HEAD?
SHE WON'T LET ANYONE NEAR HER.
IT'S A MIRACLE SHE'S EVEN ALIVE.
BUT THE AFFECTS ON HER MIND ARE EXTREME.
MISS FEATHERWIND IS CONSIDERED THE MOST DANGEROUS OF ALL THE TEACHERS.
SAY THE WRONG WORD OR PHRASE...
AND SHE'LL TURN DEADLY.

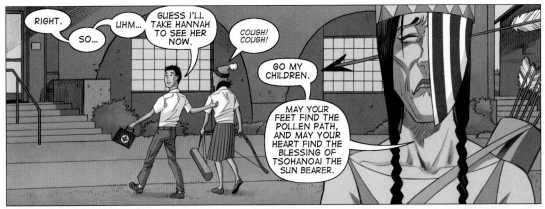

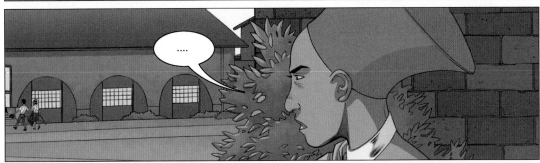

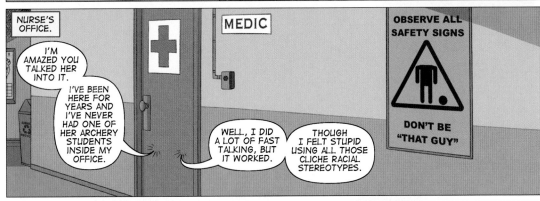

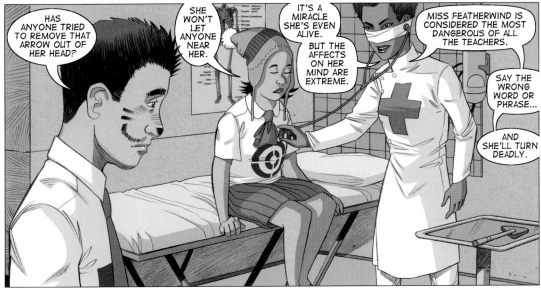

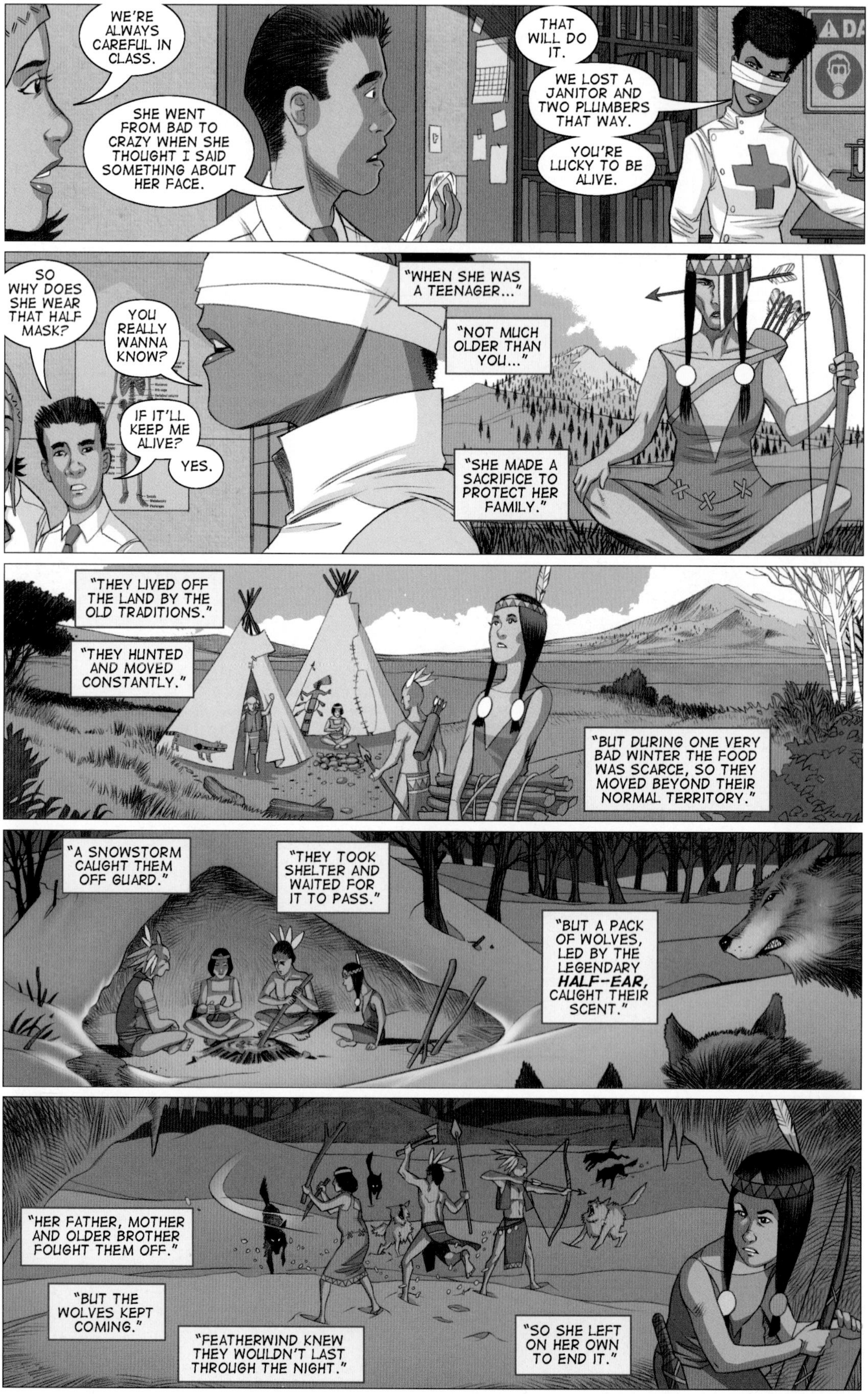
WE'RE ALWAYS CAREFUL IN CLASS.
SHE WENT FROM BAD TO CRAZY WHEN SHE THOUGHT I SAID SOMETHING ABOUT HER FACE.
THAT WILL DO IT.
WE LOST A JANITOR AND TWO PLUMBERS THAT WAY.
YOU'RE LUCKY TO BE ALIVE.
SO WHY DOES SHE WEAR THAT HALF MASK?
YOU REALLY WANNA KNOW?
IF IT'LL KEEP ME ALIVE?
YES.
"WHEN SHE WAS A TEENAGER..."
"NOT MUCH OLDER THAN YOU..."
"SHE MADE A SACRIFICE TO PROTECT HER FAMILY."
"THEY LIVED OFF THE LAND BY THE OLD TRADITIONS."
"THEY HUNTED AND MOVED CONSTANTLY."
"BUT DURING ONE VERY BAD WINTER THE FOOD WAS SCARCE, SO THEY MOVED BEYOND THEIR NORMAL TERRITORY."
"A SNOWSTORM CAUGHT THEM OFF GUARD."
"THEY TOOK SHELTER AND WAITED FOR IT TO PASS."
"BUT A PACK OF WOLVES, LED BY THE LEGENDARY HALF-EAR, CAUGHT THEIR SCENT."
"HER FATHER, MOTHER AND OLDER BROTHER FOUGHT THEM OFF."
"BUT THE WOLVES KEPT COMING."
"FEATHERWIND KNEW THEY WOULDN'T LAST THROUGH THE NIGHT."
"SO SHE LEFT ON HER OWN TO END IT."

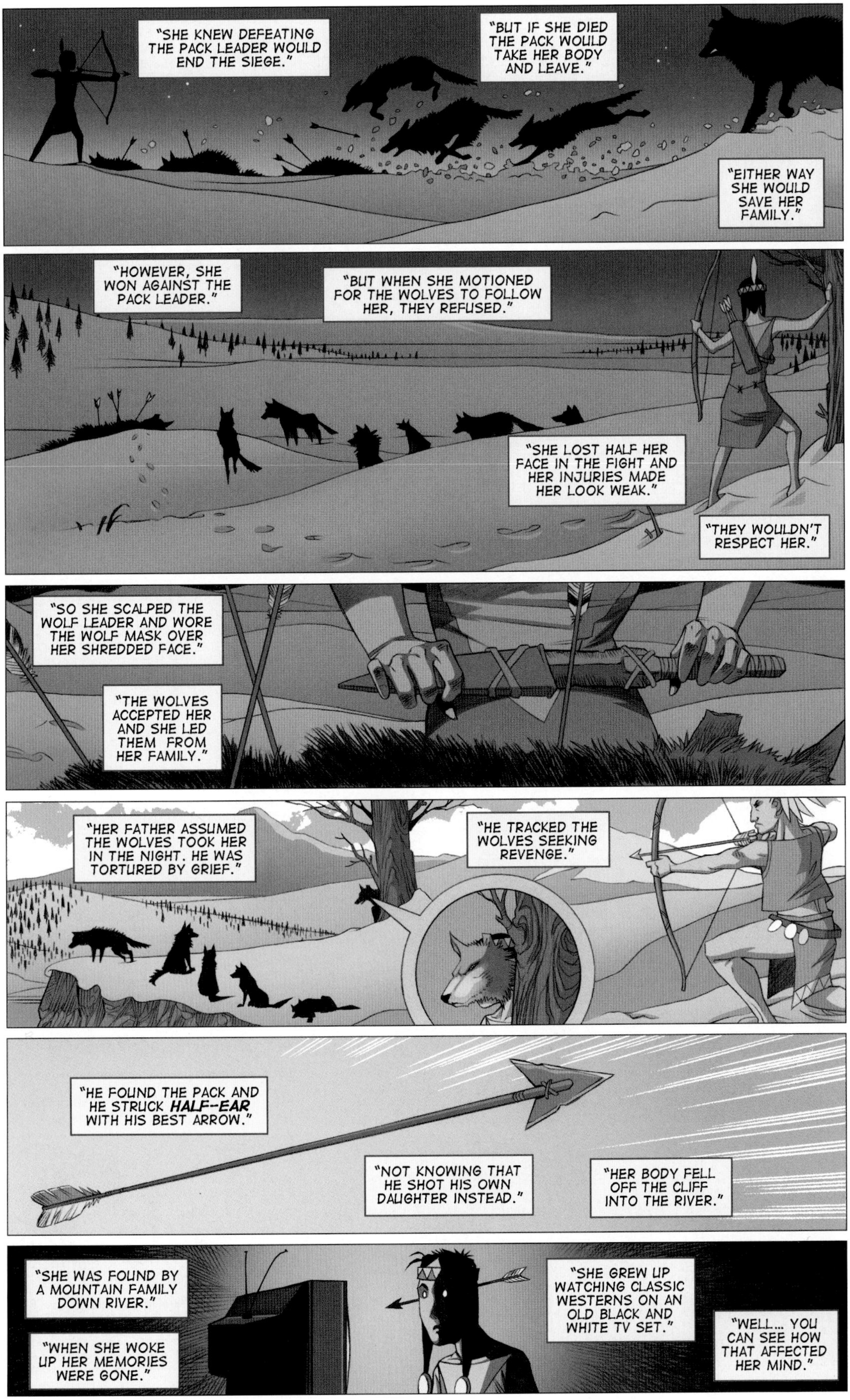
"SHE KNEW DEFEATING THE PACK LEADER WOULD END THE SIEGE."
"BUT IF SHE DIED THE PACK WOULD TAKE HER BODY AND LEAVE."
"EITHER WAY SHE WOULD SAVE HER FAMILY."
"HOWEVER, SHE WON AGAINST THE PACK LEADER."
"BUT WHEN SHE MOTIONED FOR THE WOLVES TO FOLLOW HER, THEY REFUSED."
"SHE LOST HALF HER FACE IN THE FIGHT AND HER INJURIES MADE HER LOOK WEAK."
"THEY WOULDN'T RESPECT HER."
"SO SHE SCALPED THE WOLF LEADER AND WORE THE WOLF MASK OVER HER SHREDDED FACE."
"THE WOLVES ACCEPTED HER AND SHE LED THEM FROM HER FAMILY."
"HER FATHER ASSUMED THE WOLVES TOOK HER IN THE NIGHT. HE WAS TORTURED BY GRIEF."
"HE TRACKED THE WOLVES SEEKING REVENGE."
"HE FOUND THE PACK AND HE STRUCK HALF--EAR WITH HIS BEST ARROW."
"NOT KNOWING THAT HE SHOT HIS OWN DAUGHTER INSTEAD."
"HER BODY FELL OFF THE CLIFF INTO THE RIVER."
"SHE WAS FOUND BY A MOUNTAIN FAMILY DOWN RIVER."
"WHEN SHE WOKE UP HER MEMORIES WERE GONE."
"SHE GREW UP WATCHING CLASSIC WESTERNS ON AN OLD BLACK AND WHITE TV SET."
"WELL... YOU CAN SEE HOW THAT AFFECTED HER MIND."

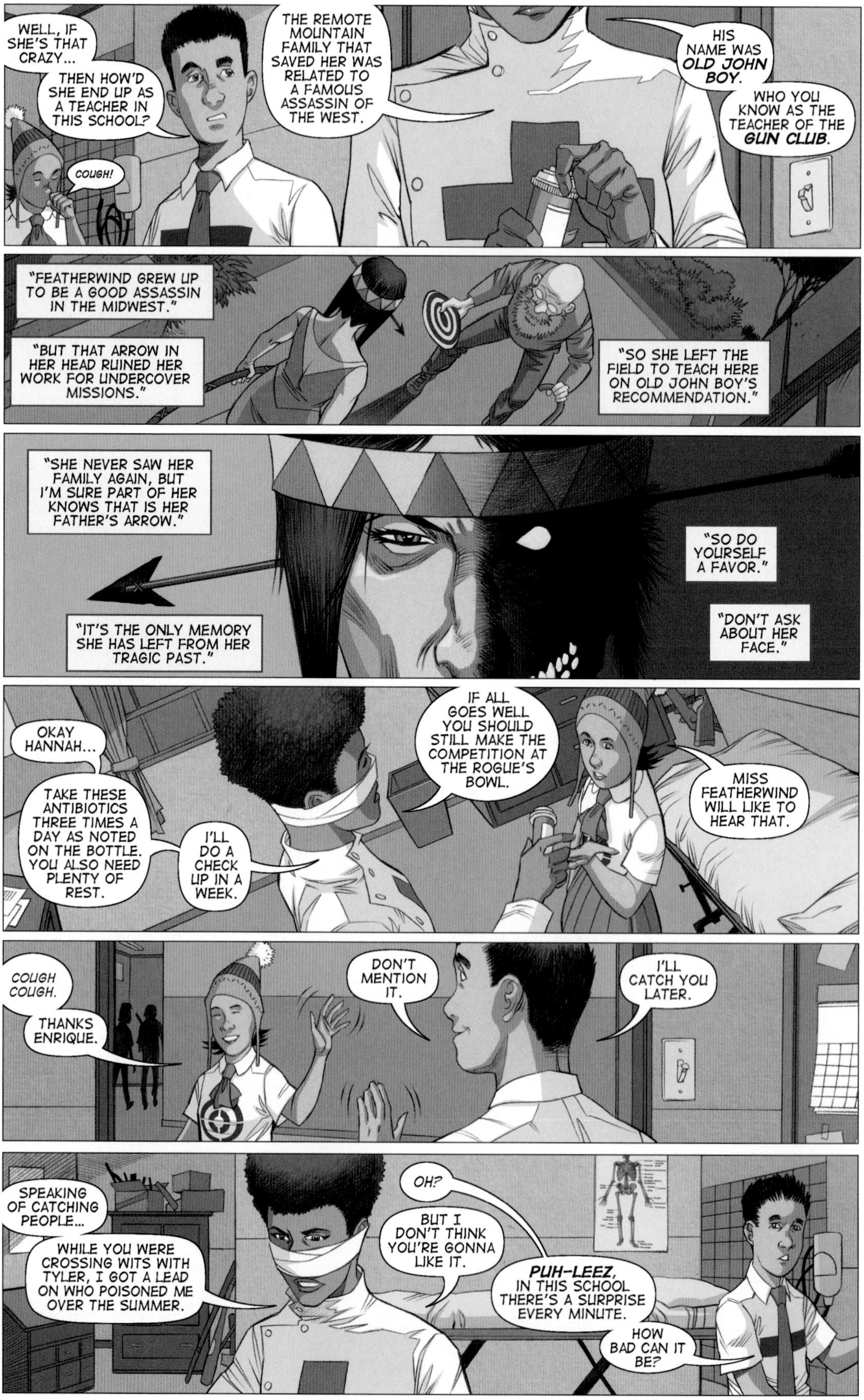
WELL, IF SHE'S THAT CRAZY...
THEN HOW'D SHE END UP AS A TEACHER IN THIS SCHOOL?
COUGH!
THE REMOTE MOUNTAIN FAMILY THAT SAVED HER WAS RELATED TO A FAMOUS ASSASSIN OF THE WEST.
HIS NAME WAS OLD JOHN BOY.
WHO YOU KNOW AS THE TEACHER OF THE GUN CLUB.
"FEATHERWIND GREW UP TO BE A GOOD ASSASSIN IN THE MIDWEST."
"BUT THAT ARROW IN HER HEAD RUINED HER WORK FOR UNDERCOVER MISSIONS."
"SO SHE LEFT THE FIELD TO TEACH HERE ON OLD JOHN BOY'S RECOMMENDATION."
"SHE NEVER SAW HER FAMILY AGAIN, BUT I'M SURE PART OF HER KNOWS THAT IS HER FATHER'S ARROW."
"IT'S THE ONLY MEMORY SHE HAS LEFT FROM HER TRAGIC PAST."
"SO DO YOURSELF A FAVOR."
"DON'T ASK ABOUT HER FACE."
OKAY HANNAH...
TAKE THESE ANTIBIOTICS THREE TIMES A DAY AS NOTED ON THE BOTTLE. YOU ALSO NEED PLENTY OF REST.
I'LL DO A CHECK UP IN A WEEK.
IF ALL GOES WELL YOU SHOULD STILL MAKE THE COMPETITION AT THE ROGUE'S BOWL.
MISS FEATHERWIND WILL LIKE TO HEAR THAT.
COUGH COUGH.
THANKS ENRIQUE.
DON'T MENTION IT.
I'LL CATCH YOU LATER.
SPEAKING OF CATCHING PEOPLE...
WHILE YOU WERE CROSSING WITS WITH TYLER, I GOT A LEAD ON WHO POISONED ME OVER THE SUMMER.
OH?
BUT I DON'T THINK YOU'RE GONNA LIKE IT.
PUH-LEEZ, IN THIS SCHOOL THERE'S A SURPRISE EVERY MINUTE.
HOW BAD CAN IT BE?

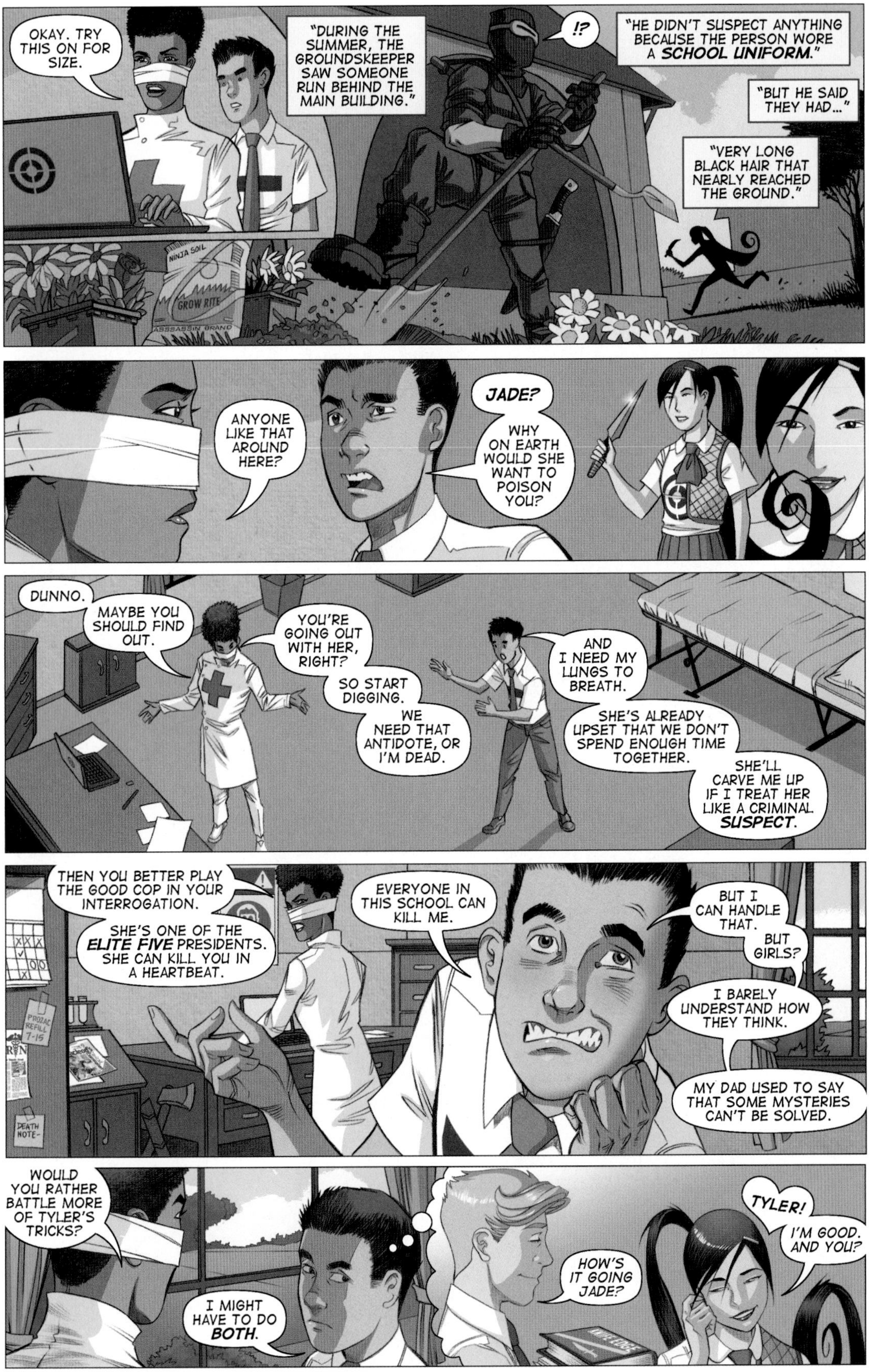
OKAY. TRY THIS ON FOR SIZE.
"DURING THE SUMMER, THE GROUNDSKEEPER SAW SOMEONE RUN BEHIND THE MAIN BUILDING."
!?
"HE DIDN'T SUSPECT ANYTHING BECAUSE THE PERSON WORE A SCHOOL UNIFORM."
"BUT HE SAID THEY HAD..."
"VERY LONG BLACK HAIR THAT NEARLY REACHED THE GROUND."
NINJA SOIL
GROW RITE
ASSSASSIN BRAND
ANYONE LIKE THAT AROUND HERE?
JADE?
WHY ON EARTH WOULD SHE WANT TO POISON YOU?
DUNNO.
MAYBE YOU SHOULD FIND OUT.
YOU'RE GOING OUT WITH HER, RIGHT?
SO START DIGGING.
WE NEED THAT ANTIDOTE, OR I'M DEAD.
AND I NEED MY LUNGS TO BREATH.
SHE'S ALREADY UPSET THAT WE DON'T SPEND ENOUGH TIME TOGETHER.
SHE'LL CARVE ME UP IF I TREAT HER LIKE A CRIMINAL SUSPECT.
THEN YOU BETTER PLAY THE GOOD COP IN YOUR INTERROGATION.
SHE'S ONE OF THE ELITE FIVE PRESIDENTS. SHE CAN KILL YOU IN A HEARTBEAT.
EVERYONE IN THIS SCHOOL CAN KILL ME.
BUT I CAN HANDLE THAT.
BUT GIRLS?
I BARELY UNDERSTAND HOW THEY THINK.
MY DAD USED TO SAY THAT SOME MYSTERIES CAN'T BE SOLVED.
PROZAC REFILL 7-15
DEATH NOTE-
WOULD YOU RATHER BATTLE MORE OF TYLER'S TRICKS?
I MIGHT HAVE TO DO BOTH.
HOW'S IT GOING JADE?
TYLER!
I'M GOOD. AND YOU?

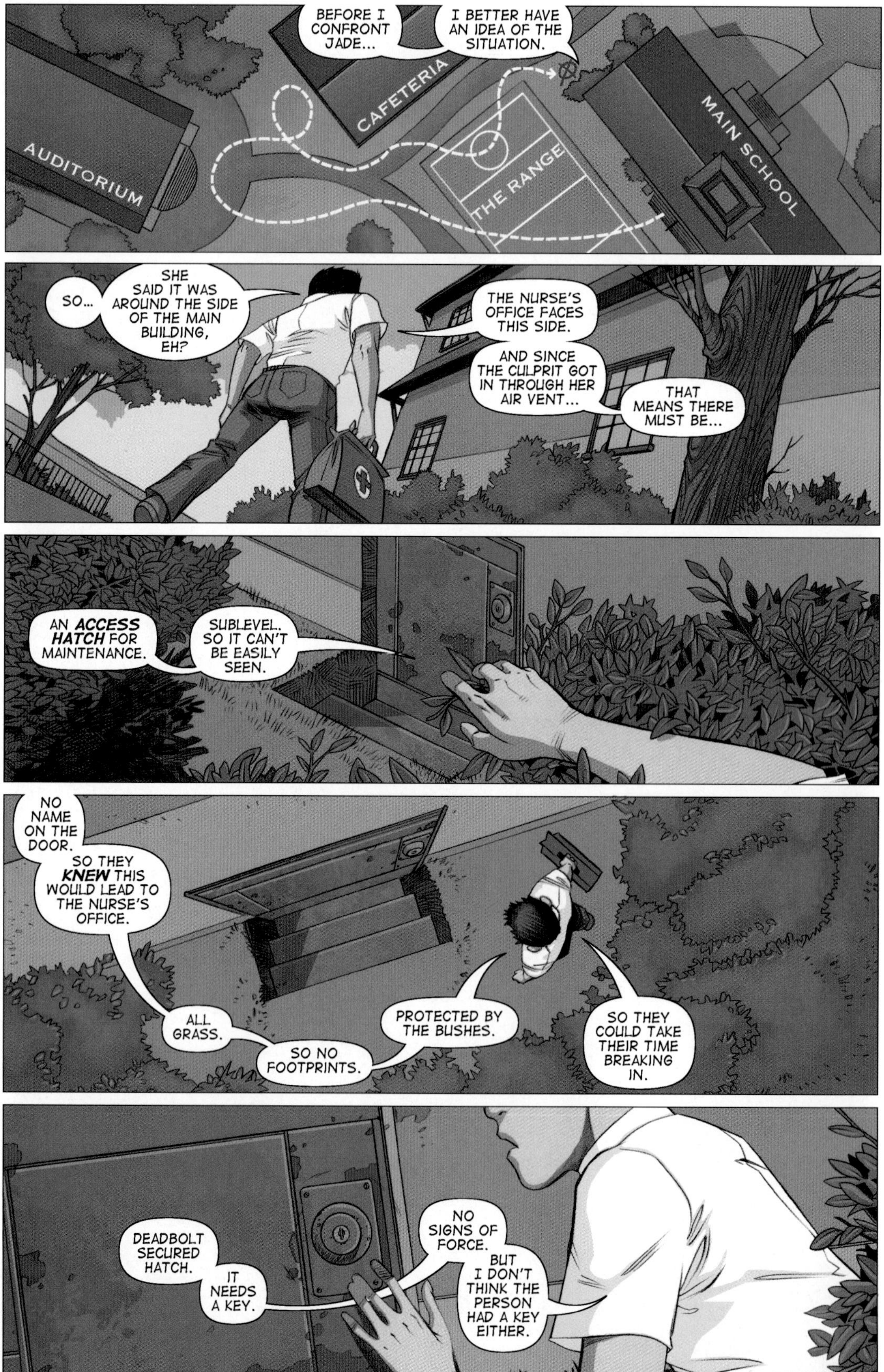
BEFORE I CONFRONT JADE...
I BETTER HAVE AN IDEA OF THE SITUATION.
AUDITORIUM
CAFETERIA
THE RANGE
MAIN SCHOOL
SO...
SHE SAID IT WAS AROUND THE SIDE OF THE MAIN BUILDING, EH?
THE NURSE'S OFFICE FACES THIS SIDE.
AND SINCE THE CULPRIT GOT IN THROUGH HER AIR VENT...
THAT MEANS THERE MUST BE...
AN ACCESS HATCH FOR MAINTENANCE.
SUBLEVEL. SO IT CAN'T BE EASILY SEEN.
NO NAME ON THE DOOR.
SO THEY KNEW THIS WOULD LEAD TO THE NURSE'S OFFICE.
ALL GRASS.
SO NO FOOTPRINTS.
PROTECTED BY THE BUSHES.
SO THEY COULD TAKE THEIR TIME BREAKING IN.
DEADBOLT SECURED HATCH.
IT NEEDS A KEY.
NO SIGNS OF FORCE.
BUT I DON'T THINK THE PERSON HAD A KEY EITHER.

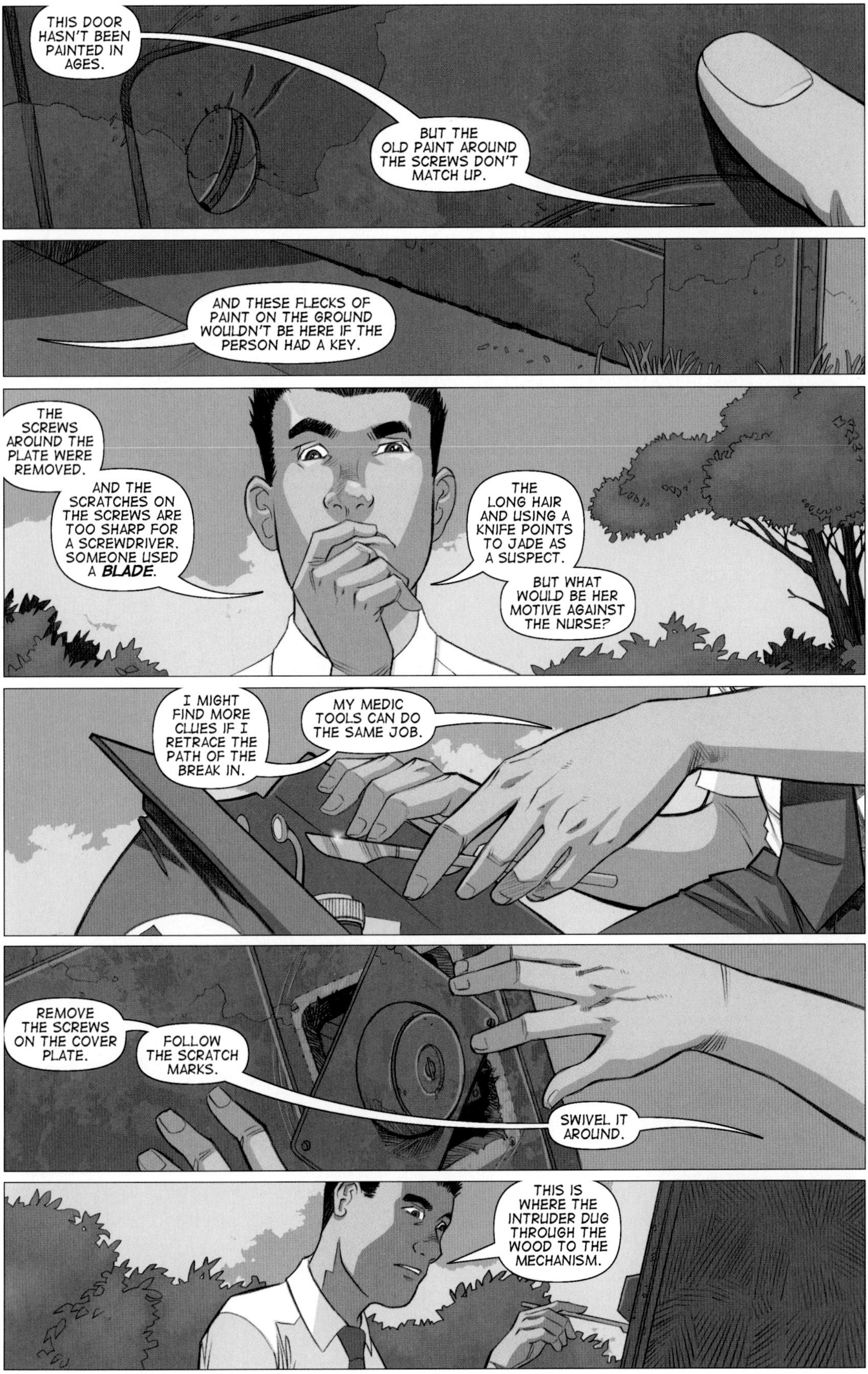
THIS DOOR HASN'T BEEN PAINTED IN AGES.
BUT THE OLD PAINT AROUND THE SCREWS DON'T MATCH UP.
AND THESE FLECKS OF PAINT ON THE GROUND WOULDN'T BE HERE IF THE PERSON HAD A KEY.
THE SCREWS AROUND THE PLATE WERE REMOVED.
AND THE SCRATCHES ON THE SCREWS ARE TOO SHARP FOR A SCREWDRIVER. SOMEONE USED A **BLADE**.
THE LONG HAIR AND USING A KNIFE POINTS TO JADE AS A SUSPECT.
BUT WHAT WOULD BE HER MOTIVE AGAINST THE NURSE?
I MIGHT FIND MORE CLUES IF I RETRACE THE PATH OF THE BREAK IN.
MY MEDIC TOOLS CAN DO THE SAME JOB.
REMOVE THE SCREWS ON THE COVER PLATE.
FOLLOW THE SCRATCH MARKS.
SWIVEL IT AROUND.
THIS IS WHERE THE INTRUDER DUG THROUGH THE WOOD TO THE MECHANISM.

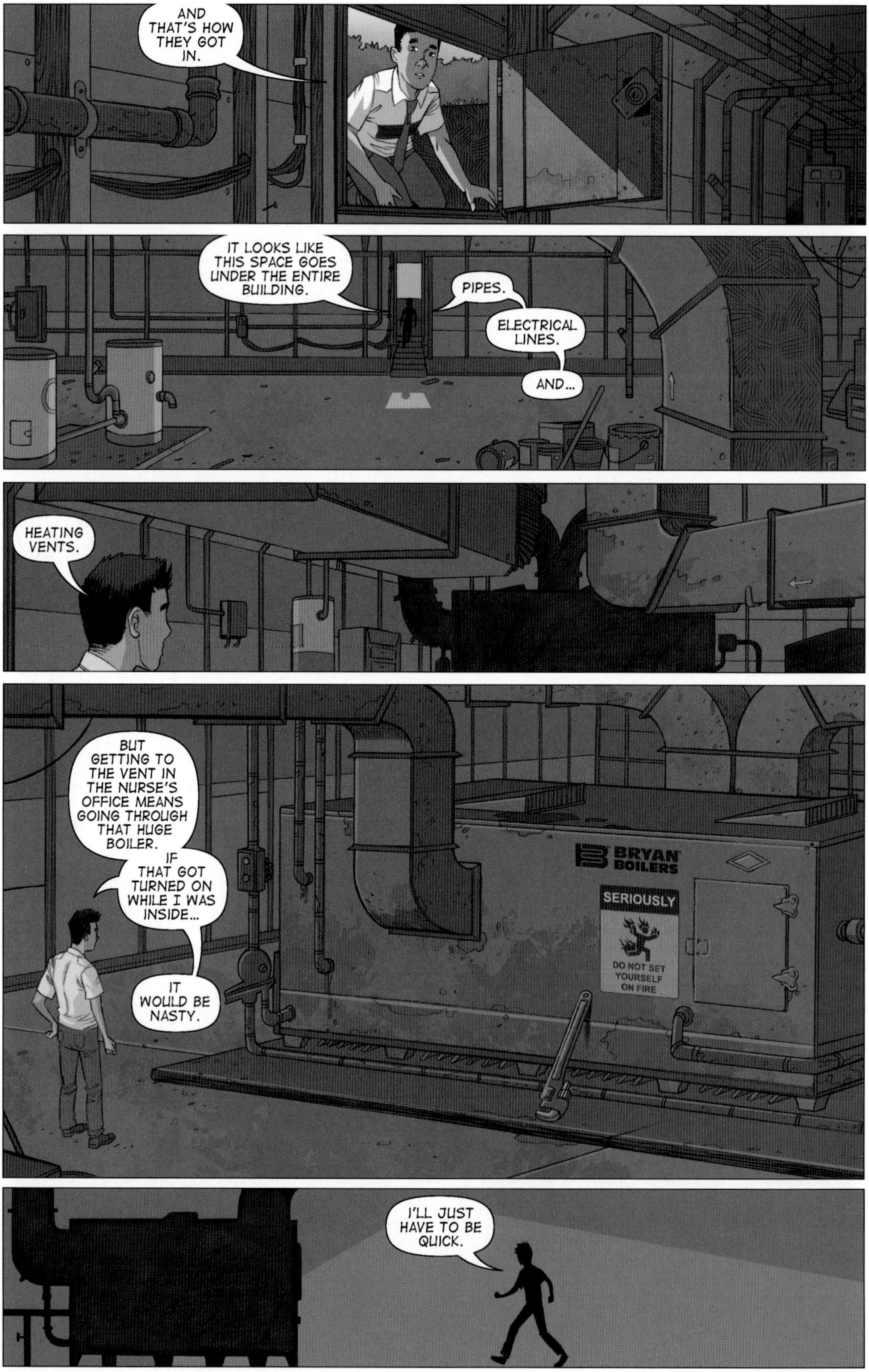
AND THAT'S HOW THEY GOT IN.
IT LOOKS LIKE THIS SPACE GOES UNDER THE ENTIRE BUILDING.
PIPES.
ELECTRICAL LINES.
AND...
HEATING VENTS.
BUT GETTING TO THE VENT IN THE NURSE'S OFFICE MEANS GOING THROUGH THAT HUGE BOILER.
BRYAN BOILERS
SERIOUSLY
DO NOT SET YOURSELF ON FIRE
IF THAT GOT TURNED ON WHILE I WAS INSIDE...
IT WOULD BE NASTY.
I'LL JUST HAVE TO BE QUICK.

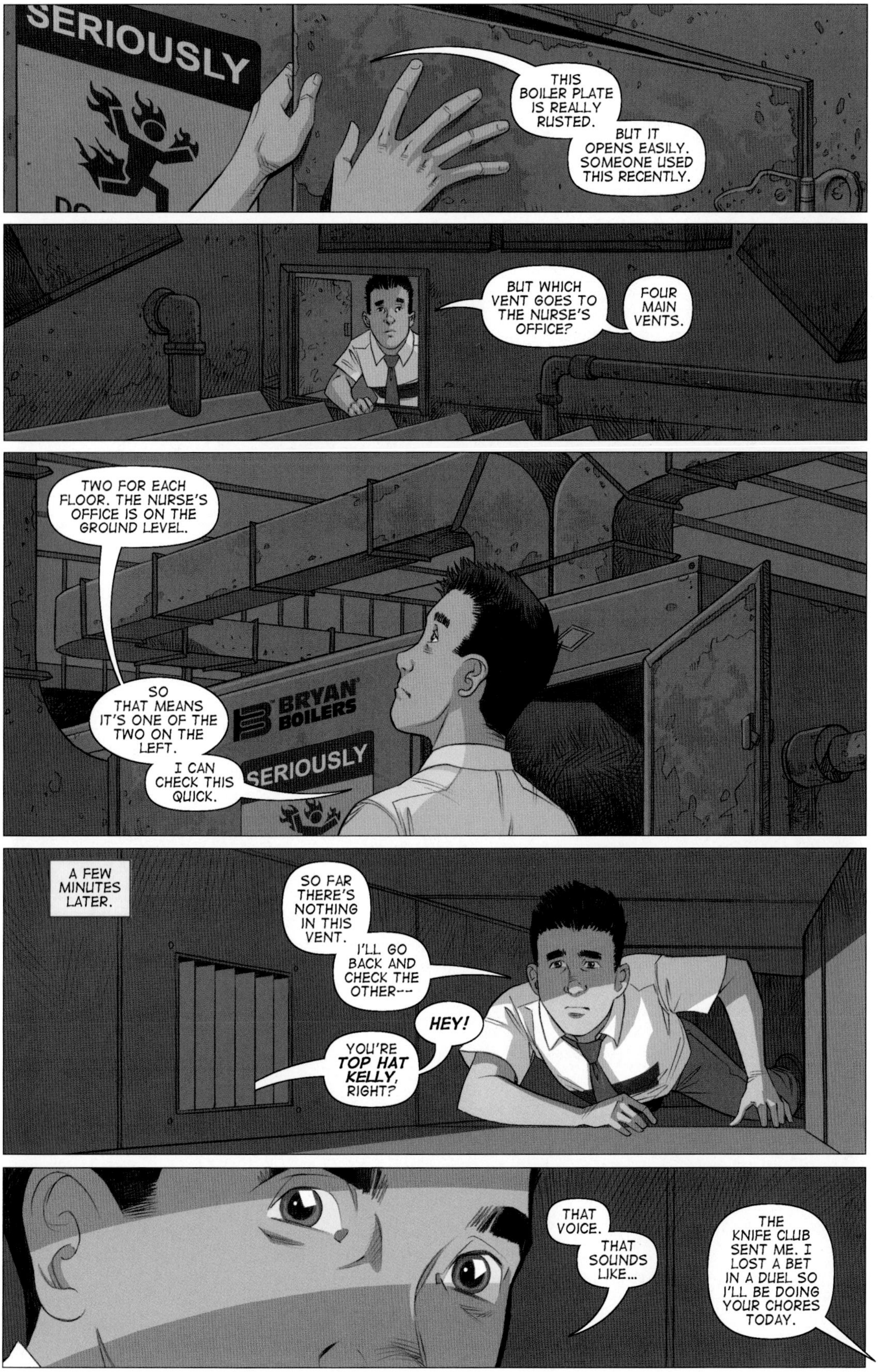
SERIOUSLY
THIS BOILER PLATE IS REALLY RUSTED.
BUT IT OPENS EASILY. SOMEONE USED THIS RECENTLY.
BUT WHICH VENT GOES TO THE NURSE'S OFFICE?
FOUR MAIN VENTS.
TWO FOR EACH FLOOR. THE NURSE'S OFFICE IS ON THE GROUND LEVEL.
SO THAT MEANS IT'S ONE OF THE TWO ON THE LEFT.
I CAN CHECK THIS QUICK.
BRYAN BOILERS
SERIOUSLY
A FEW MINUTES LATER.
SO FAR THERE'S NOTHING IN THIS VENT.
I'LL GO BACK AND CHECK THE OTHER--
HEY!
YOU'RE TOP HAT KELLY, RIGHT?
THAT VOICE.
THAT SOUNDS LIKE...
THE KNIFE CLUB SENT ME. I LOST A BET IN A DUEL SO I'LL BE DOING YOUR CHORES TODAY.

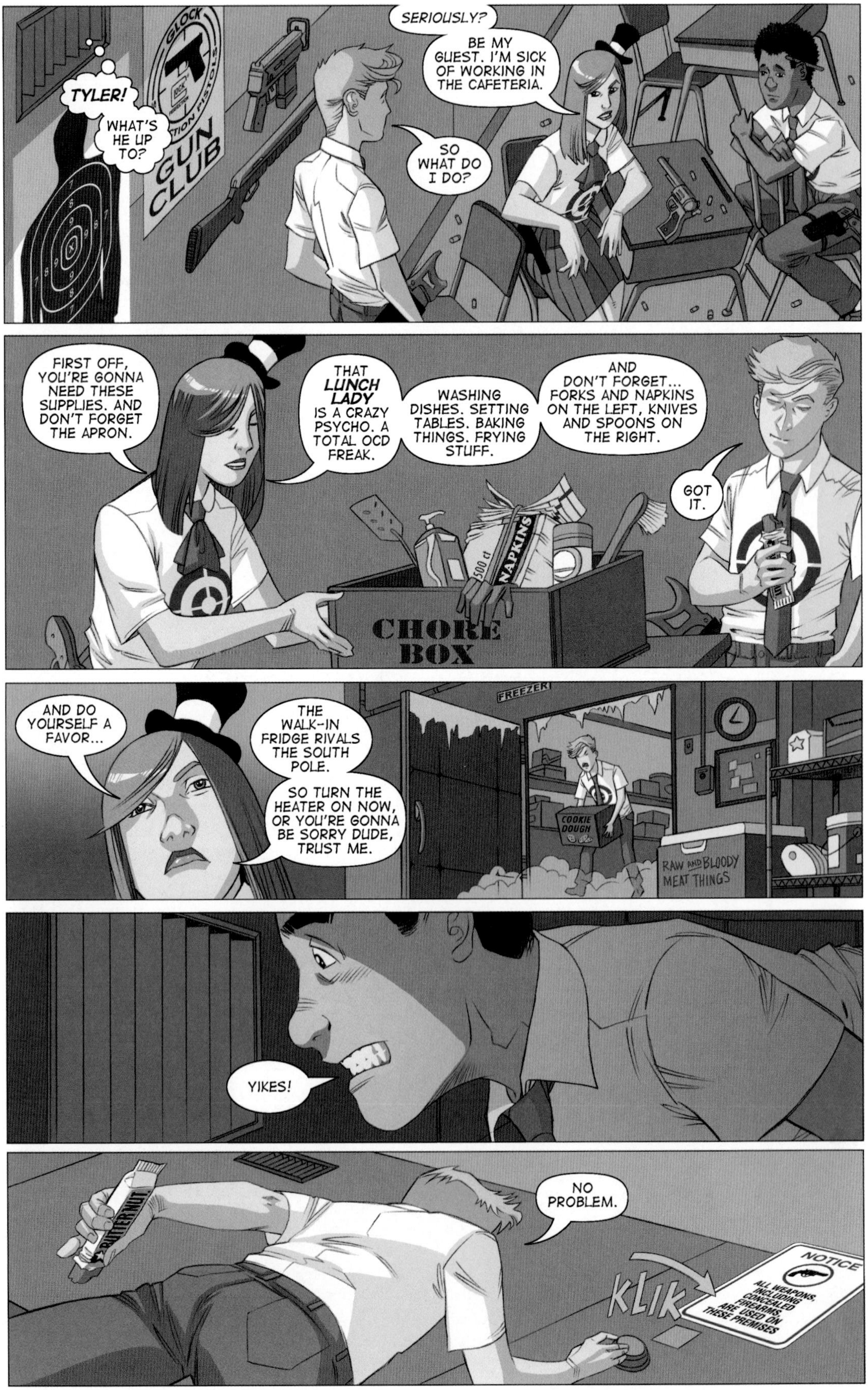
TYLER!
WHAT'S HE UP TO?
GLOCK
GUN CLUB
SERIOUSLY?
BE MY GUEST. I'M SICK OF WORKING IN THE CAFETERIA.
SO WHAT DO I DO?
FIRST OFF, YOU'RE GONNA NEED THESE SUPPLIES. AND DON'T FORGET THE APRON.
THAT LUNCH LADY IS A CRAZY PSYCHO. A TOTAL OCD FREAK.
WASHING DISHES. SETTING TABLES. BAKING THINGS. FRYING STUFF.
AND DON'T FORGET... FORKS AND NAPKINS ON THE LEFT, KNIVES AND SPOONS ON THE RIGHT.
GOT IT.
NAPKINS
CHORE BOX
AND DO YOURSELF A FAVOR...
THE WALK-IN FRIDGE RIVALS THE SOUTH POLE.
SO TURN THE HEATER ON NOW, OR YOU'RE GONNA BE SORRY DUDE, TRUST ME.
FREEZER
COOKIE DOUGH
RAW AND BLOODY MEAT THINGS
YIKES!
NO PROBLEM.
BUTTERNUT
KLIK
NOTICE
ALL WEAPONS, INCLUDING CONCEALED FIREARMS, ARE USED ON THESE PREMISES

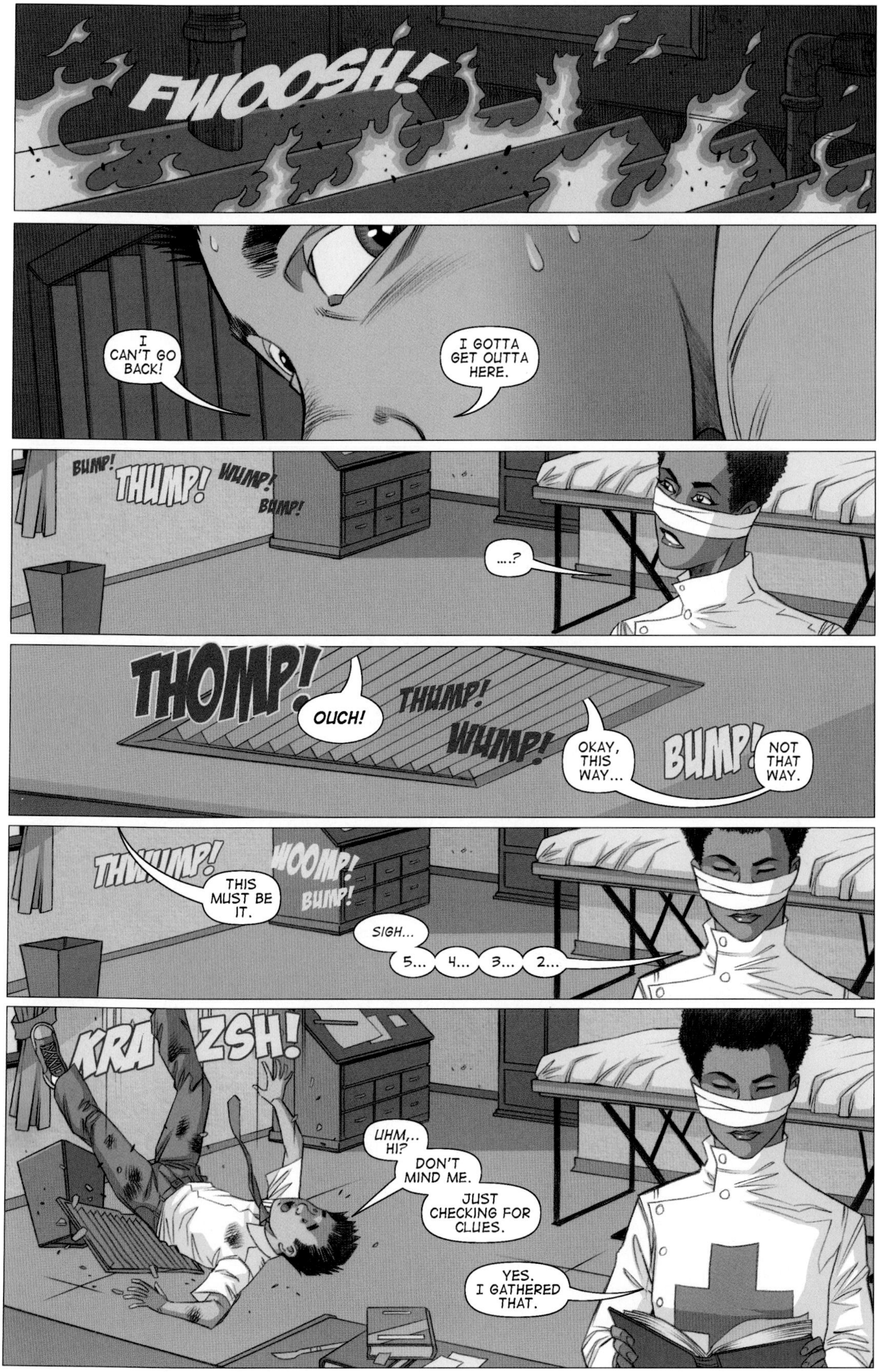
FWOOSH!
I CAN'T GO BACK!
I GOTTA GET OUTTA HERE.
BUMP!
THUMP!
WUMP!
BUMP!
....?
THOMP!
OUCH!
THUMP!
WUMP!
OKAY, THIS WAY...
BUMP!
NOT THAT WAY.
THWUMP!
THIS MUST BE IT.
WOOMP!
BUMP!
SIGH...
5...
4...
3...
2...
KRA ZSH!
UHM,.. HI?
DON'T MIND ME.
JUST CHECKING FOR CLUES.
YES. I GATHERED THAT.

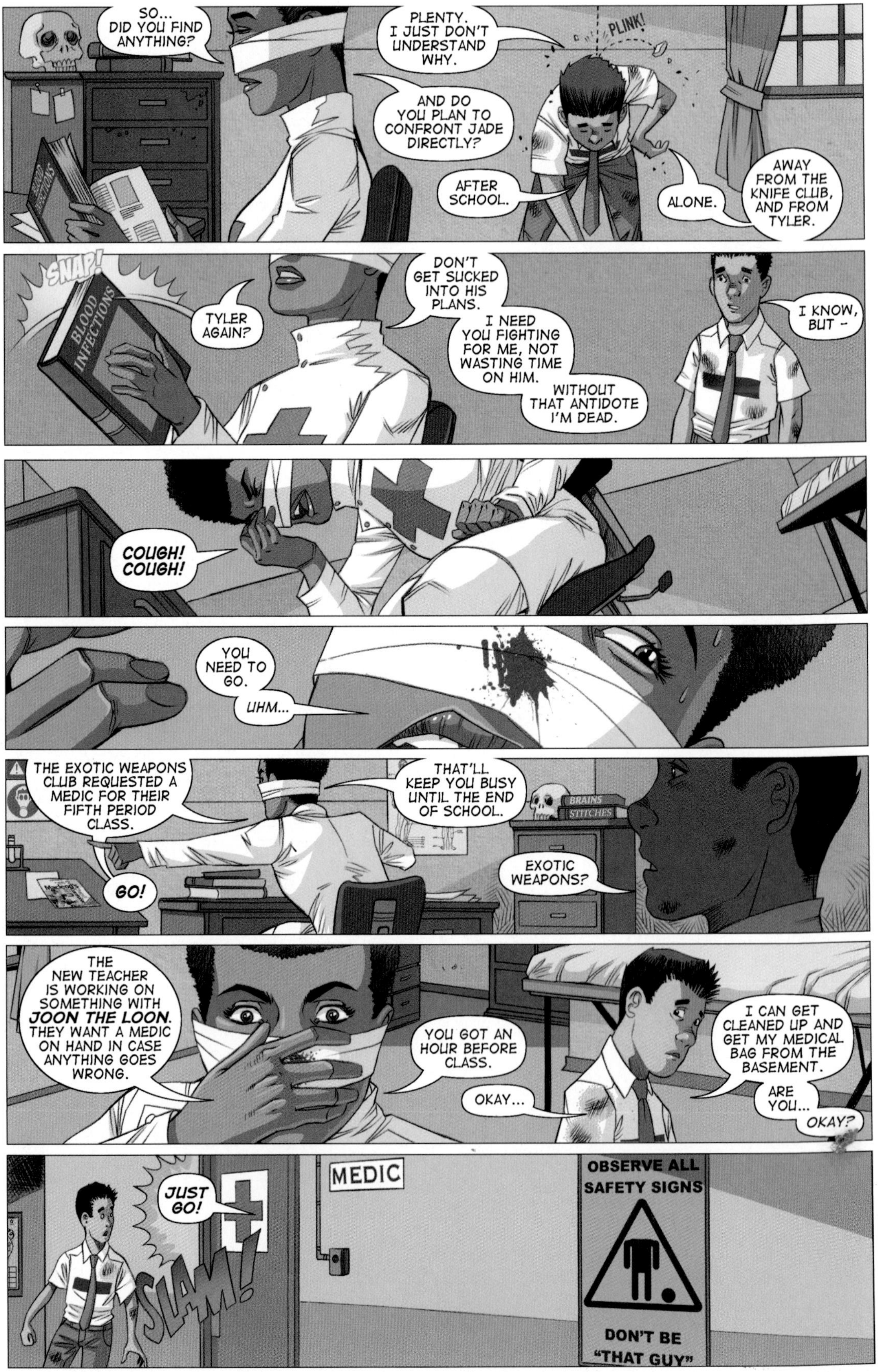
SO... DID YOU FIND ANYTHING?
PLENTY. I JUST DON'T UNDERSTAND WHY.
PLINK!
AND DO YOU PLAN TO CONFRONT JADE DIRECTLY?
AFTER SCHOOL.
ALONE.
AWAY FROM THE KNIFE CLUB, AND FROM TYLER.
BLOOD INFECTIONS
SNAP!
TYLER AGAIN?
DON'T GET SUCKED INTO HIS PLANS.
I NEED YOU FIGHTING FOR ME, NOT WASTING TIME ON HIM.
WITHOUT THAT ANTIDOTE I'M DEAD.
I KNOW, BUT --
COUGH! COUGH!
YOU NEED TO GO.
UHM...
THE EXOTIC WEAPONS CLUB REQUESTED A MEDIC FOR THEIR FIFTH PERIOD CLASS.
THAT'LL KEEP YOU BUSY UNTIL THE END OF SCHOOL.
BRAINS
STITCHES
EXOTIC WEAPONS?
GO!
THE NEW TEACHER IS WORKING ON SOMETHING WITH **JOON THE LOON**. THEY WANT A MEDIC ON HAND IN CASE ANYTHING GOES WRONG.
YOU GOT AN HOUR BEFORE CLASS.
OKAY...
I CAN GET CLEANED UP AND GET MY MEDICAL BAG FROM THE BASEMENT.
ARE YOU... OKAY?
JUST GO!
SLAM!
MEDIC
OBSERVE ALL SAFETY SIGNS
DON'T BE "THAT GUY"

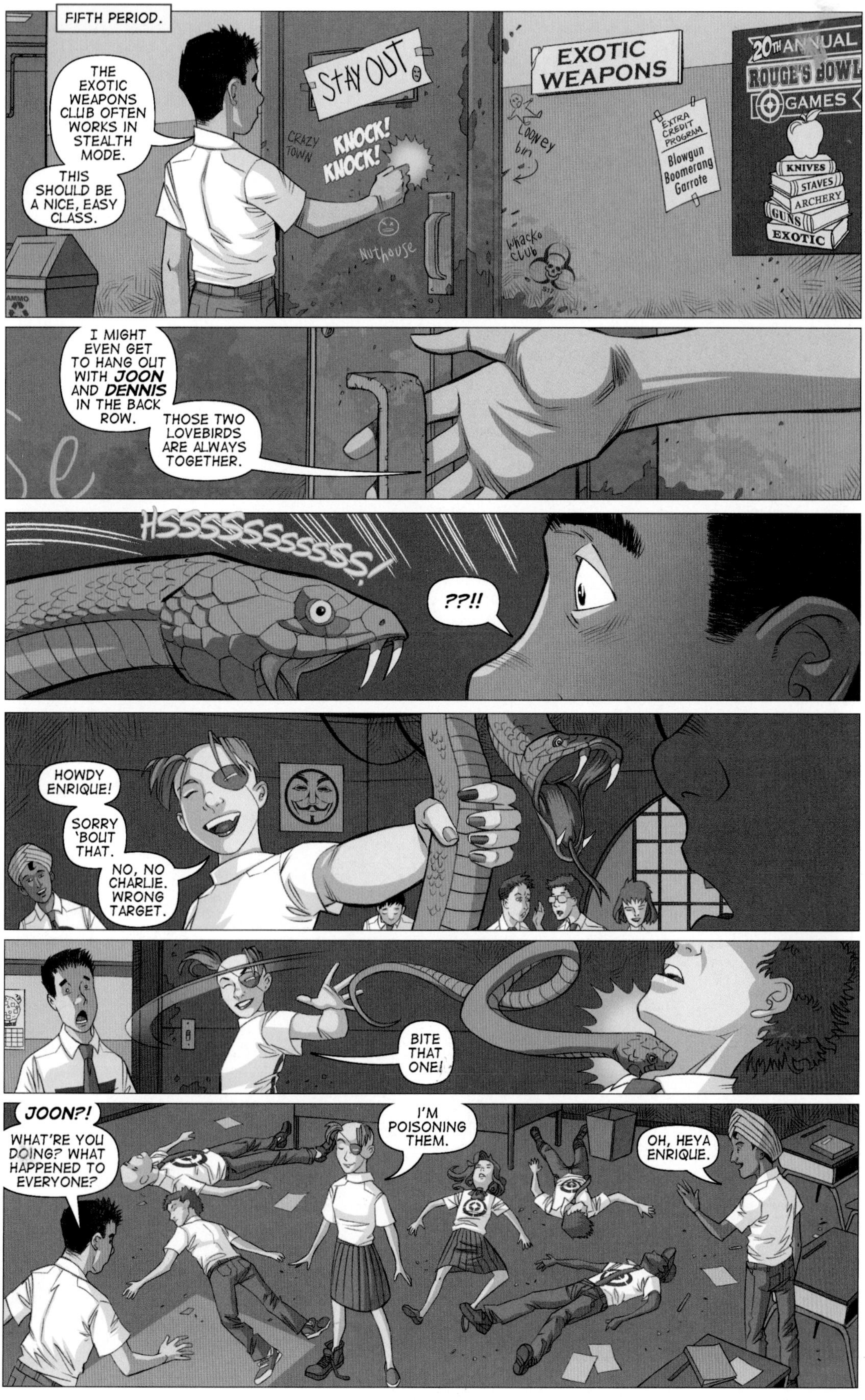
FIFTH PERIOD.
THE EXOTIC WEAPONS CLUB OFTEN WORKS IN STEALTH MODE.
THIS SHOULD BE A NICE, EASY CLASS.
STAY OUT
KNOCK! KNOCK!
CRAZY TOWN
Nuthouse
EXOTIC WEAPONS
Looney bin
Whacko club
EXTRA CREDIT PROGRAM
Blowgun
Boomerang
Garrote
20TH ANNUAL
ROUGE'S BOWL
GAMES
KNIVES
STAVES
ARCHERY
GUNS
EXOTIC
AMMO
I MIGHT EVEN GET TO HANG OUT WITH JOON AND DENNIS IN THE BACK ROW.
THOSE TWO LOVEBIRDS ARE ALWAYS TOGETHER.
HSSSSSSSSSSS!
??!!
HOWDY ENRIQUE!
SORRY 'BOUT THAT.
NO, NO CHARLIE. WRONG TARGET.
BITE THAT ONE!
JOON?!
WHAT'RE YOU DOING? WHAT HAPPENED TO EVERYONE?
I'M POISONING THEM.
OH, HEYA ENRIQUE.

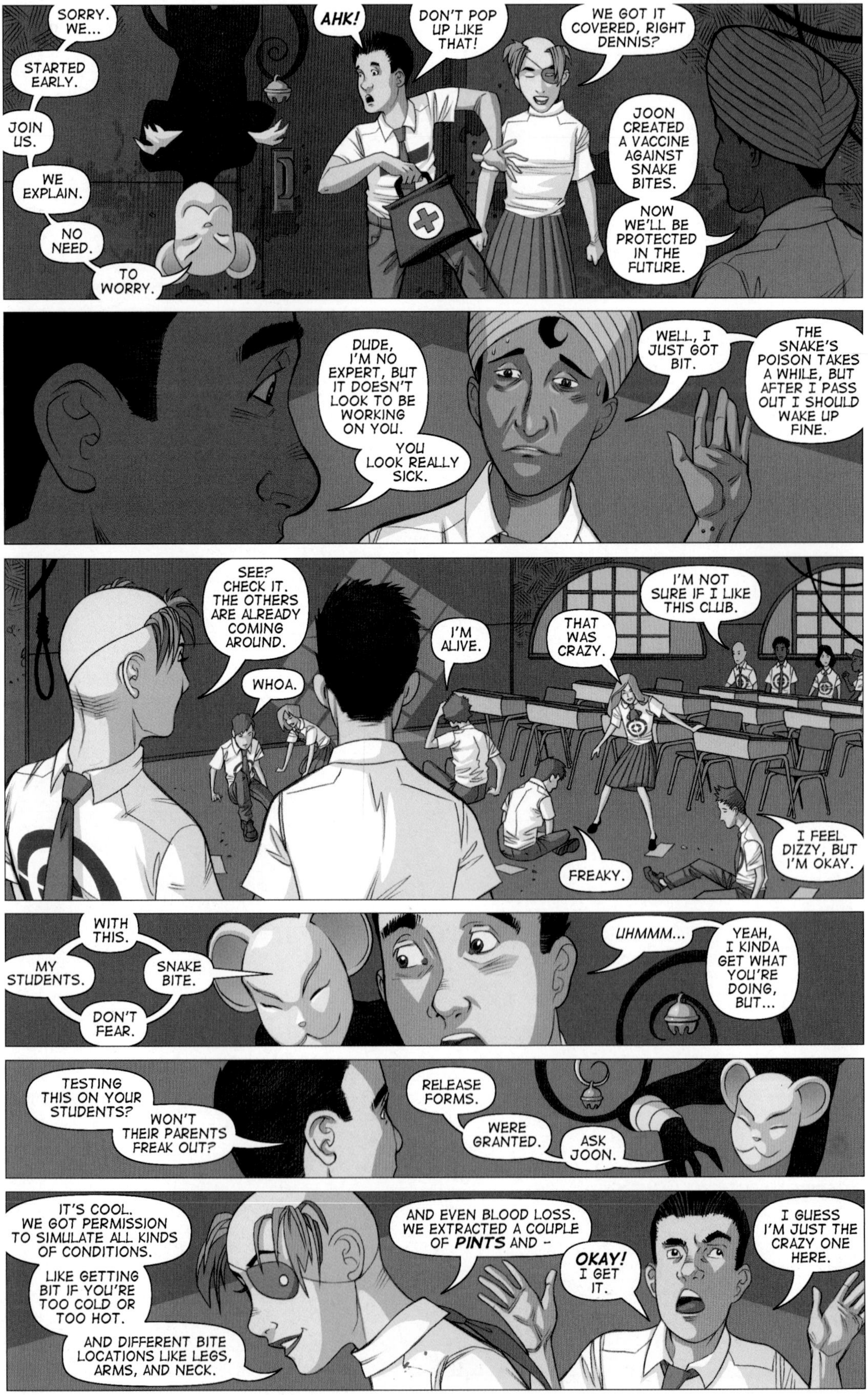
SORRY. WE...
STARTED EARLY.
JOIN US.
WE EXPLAIN.
NO NEED.
TO WORRY.
AHK!
DON'T POP UP LIKE THAT!
WE GOT IT COVERED, RIGHT DENNIS?
JOON CREATED A VACCINE AGAINST SNAKE BITES.
NOW WE'LL BE PROTECTED IN THE FUTURE.
DUDE, I'M NO EXPERT, BUT IT DOESN'T LOOK TO BE WORKING ON YOU.
YOU LOOK REALLY SICK.
WELL, I JUST GOT BIT.
THE SNAKE'S POISON TAKES A WHILE, BUT AFTER I PASS OUT I SHOULD WAKE UP FINE.
SEE? CHECK IT. THE OTHERS ARE ALREADY COMING AROUND.
WHOA.
I'M ALIVE.
THAT WAS CRAZY.
I'M NOT SURE IF I LIKE THIS CLUB.
FREAKY.
I FEEL DIZZY, BUT I'M OKAY.
WITH THIS.
SNAKE BITE.
DON'T FEAR.
MY STUDENTS.
UHMMM...
YEAH, I KINDA GET WHAT YOU'RE DOING, BUT...
TESTING THIS ON YOUR STUDENTS?
WON'T THEIR PARENTS FREAK OUT?
RELEASE FORMS.
WERE GRANTED.
ASK JOON.
IT'S COOL. WE GOT PERMISSION TO SIMULATE ALL KINDS OF CONDITIONS.
LIKE GETTING BIT IF YOU'RE TOO COLD OR TOO HOT.
AND DIFFERENT BITE LOCATIONS LIKE LEGS, ARMS, AND NECK.
AND EVEN BLOOD LOSS. WE EXTRACTED A COUPLE OF PINTS AND -
OKAY! I GET IT.
I GUESS I'M JUST THE CRAZY ONE HERE.

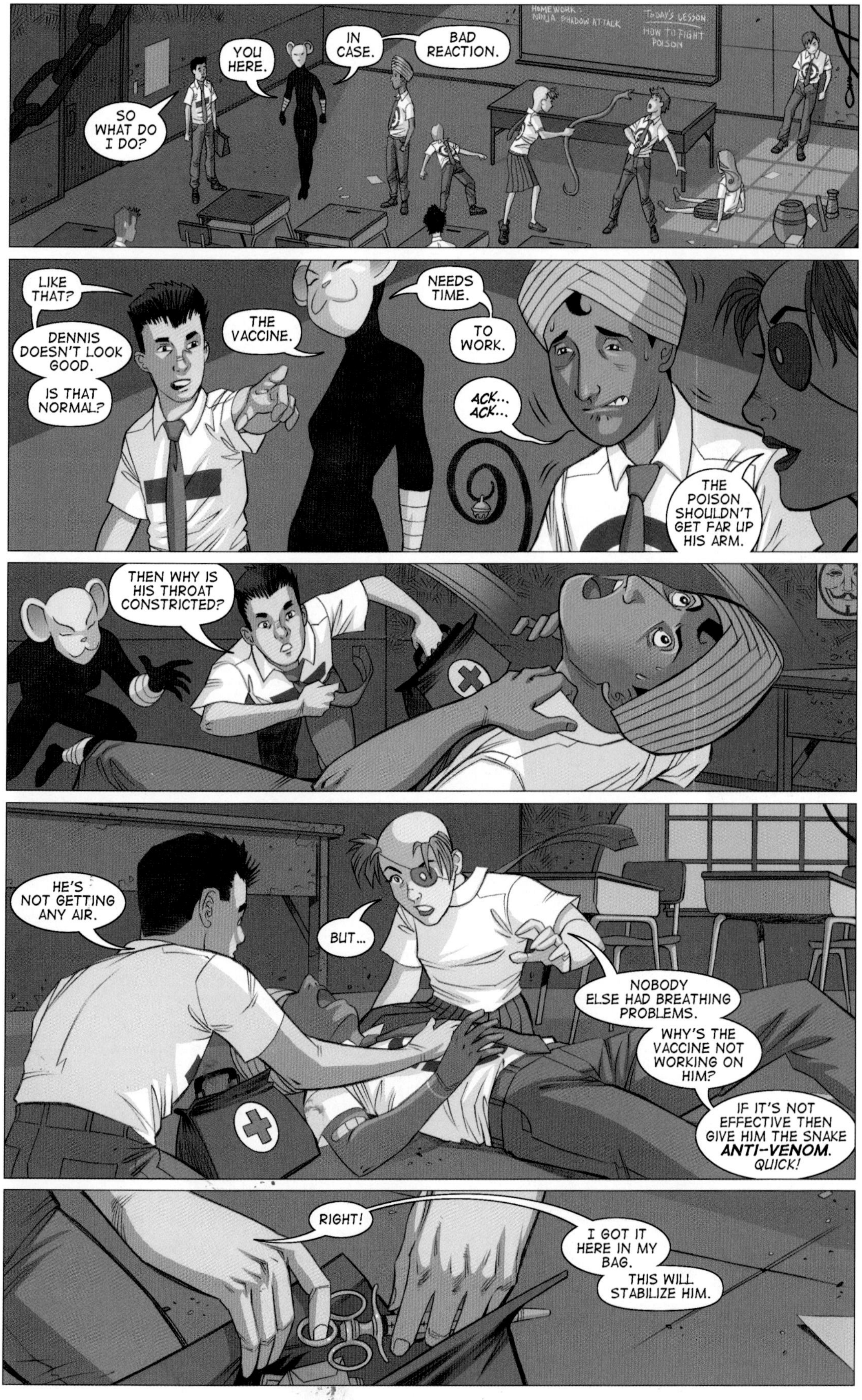
HOMEWORK: NINJA SHADOW ATTACK
TODAY'S LESSON HOW TO FIGHT POISON
SO WHAT DO I DO?
YOU HERE.
IN CASE.
BAD REACTION.
LIKE THAT?
DENNIS DOESN'T LOOK GOOD.
IS THAT NORMAL?
THE VACCINE.
NEEDS TIME.
TO WORK.
ACK... ACK...
THE POISON SHOULDN'T GET FAR UP HIS ARM.
THEN WHY IS HIS THROAT CONSTRICTED?
HE'S NOT GETTING ANY AIR.
BUT...
NOBODY ELSE HAD BREATHING PROBLEMS.
WHY'S THE VACCINE NOT WORKING ON HIM?
IF IT'S NOT EFFECTIVE THEN GIVE HIM THE SNAKE ***ANTI-VENOM***. *QUICK!*
RIGHT!
I GOT IT HERE IN MY BAG.
THIS WILL STABILIZE HIM.

HOLD ON DENNIS, WE'LL GET YOU FIXED UP IN A –

....?

WAIT. I GOT SOME QUESTIONS.

HE'S GONNA DIE. GIVE HIM THE ANTI-VENOM NOW.

SERIOUSLY?

NO.

WHA–? WHY?

SOMETHING'S NOT RIGHT.

YOU'RE CRAZY. HELP HIM!

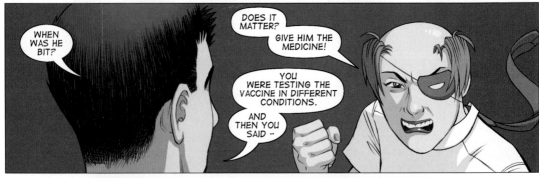

WHEN WAS HE BIT?

DOES IT MATTER? GIVE HIM THE MEDICINE!

YOU WERE TESTING THE VACCINE IN DIFFERENT CONDITIONS.

AND THEN YOU SAID –

OH I GET IT.

THIS IS JUST WHAT RICK THE STICK WAS TALKIN' ABOUT.

YOU'RE SHOWING OFF!

YOU EMBARRASSED THE STICK CLUB AND THE GUN CLUB, THEN YOU PISSED OFF THE ARCHERY CLUB. NOW YOU'RE AFTER MY CLASS.

JOON, NONE OF THAT IS TRUE.

THAT WAS ALL TYLER. HE WAS...

NEVER MIND ANY OF THAT.

THIS IS NOT ABOUT ME.

I NEED TO KNOW THE DETAILS ABOUT DENNIS.

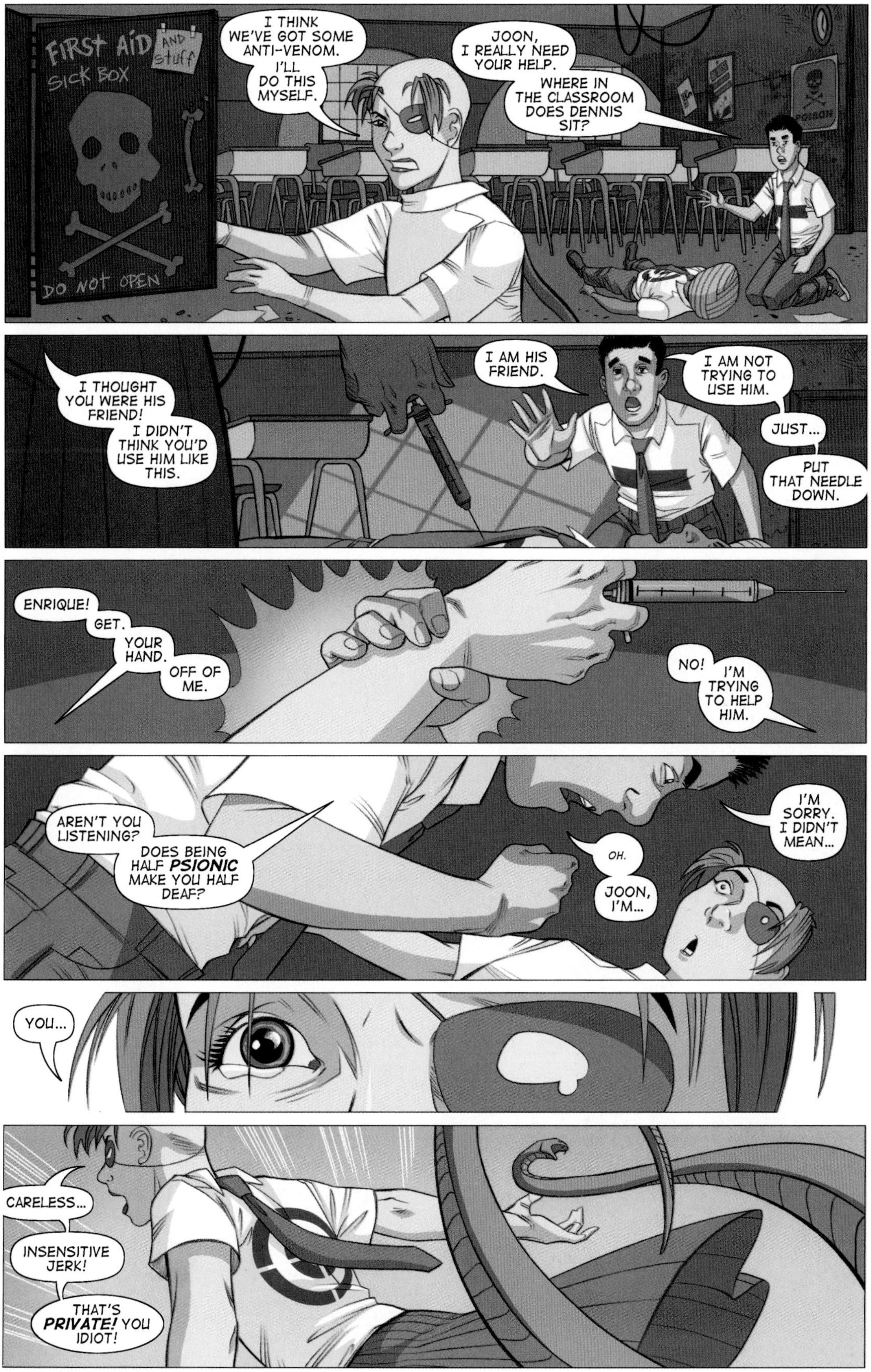
FIRST AID AND stuff
SICK BOX
DO NOT OPEN
I THINK WE'VE GOT SOME ANTI-VENOM.
I'LL DO THIS MYSELF.
JOON, I REALLY NEED YOUR HELP.
WHERE IN THE CLASSROOM DOES DENNIS SIT?
POISON
I THOUGHT YOU WERE HIS FRIEND!
I DIDN'T THINK YOU'D USE HIM LIKE THIS.
I AM HIS FRIEND.
I AM NOT TRYING TO USE HIM.
JUST...
PUT THAT NEEDLE DOWN.
ENRIQUE!
GET.
YOUR HAND.
OFF OF ME.
NO!
I'M TRYING TO HELP HIM.
AREN'T YOU LISTENING?
DOES BEING HALF **PSIONIC** MAKE YOU HALF DEAF?
OH.
JOON, I'M...
I'M SORRY. I DIDN'T MEAN...
YOU...
CARELESS...
INSENSITIVE JERK!
THAT'S **PRIVATE!** YOU IDIOT!

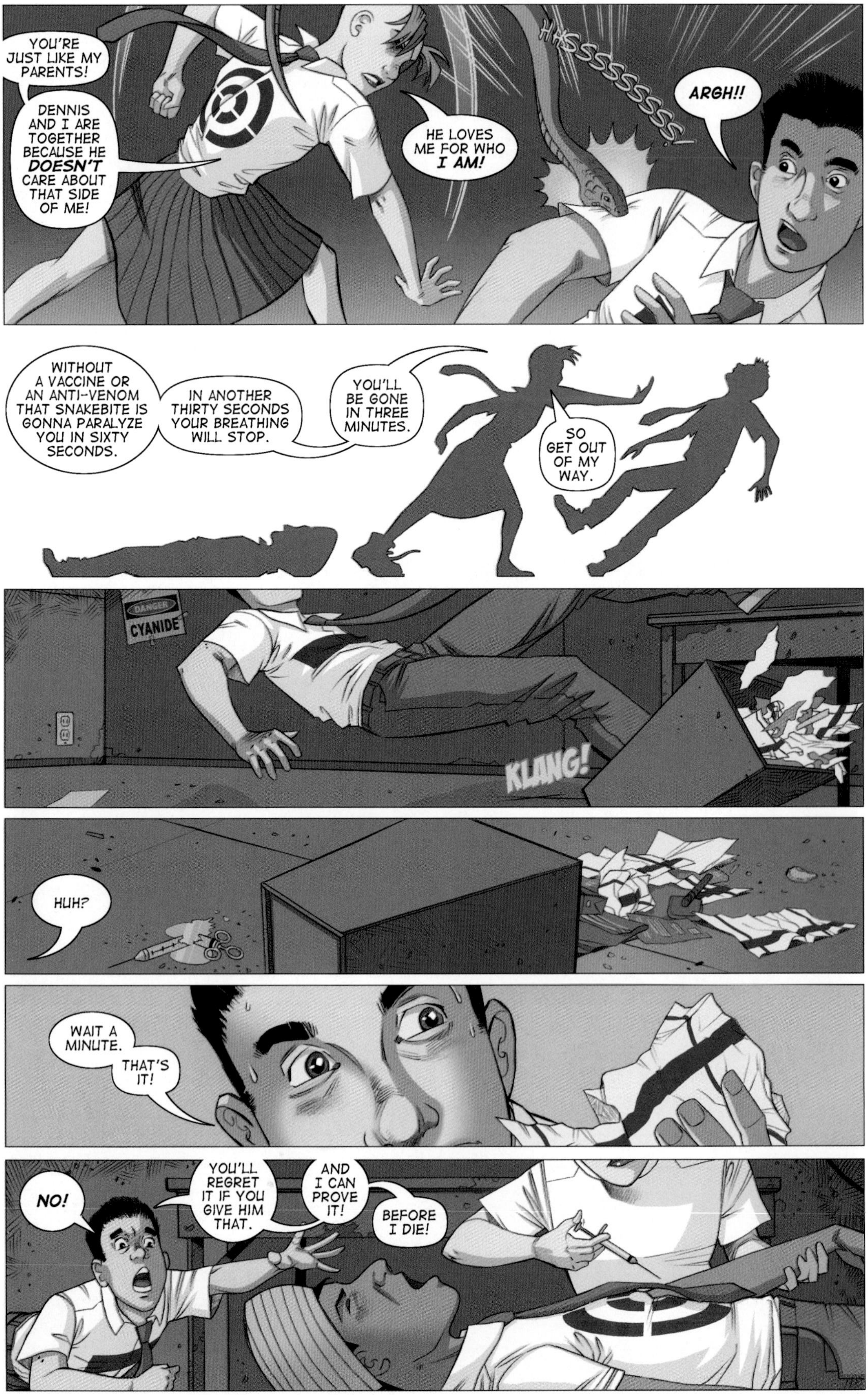
YOU'RE JUST LIKE MY PARENTS!
DENNIS AND I ARE TOGETHER BECAUSE HE DOESN'T CARE ABOUT THAT SIDE OF ME!
HE LOVES ME FOR WHO I AM!
HISSSSSSSSS!
ARGH!!
WITHOUT A VACCINE OR AN ANTI-VENOM THAT SNAKEBITE IS GONNA PARALYZE YOU IN SIXTY SECONDS.
IN ANOTHER THIRTY SECONDS YOUR BREATHING WILL STOP.
YOU'LL BE GONE IN THREE MINUTES.
SO GET OUT OF MY WAY.
DANGER
CYANIDE
KLANG!
HUH?
WAIT A MINUTE.
THAT'S IT!
NO!
YOU'LL REGRET IT IF YOU GIVE HIM THAT.
AND I CAN PROVE IT!
BEFORE I DIE!

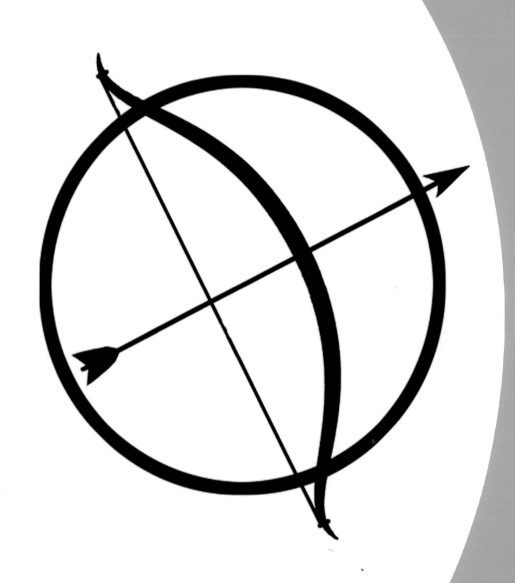

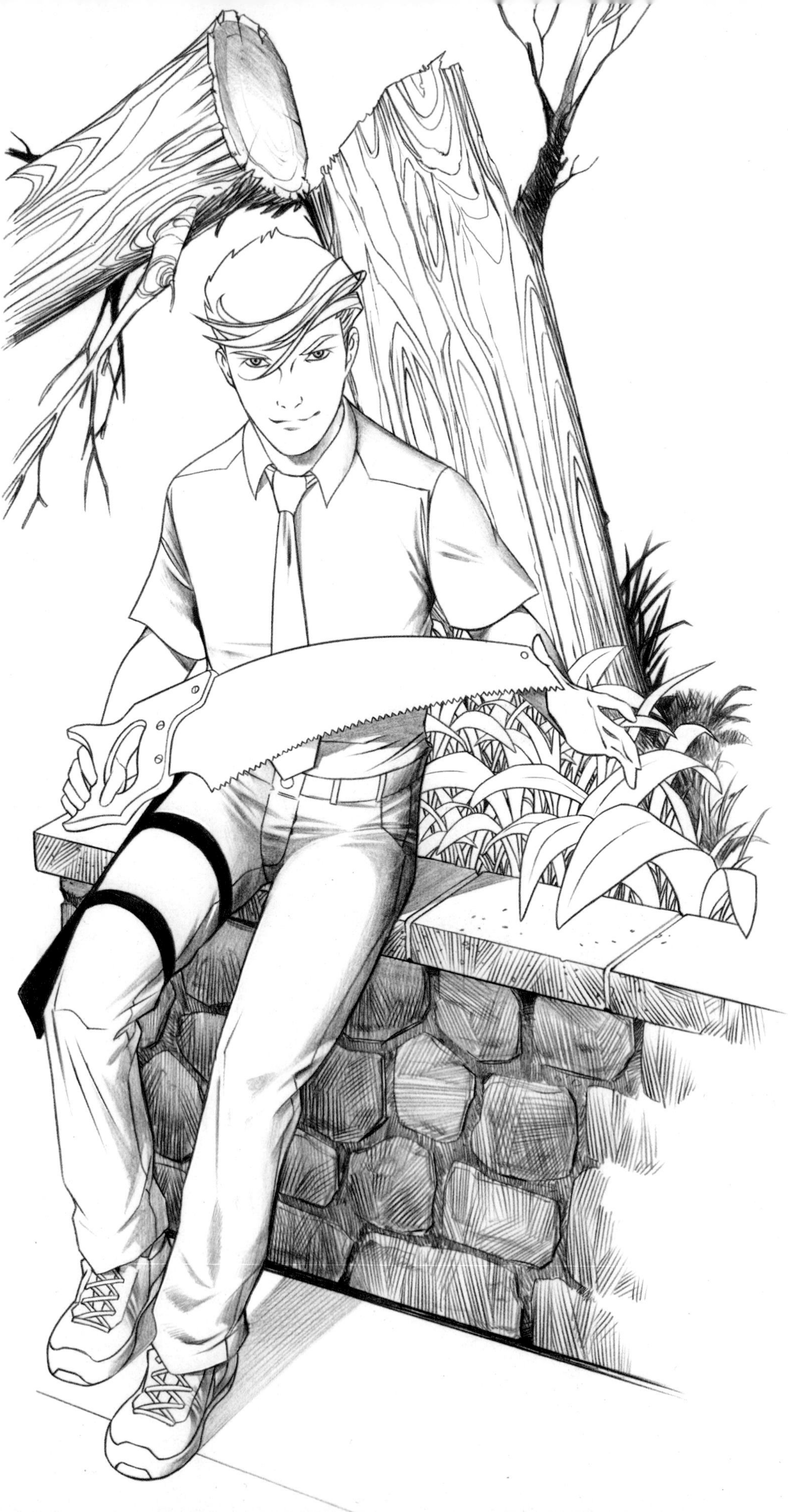

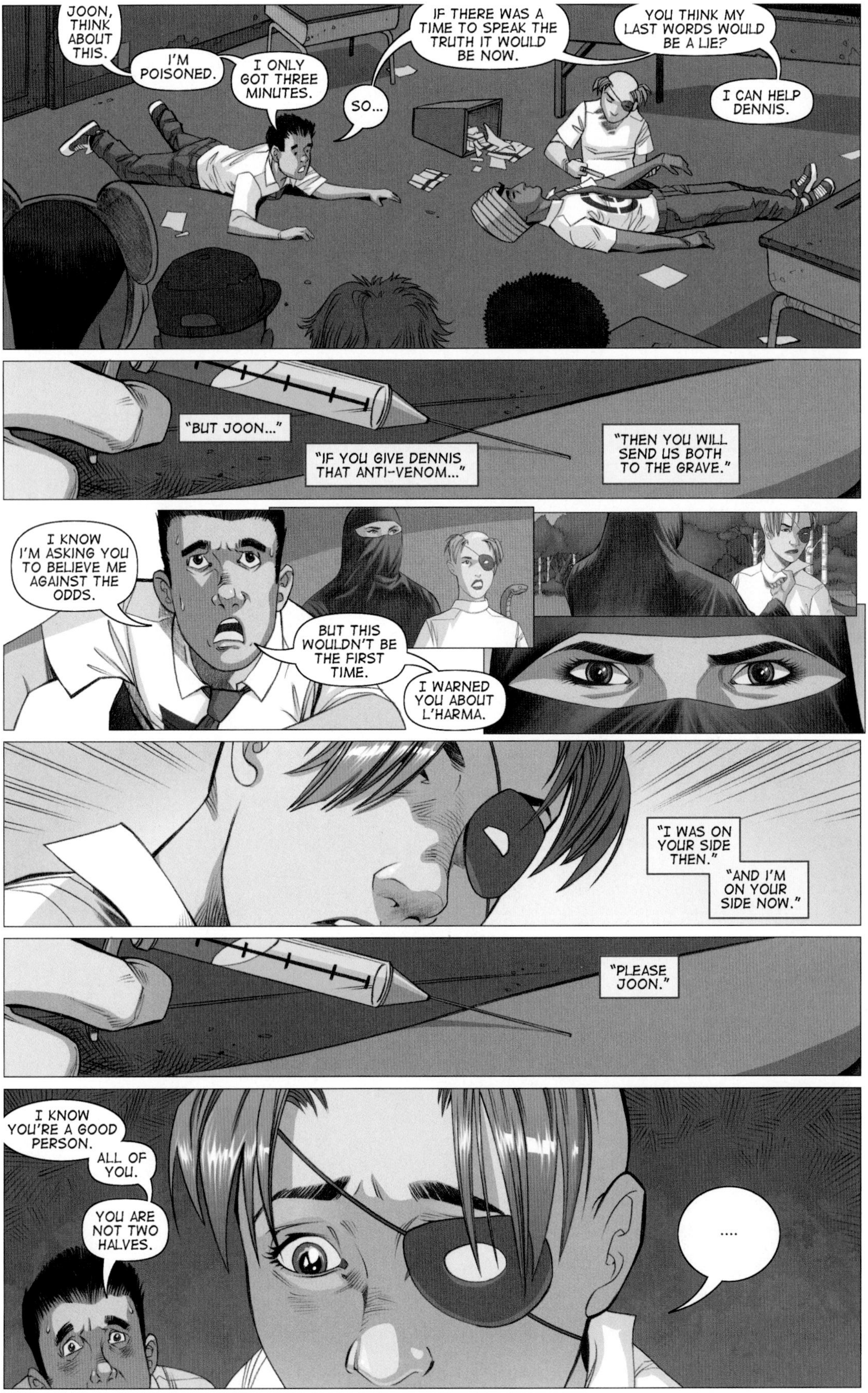
JOON, THINK ABOUT THIS.
I'M POISONED.
I ONLY GOT THREE MINUTES.
SO...
IF THERE WAS A TIME TO SPEAK THE TRUTH IT WOULD BE NOW.
YOU THINK MY LAST WORDS WOULD BE A LIE?
I CAN HELP DENNIS.
"BUT JOON..."
"IF YOU GIVE DENNIS THAT ANTI-VENOM..."
"THEN YOU WILL SEND US BOTH TO THE GRAVE."
I KNOW I'M ASKING YOU TO BELIEVE ME AGAINST THE ODDS.
BUT THIS WOULDN'T BE THE FIRST TIME.
I WARNED YOU ABOUT L'HARMA.
"I WAS ON YOUR SIDE THEN."
"AND I'M ON YOUR SIDE NOW."
"PLEASE JOON."
I KNOW YOU'RE A GOOD PERSON.
ALL OF YOU.
YOU ARE NOT TWO HALVES.
....

THAT DESK.
WITH THE BACKPACK.
SOMETHING THIS IMPORTANT TO DENNIS...
DANGER
CYANIDE
WOULDN'T BE BURIED.
WOULDN'T BE HIDDEN.
ALWAYS AT HIS SIDE.
HE'D HAVE IT ACCESSIBLE AT ALL TIMES.
SCHOOL BACKPACK.
AND EASY TO GRAB.
SNAP!
THE EPI-PEN.
CAP OFF.
POINT DOWN.

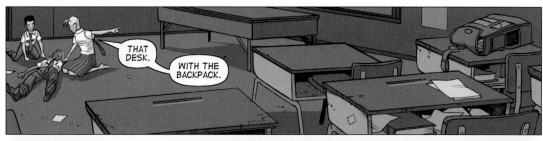

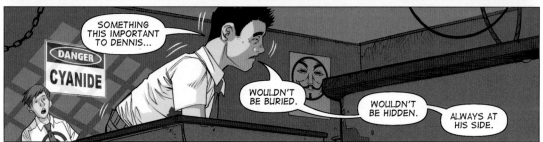

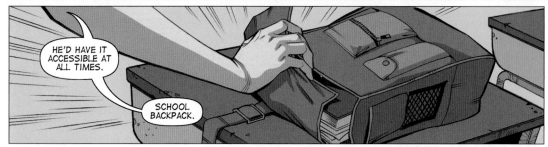

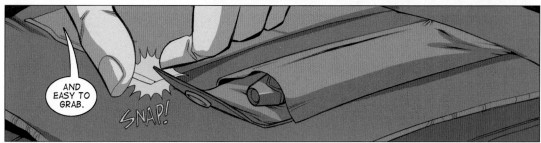

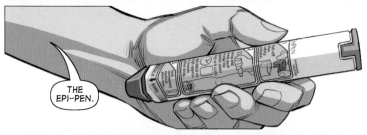

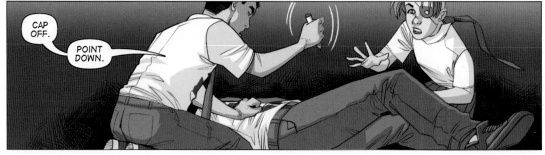

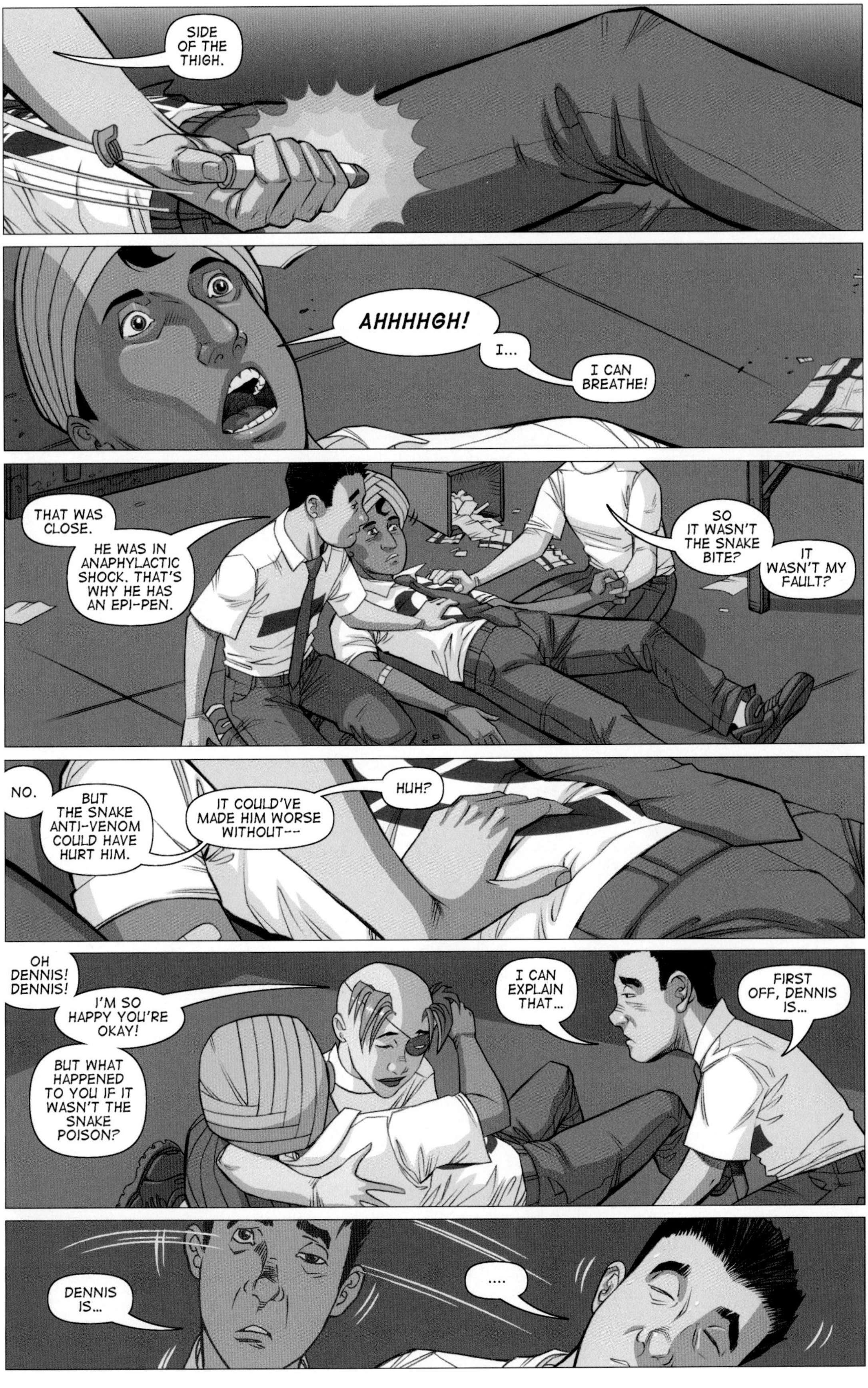
SIDE OF THE THIGH.
AHHHHGH!
I...
I CAN BREATHE!
THAT WAS CLOSE.
HE WAS IN ANAPHYLACTIC SHOCK. THAT'S WHY HE HAS AN EPI-PEN.
SO IT WASN'T THE SNAKE BITE?
IT WASN'T MY FAULT?
NO.
BUT THE SNAKE ANTI-VENOM COULD HAVE HURT HIM.
IT COULD'VE MADE HIM WORSE WITHOUT--
HUH?
OH DENNIS! DENNIS!
I'M SO HAPPY YOU'RE OKAY!
BUT WHAT HAPPENED TO YOU IF IT WASN'T THE SNAKE POISON?
I CAN EXPLAIN THAT...
FIRST OFF, DENNIS IS...
DENNIS IS...
....

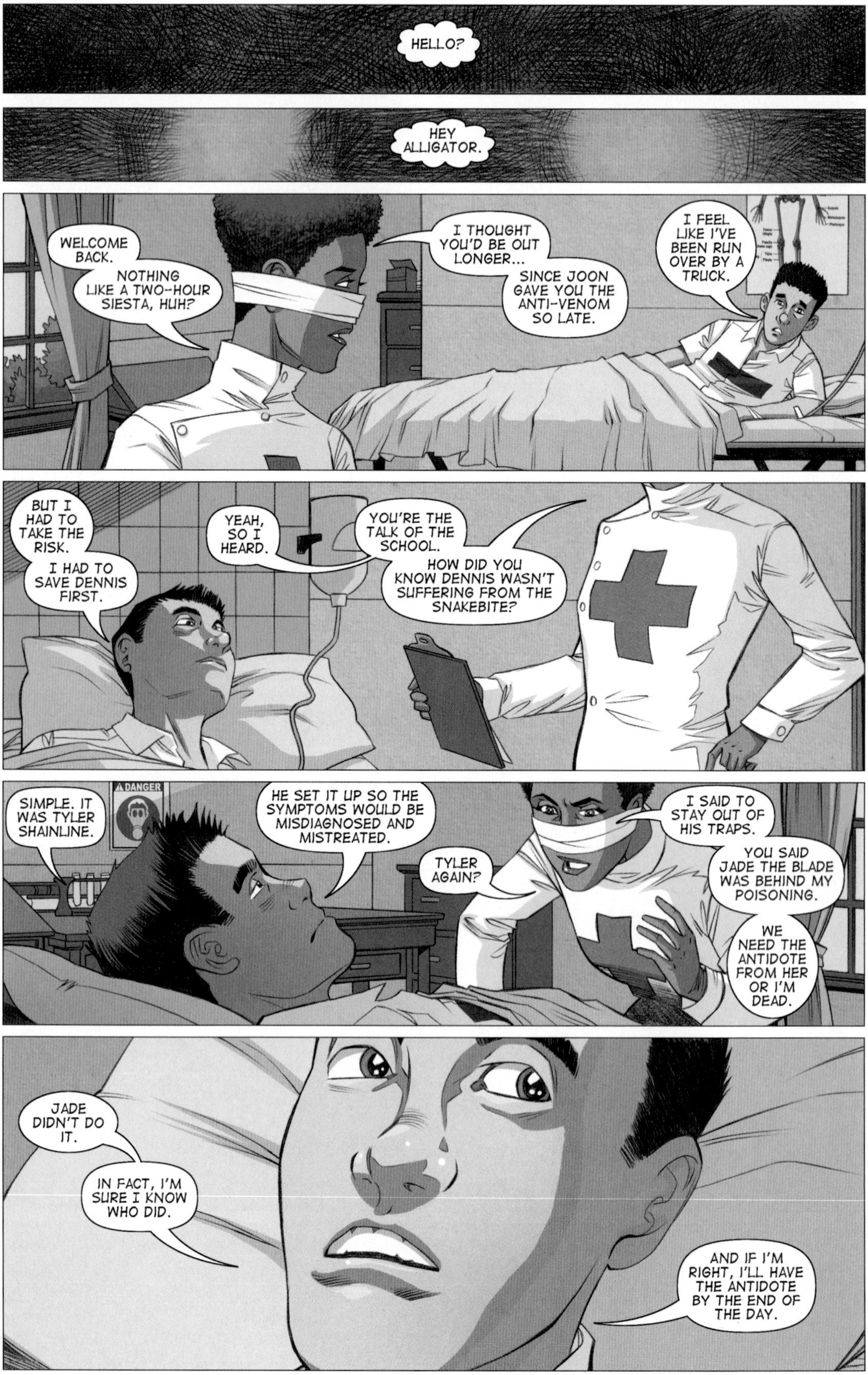
HELLO?
HEY ALLIGATOR.
WELCOME BACK.
NOTHING LIKE A TWO-HOUR SIESTA, HUH?
I THOUGHT YOU'D BE OUT LONGER...
SINCE JOON GAVE YOU THE ANTI-VENOM SO LATE.
I FEEL LIKE I'VE BEEN RUN OVER BY A TRUCK.
BUT I HAD TO TAKE THE RISK.
I HAD TO SAVE DENNIS FIRST.
YEAH, SO I HEARD.
YOU'RE THE TALK OF THE SCHOOL.
HOW DID YOU KNOW DENNIS WASN'T SUFFERING FROM THE SNAKEBITE?
SIMPLE. IT WAS TYLER SHAINLINE.
DANGER
HE SET IT UP SO THE SYMPTOMS WOULD BE MISDIAGNOSED AND MISTREATED.
TYLER AGAIN?
I SAID TO STAY OUT OF HIS TRAPS.
YOU SAID JADE THE BLADE WAS BEHIND MY POISONING.
WE NEED THE ANTIDOTE FROM HER OR I'M DEAD.
JADE DIDN'T DO IT.
IN FACT, I'M SURE I KNOW WHO DID.
AND IF I'M RIGHT, I'LL HAVE THE ANTIDOTE BY THE END OF THE DAY.

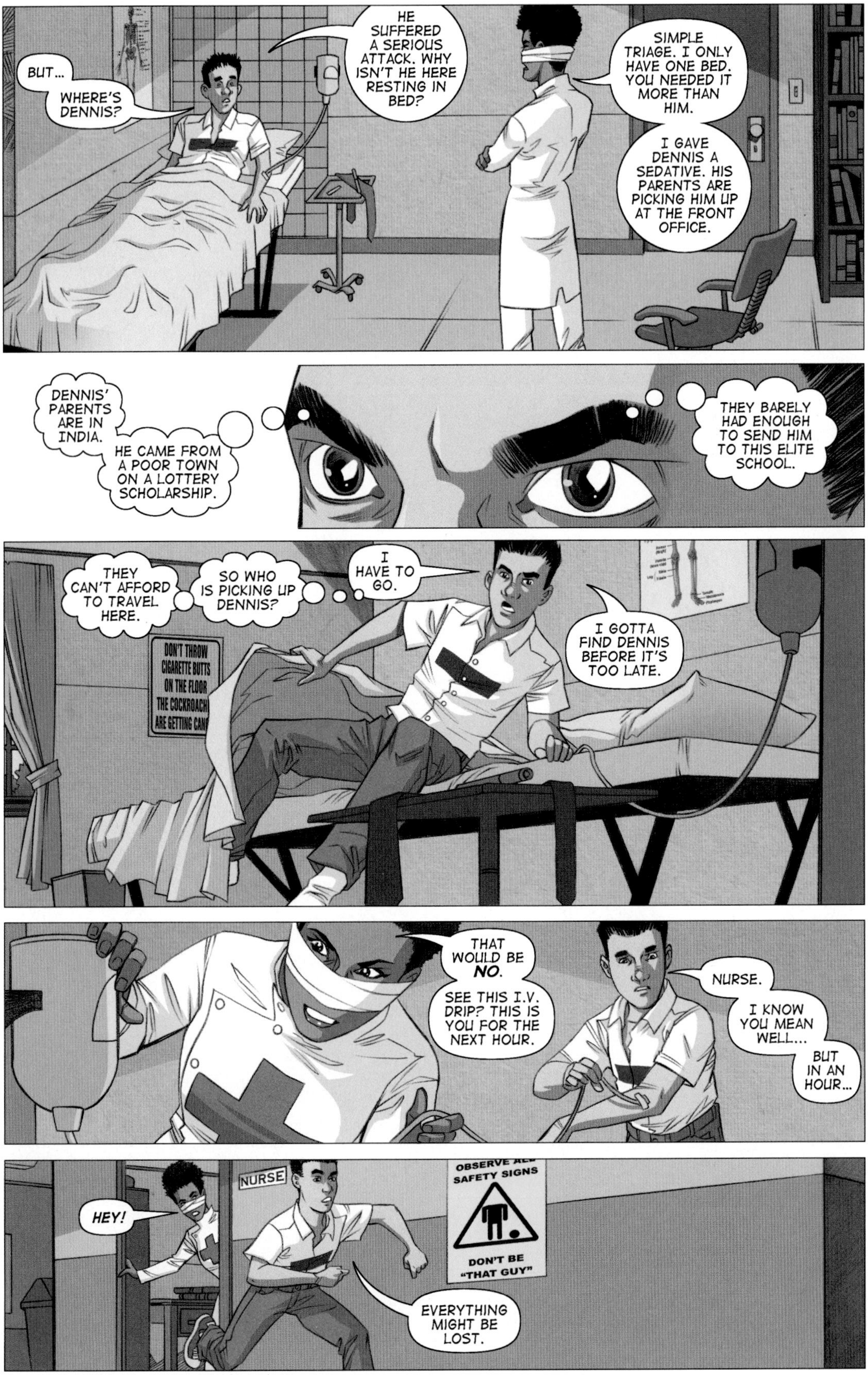
BUT... WHERE'S DENNIS?
HE SUFFERED A SERIOUS ATTACK. WHY ISN'T HE HERE RESTING IN BED?
SIMPLE TRIAGE. I ONLY HAVE ONE BED. YOU NEEDED IT MORE THAN HIM.
I GAVE DENNIS A SEDATIVE. HIS PARENTS ARE PICKING HIM UP AT THE FRONT OFFICE.
DENNIS' PARENTS ARE IN INDIA.
HE CAME FROM A POOR TOWN ON A LOTTERY SCHOLARSHIP.
THEY BARELY HAD ENOUGH TO SEND HIM TO THIS ELITE SCHOOL.
THEY CAN'T AFFORD TO TRAVEL HERE.
SO WHO IS PICKING UP DENNIS?
I HAVE TO GO.
DON'T THROW CIGARETTE BUTTS ON THE FLOOR THE COCKROACH ARE GETTING CAN
I GOTTA FIND DENNIS BEFORE IT'S TOO LATE.
THAT WOULD BE ***NO***.
SEE THIS I.V. DRIP? THIS IS YOU FOR THE NEXT HOUR.
NURSE.
I KNOW YOU MEAN WELL...
BUT IN AN HOUR...
NURSE
HEY!
OBSERVE ALL SAFETY SIGNS
DON'T BE “THAT GUY”
EVERYTHING MIGHT BE LOST.

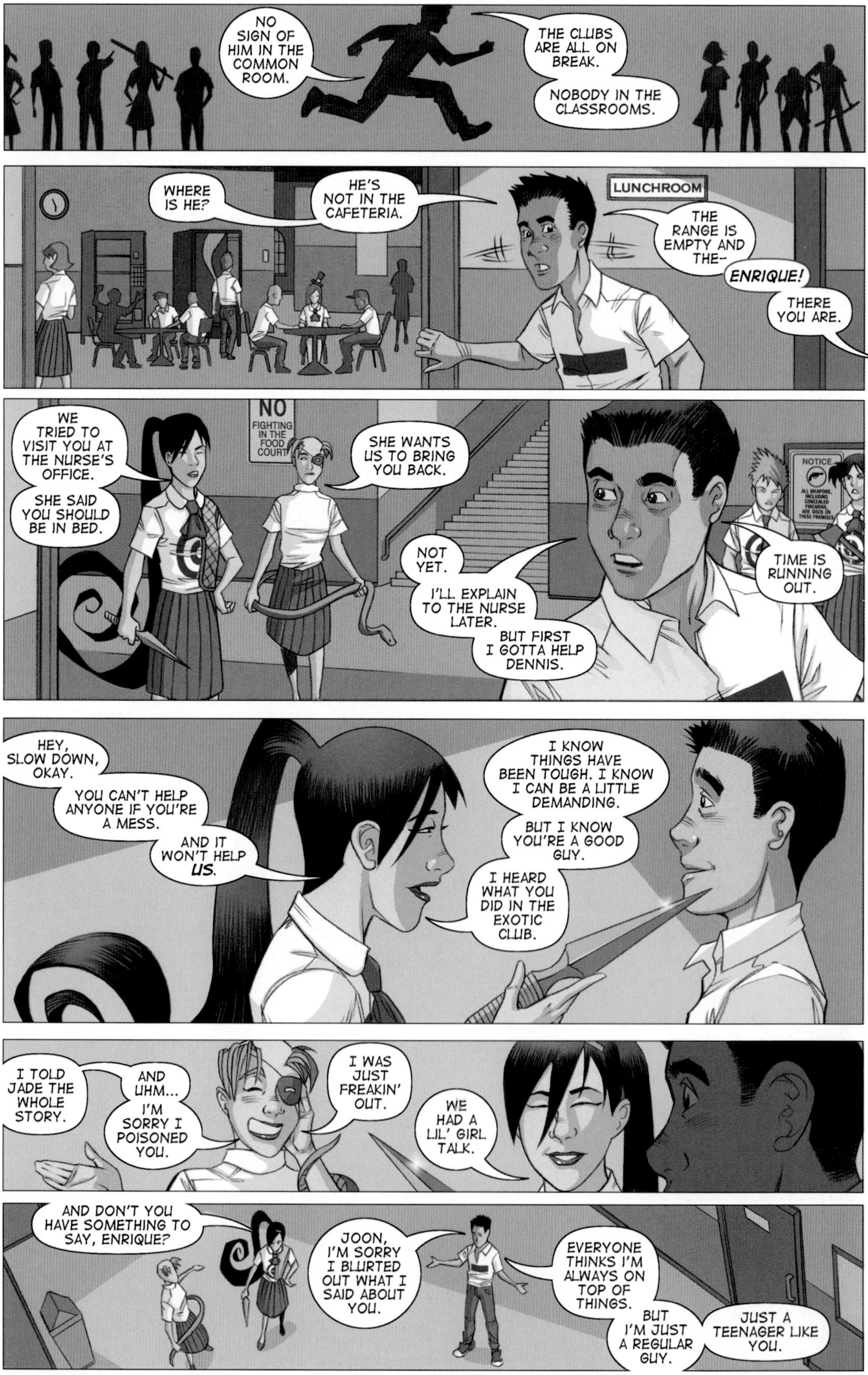
NO SIGN OF HIM IN THE COMMON ROOM.
THE CLUBS ARE ALL ON BREAK.
NOBODY IN THE CLASSROOMS.
WHERE IS HE?
HE'S NOT IN THE CAFETERIA.
LUNCHROOM
THE RANGE IS EMPTY AND THE-
ENRIQUE!
THERE YOU ARE.
WE TRIED TO VISIT YOU AT THE NURSE'S OFFICE.
SHE SAID YOU SHOULD BE IN BED.
NO FIGHTING IN THE FOOD COURT
SHE WANTS US TO BRING YOU BACK.
NOT YET.
I'LL EXPLAIN TO THE NURSE LATER.
BUT FIRST I GOTTA HELP DENNIS.
TIME IS RUNNING OUT.
HEY, SLOW DOWN, OKAY.
YOU CAN'T HELP ANYONE IF YOU'RE A MESS.
AND IT WON'T HELP US.
I KNOW THINGS HAVE BEEN TOUGH. I KNOW I CAN BE A LITTLE DEMANDING.
BUT I KNOW YOU'RE A GOOD GUY.
I HEARD WHAT YOU DID IN THE EXOTIC CLUB.
I TOLD JADE THE WHOLE STORY.
AND UHM... I'M SORRY I POISONED YOU.
I WAS JUST FREAKIN' OUT.
WE HAD A LIL' GIRL TALK.
AND DON'T YOU HAVE SOMETHING TO SAY, ENRIQUE?
JOON, I'M SORRY I BLURTED OUT WHAT I SAID ABOUT YOU.
EVERYONE THINKS I'M ALWAYS ON TOP OF THINGS.
BUT I'M JUST A REGULAR GUY.
JUST A TEENAGER LIKE YOU.

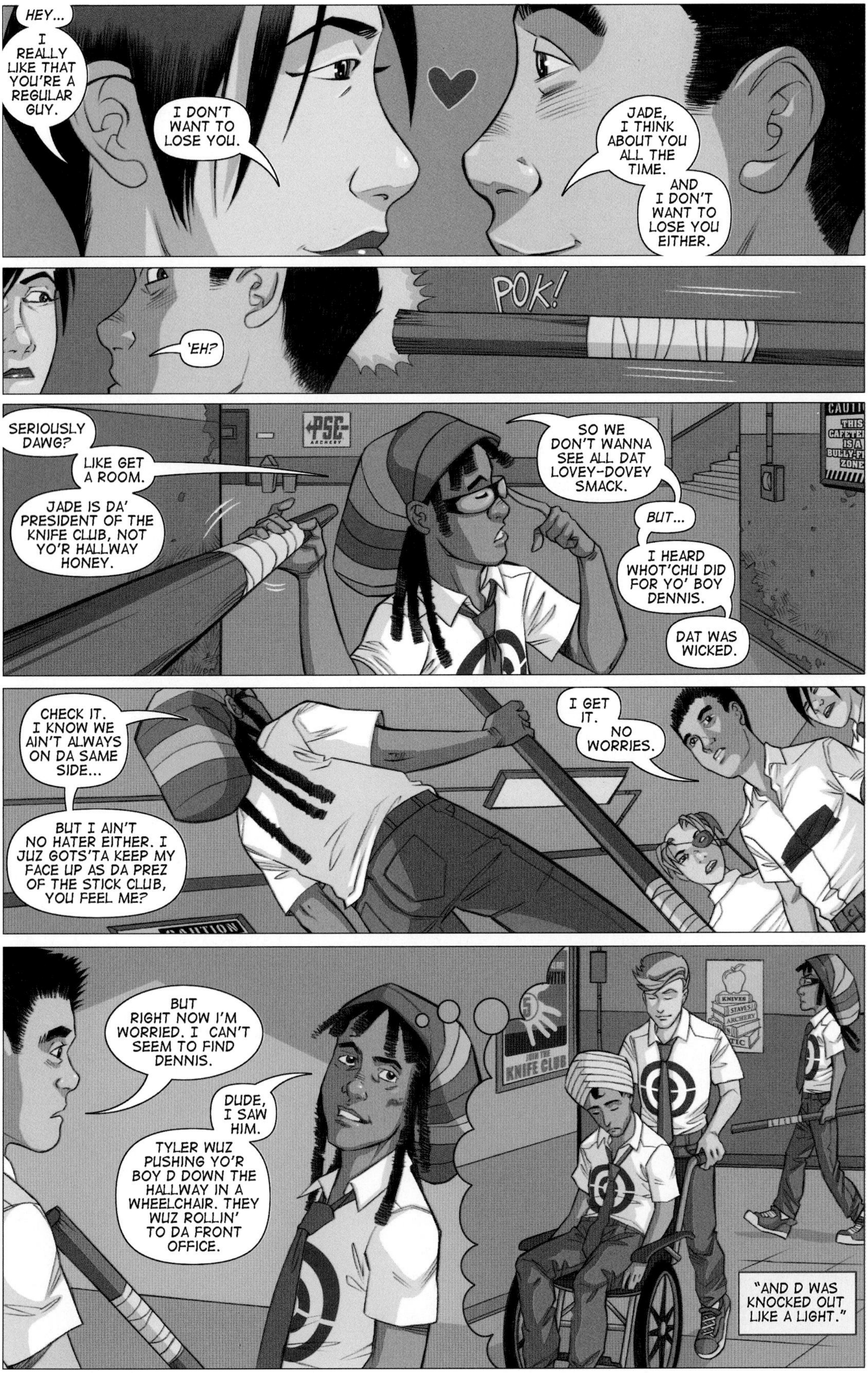
HEY...
I REALLY LIKE THAT YOU'RE A REGULAR GUY.
I DON'T WANT TO LOSE YOU.
JADE, I THINK ABOUT YOU ALL THE TIME.
AND I DON'T WANT TO LOSE YOU EITHER.
POK!
'EH?
SERIOUSLY DAWG?
LIKE GET A ROOM.
JADE IS DA' PRESIDENT OF THE KNIFE CLUB, NOT YO'R HALLWAY HONEY.
SO WE DON'T WANNA SEE ALL DAT LOVEY-DOVEY SMACK.
BUT...
I HEARD WHOT'CHU DID FOR YO' BOY DENNIS.
DAT WAS WICKED.
CHECK IT. I KNOW WE AIN'T ALWAYS ON DA SAME SIDE...
BUT I AIN'T NO HATER EITHER. I JUZ GOTS'TA KEEP MY FACE UP AS DA PREZ OF THE STICK CLUB, YOU FEEL ME?
I GET IT.
NO WORRIES.
BUT RIGHT NOW I'M WORRIED. I CAN'T SEEM TO FIND DENNIS.
DUDE, I SAW HIM.
TYLER WUZ PUSHING YO'R BOY D DOWN THE HALLWAY IN A WHEELCHAIR. THEY WUZ ROLLIN' TO DA FRONT OFFICE.
JOIN THE KNIFE CLUB
"AND D WAS KNOCKED OUT LIKE A LIGHT."

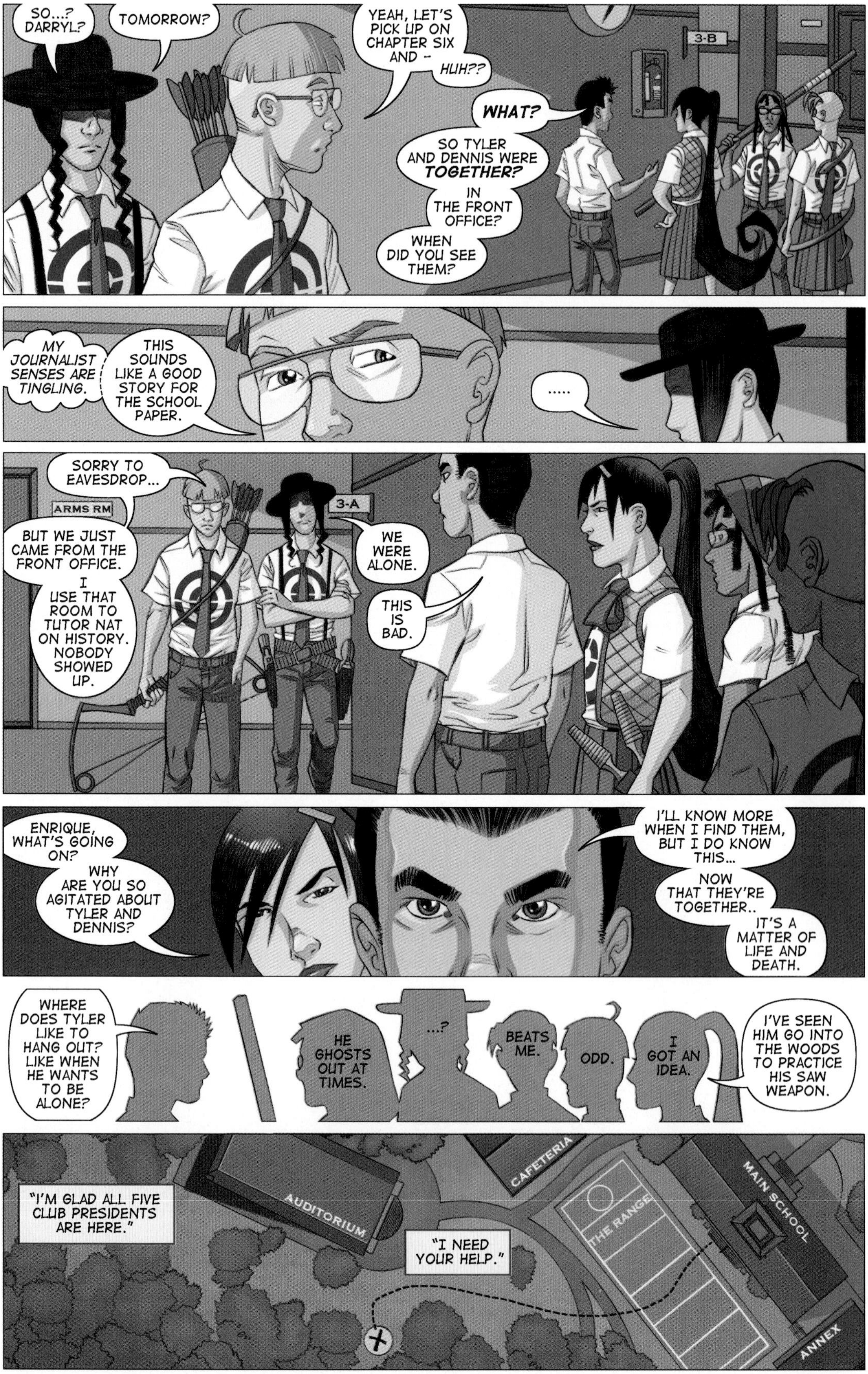
SO...? DARRYL?
TOMORROW?
YEAH, LET'S PICK UP ON CHAPTER SIX AND -
HUH??
WHAT?
SO TYLER AND DENNIS WERE TOGETHER?
IN THE FRONT OFFICE?
WHEN DID YOU SEE THEM?
3-B
MY JOURNALIST SENSES ARE TINGLING.
THIS SOUNDS LIKE A GOOD STORY FOR THE SCHOOL PAPER.
.....
SORRY TO EAVESDROP...
BUT WE JUST CAME FROM THE FRONT OFFICE.
I USE THAT ROOM TO TUTOR NAT ON HISTORY. NOBODY SHOWED UP.
ARMS RM
3-A
WE WERE ALONE.
THIS IS BAD.
ENRIQUE, WHAT'S GOING ON?
WHY ARE YOU SO AGITATED ABOUT TYLER AND DENNIS?
I'LL KNOW MORE WHEN I FIND THEM, BUT I DO KNOW THIS...
NOW THAT THEY'RE TOGETHER..
IT'S A MATTER OF LIFE AND DEATH.
WHERE DOES TYLER LIKE TO HANG OUT? LIKE WHEN HE WANTS TO BE ALONE?
HE GHOSTS OUT AT TIMES.
...?
BEATS ME.
ODD.
I GOT AN IDEA.
I'VE SEEN HIM GO INTO THE WOODS TO PRACTICE HIS SAW WEAPON.
"I'M GLAD ALL FIVE CLUB PRESIDENTS ARE HERE."
AUDITORIUM
CAFETERIA
MAIN SCHOOL
THE RANGE
"I NEED YOUR HELP."
ANNEX

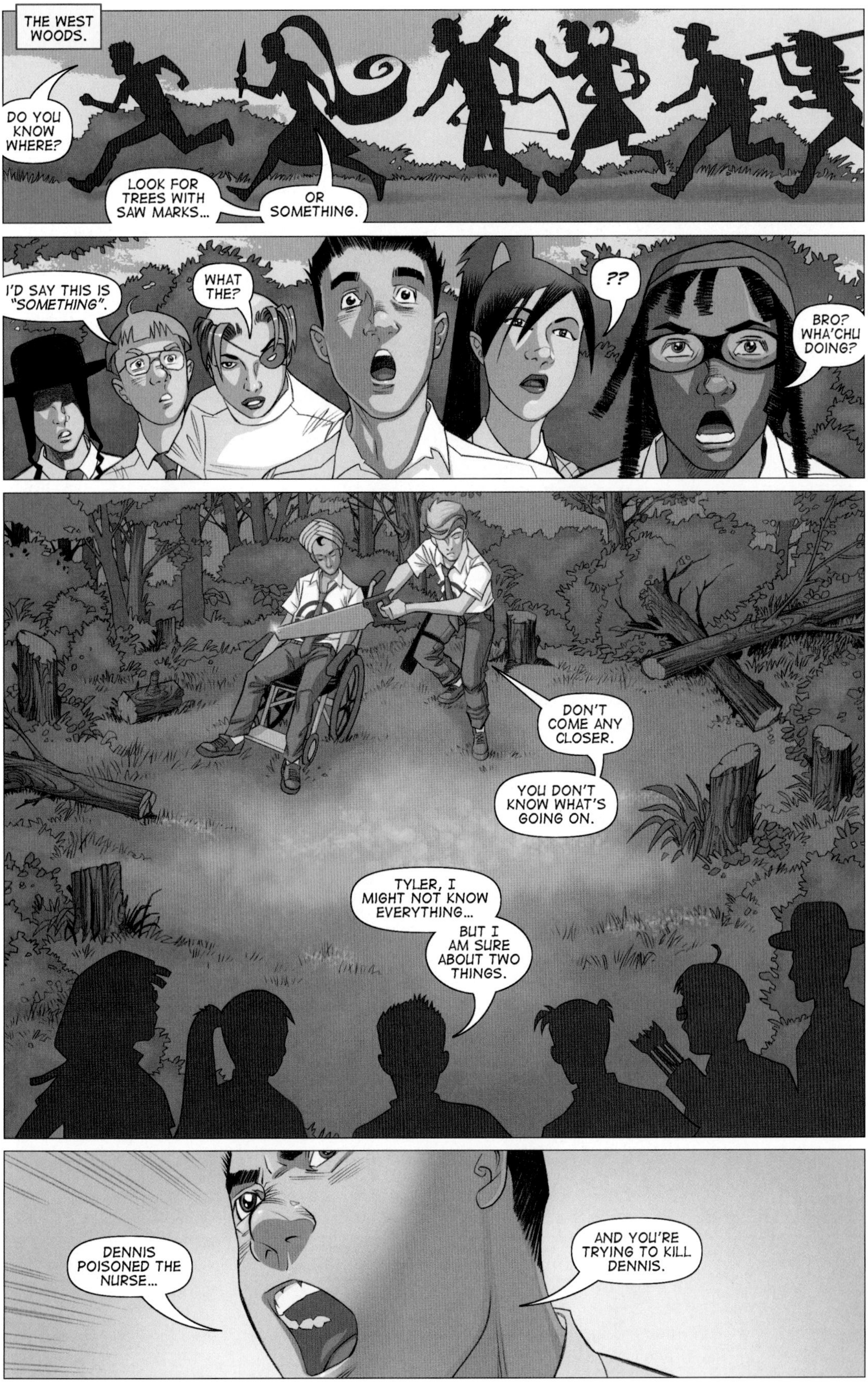
THE WEST WOODS.
DO YOU KNOW WHERE?
LOOK FOR TREES WITH SAW MARKS...
OR SOMETHING.
I'D SAY THIS IS "SOMETHING".
WHAT THE?
??
BRO? WHA'CHU DOING?
DON'T COME ANY CLOSER.
YOU DON'T KNOW WHAT'S GOING ON.
TYLER, I MIGHT NOT KNOW EVERYTHING...
BUT I AM SURE ABOUT TWO THINGS.
DENNIS POISONED THE NURSE...
AND YOU'RE TRYING TO KILL DENNIS.

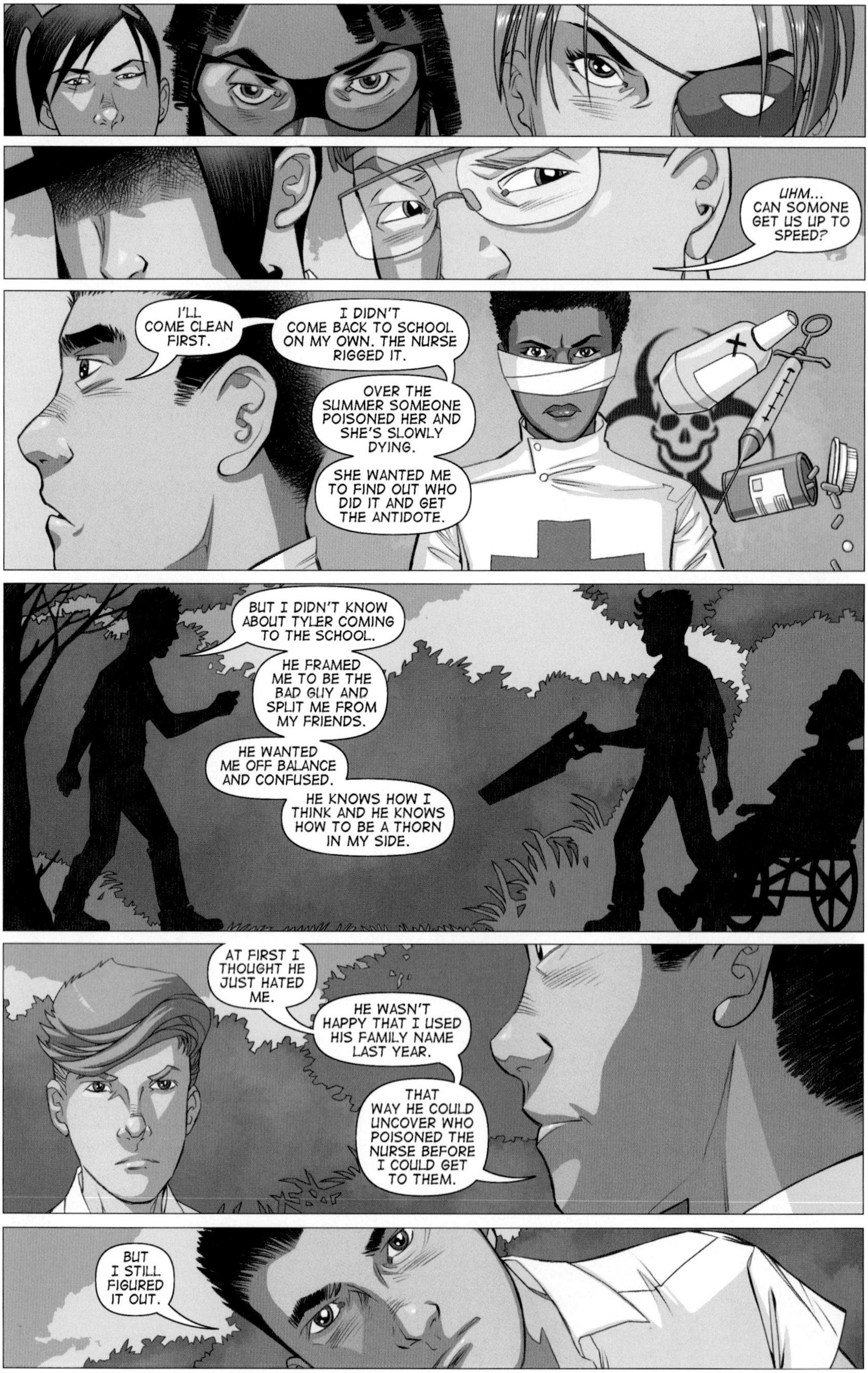
UHM... CAN SOMONE GET US UP TO SPEED?
I'LL COME CLEAN FIRST.
I DIDN'T COME BACK TO SCHOOL ON MY OWN. THE NURSE RIGGED IT.
OVER THE SUMMER SOMEONE POISONED HER AND SHE'S SLOWLY DYING.
SHE WANTED ME TO FIND OUT WHO DID IT AND GET THE ANTIDOTE.
BUT I DIDN'T KNOW ABOUT TYLER COMING TO THE SCHOOL.
HE FRAMED ME TO BE THE BAD GUY AND SPLIT ME FROM MY FRIENDS.
HE WANTED ME OFF BALANCE AND CONFUSED.
HE KNOWS HOW I THINK AND HE KNOWS HOW TO BE A THORN IN MY SIDE.
AT FIRST I THOUGHT HE JUST HATED ME.
HE WASN'T HAPPY THAT I USED HIS FAMILY NAME LAST YEAR.
THAT WAY HE COULD UNCOVER WHO POISONED THE NURSE BEFORE I COULD GET TO THEM.
BUT I STILL FIGURED IT OUT.

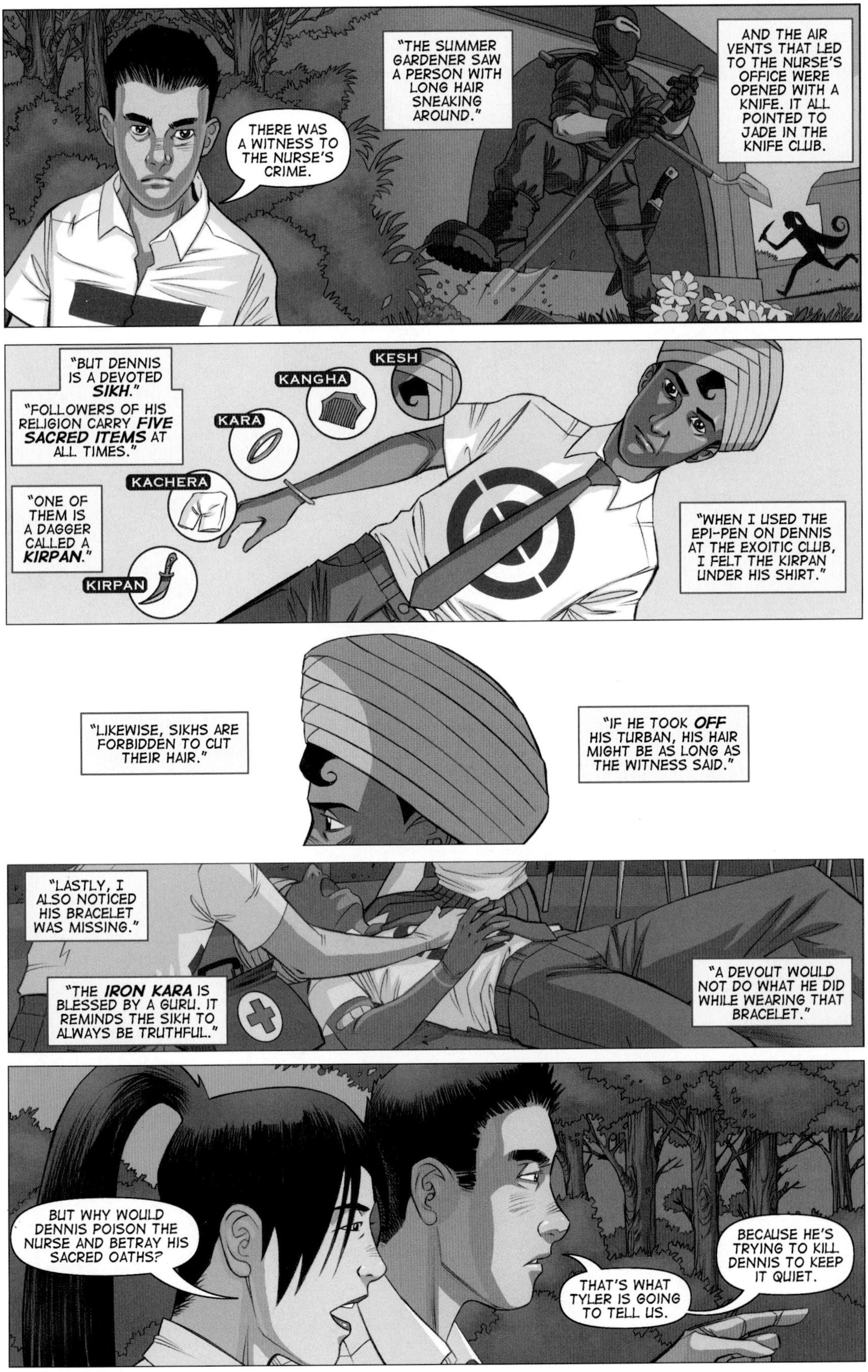
THERE WAS A WITNESS TO THE NURSE'S CRIME.
"THE SUMMER GARDENER SAW A PERSON WITH LONG HAIR SNEAKING AROUND."
AND THE AIR VENTS THAT LED TO THE NURSE'S OFFICE WERE OPENED WITH A KNIFE. IT ALL POINTED TO JADE IN THE KNIFE CLUB.
"BUT DENNIS IS A DEVOTED SIKH."
"FOLLOWERS OF HIS RELIGION CARRY FIVE SACRED ITEMS AT ALL TIMES."
KESH
KANGHA
KARA
KACHERA
KIRPAN
"ONE OF THEM IS A DAGGER CALLED A KIRPAN."
"WHEN I USED THE EPI-PEN ON DENNIS AT THE EXOITIC CLUB, I FELT THE KIRPAN UNDER HIS SHIRT."
"LIKEWISE, SIKHS ARE FORBIDDEN TO CUT THEIR HAIR."
"IF HE TOOK OFF HIS TURBAN, HIS HAIR MIGHT BE AS LONG AS THE WITNESS SAID."
"LASTLY, I ALSO NOTICED HIS BRACELET WAS MISSING."
"THE IRON KARA IS BLESSED BY A GURU. IT REMINDS THE SIKH TO ALWAYS BE TRUTHFUL."
"A DEVOUT WOULD NOT DO WHAT HE DID WHILE WEARING THAT BRACELET."
BUT WHY WOULD DENNIS POISON THE NURSE AND BETRAY HIS SACRED OATHS?
THAT'S WHAT TYLER IS GOING TO TELL US.
BECAUSE HE'S TRYING TO KILL DENNIS TO KEEP IT QUIET.

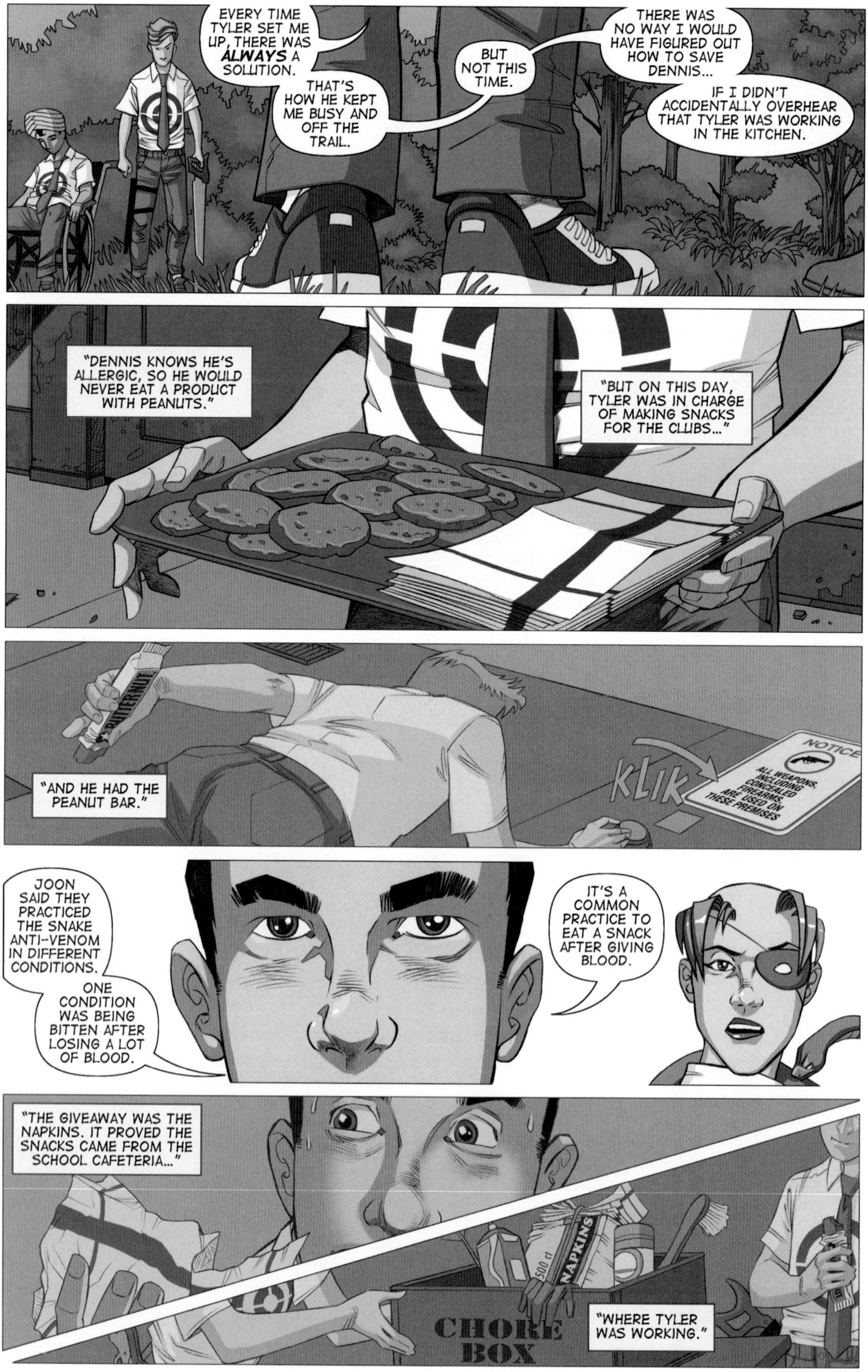
EVERY TIME TYLER SET ME UP, THERE WAS ALWAYS A SOLUTION.
THAT'S HOW HE KEPT ME BUSY AND OFF THE TRAIL.
BUT NOT THIS TIME.
THERE WAS NO WAY I WOULD HAVE FIGURED OUT HOW TO SAVE DENNIS...
IF I DIDN'T ACCIDENTALLY OVERHEAR THAT TYLER WAS WORKING IN THE KITCHEN.
"DENNIS KNOWS HE'S ALLERGIC, SO HE WOULD NEVER EAT A PRODUCT WITH PEANUTS."
"BUT ON THIS DAY, TYLER WAS IN CHARGE OF MAKING SNACKS FOR THE CLUBS..."
"AND HE HAD THE PEANUT BAR."
BUTTERNUT
KLIK
NOTICE
ALL WEAPONS, INCLUDING CONCEALED FIREARMS, ARE USED ON THESE PREMISES
JOON SAID THEY PRACTICED THE SNAKE ANTI-VENOM IN DIFFERENT CONDITIONS.
ONE CONDITION WAS BEING BITTEN AFTER LOSING A LOT OF BLOOD.
IT'S A COMMON PRACTICE TO EAT A SNACK AFTER GIVING BLOOD.
"THE GIVEAWAY WAS THE NAPKINS. IT PROVED THE SNACKS CAME FROM THE SCHOOL CAFETERIA..."
NAPKINS
500 ct
CHORE BOX
"WHERE TYLER WAS WORKING."

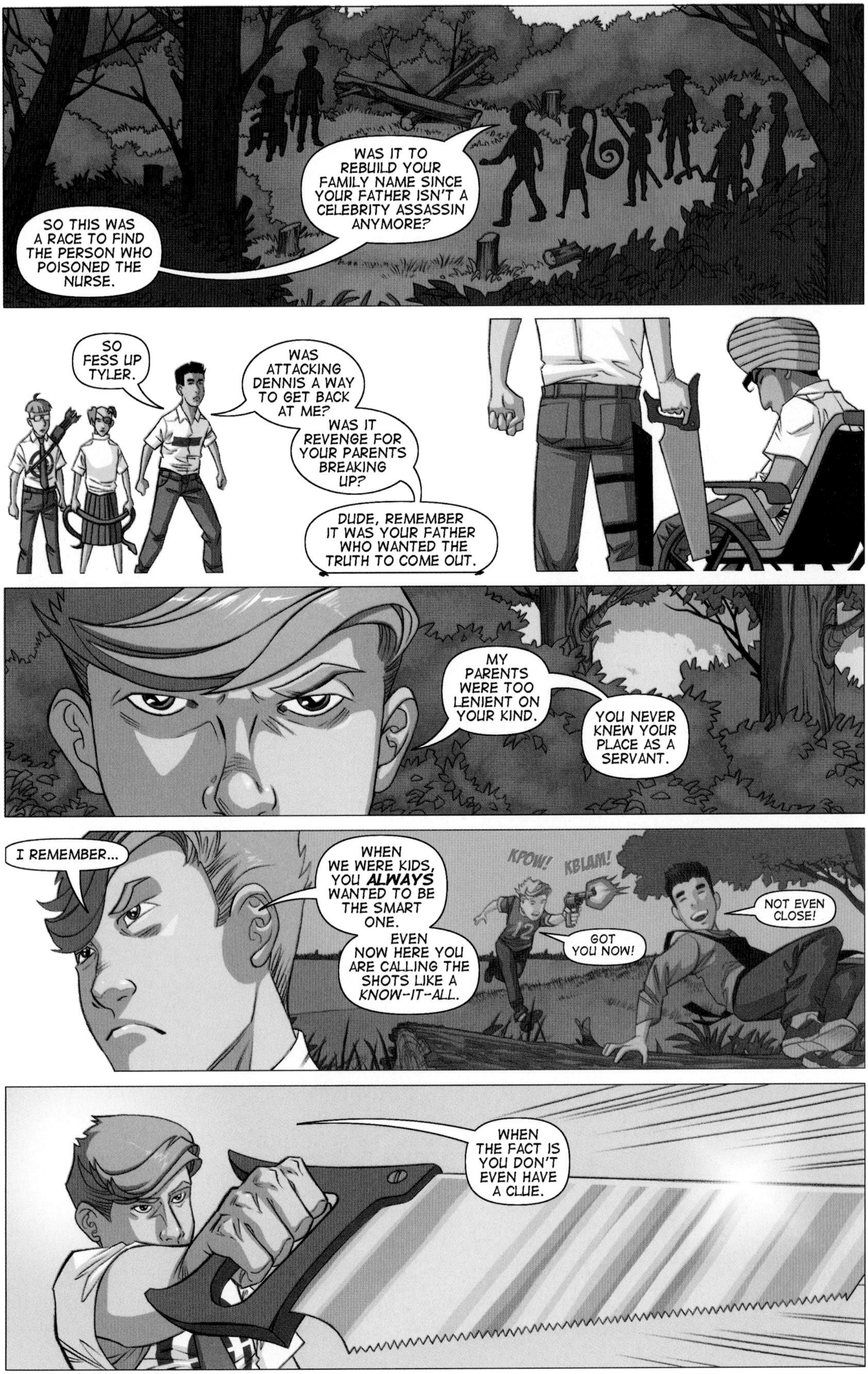
SO THIS WAS A RACE TO FIND THE PERSON WHO POISONED THE NURSE.
WAS IT TO REBUILD YOUR FAMILY NAME SINCE YOUR FATHER ISN'T A CELEBRITY ASSASSIN ANYMORE?
SO FESS UP TYLER.
WAS ATTACKING DENNIS A WAY TO GET BACK AT ME?
WAS IT REVENGE FOR YOUR PARENTS BREAKING UP?
DUDE, REMEMBER IT WAS YOUR FATHER WHO WANTED THE TRUTH TO COME OUT.
MY PARENTS WERE TOO LENIENT ON YOUR KIND.
YOU NEVER KNEW YOUR PLACE AS A SERVANT.
I REMEMBER...
WHEN WE WERE KIDS, YOU ***ALWAYS*** WANTED TO BE THE SMART ONE.
EVEN NOW HERE YOU ARE CALLING THE SHOTS LIKE A *KNOW-IT-ALL.*
KPOW!
KBLAM!
GOT YOU NOW!
NOT EVEN CLOSE!
WHEN THE FACT IS YOU DON'T EVEN HAVE A CLUE.

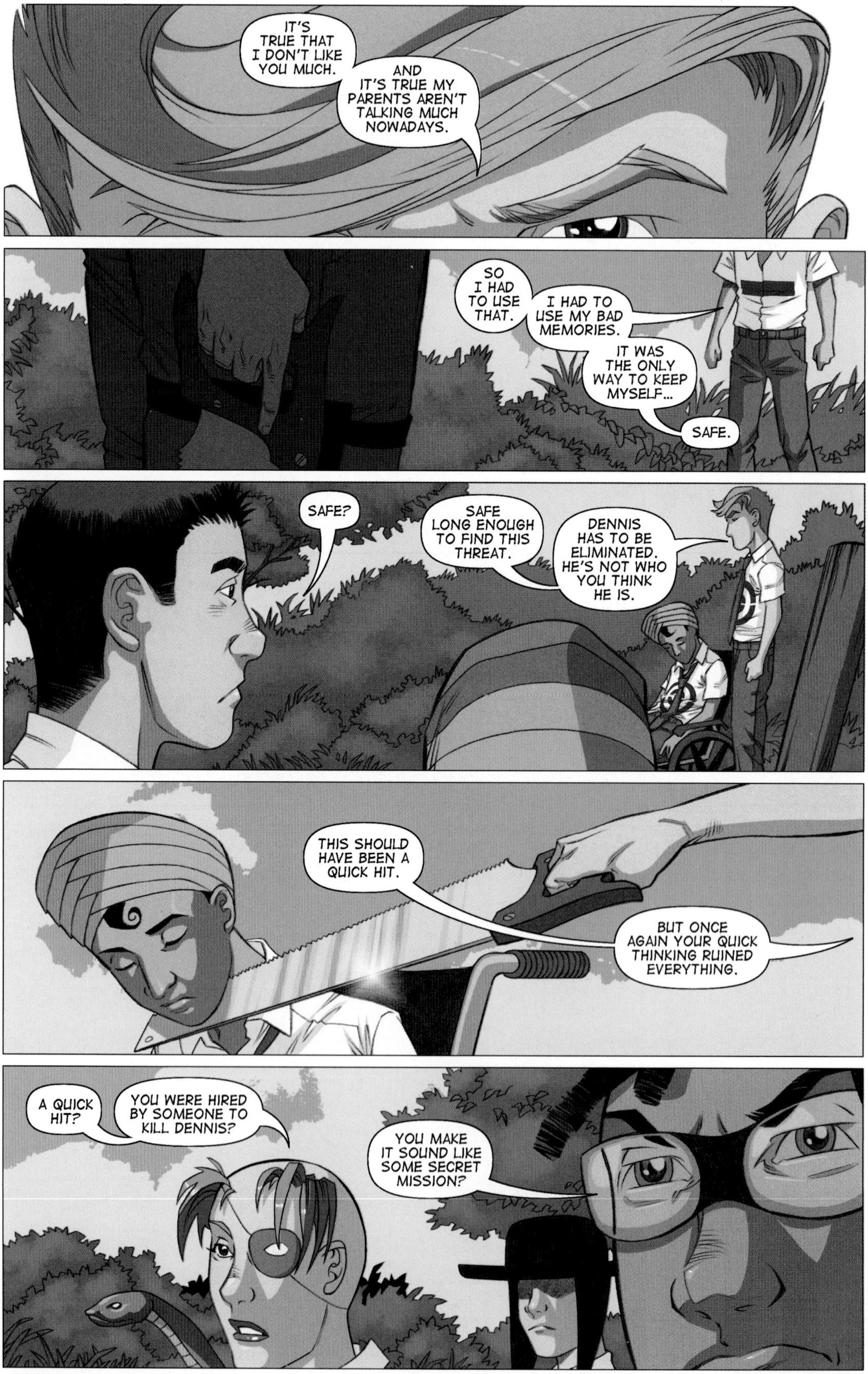
IT'S TRUE THAT I DON'T LIKE YOU MUCH.
AND IT'S TRUE MY PARENTS AREN'T TALKING MUCH NOWADAYS.
SO I HAD TO USE THAT.
I HAD TO USE MY BAD MEMORIES.
IT WAS THE ONLY WAY TO KEEP MYSELF...
SAFE.
SAFE?
SAFE LONG ENOUGH TO FIND THIS THREAT.
DENNIS HAS TO BE ELIMINATED. HE'S NOT WHO YOU THINK HE IS.
THIS SHOULD HAVE BEEN A QUICK HIT.
BUT ONCE AGAIN YOUR QUICK THINKING RUINED EVERYTHING.
A QUICK HIT?
YOU WERE HIRED BY SOMEONE TO KILL DENNIS?
YOU MAKE IT SOUND LIKE SOME SECRET MISSION?

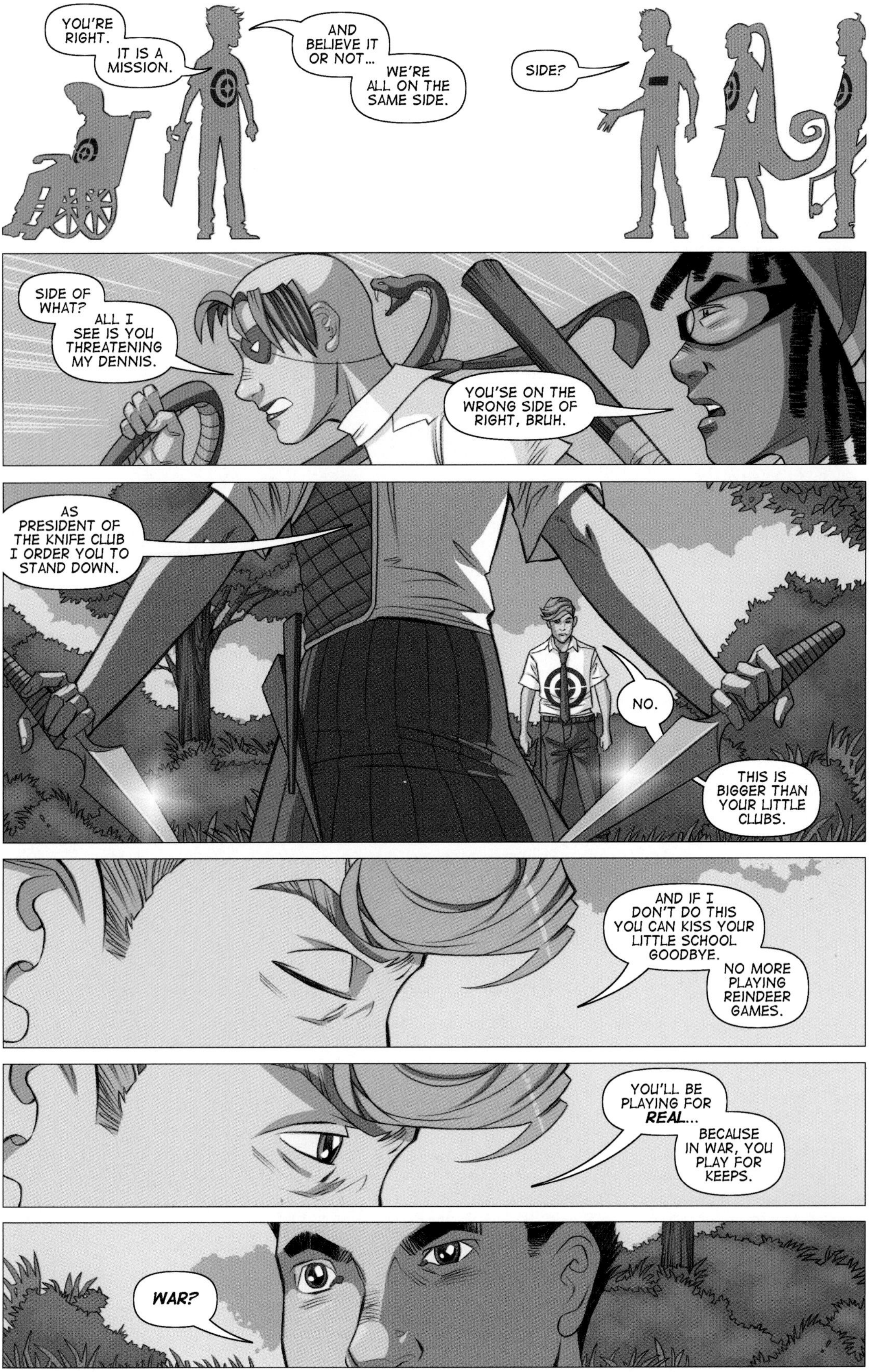
YOU'RE RIGHT.
IT IS A MISSION.
AND BELIEVE IT OR NOT...
WE'RE ALL ON THE SAME SIDE.
SIDE?
SIDE OF WHAT?
ALL I SEE IS YOU THREATENING MY DENNIS.
YOU'SE ON THE WRONG SIDE OF RIGHT, BRUH.
AS PRESIDENT OF THE KNIFE CLUB I ORDER YOU TO STAND DOWN.
NO.
THIS IS BIGGER THAN YOUR LITTLE CLUBS.
AND IF I DON'T DO THIS YOU CAN KISS YOUR LITTLE SCHOOL GOODBYE.
NO MORE PLAYING REINDEER GAMES.
YOU'LL BE PLAYING FOR REAL...
BECAUSE IN WAR, YOU PLAY FOR KEEPS.
WAR?

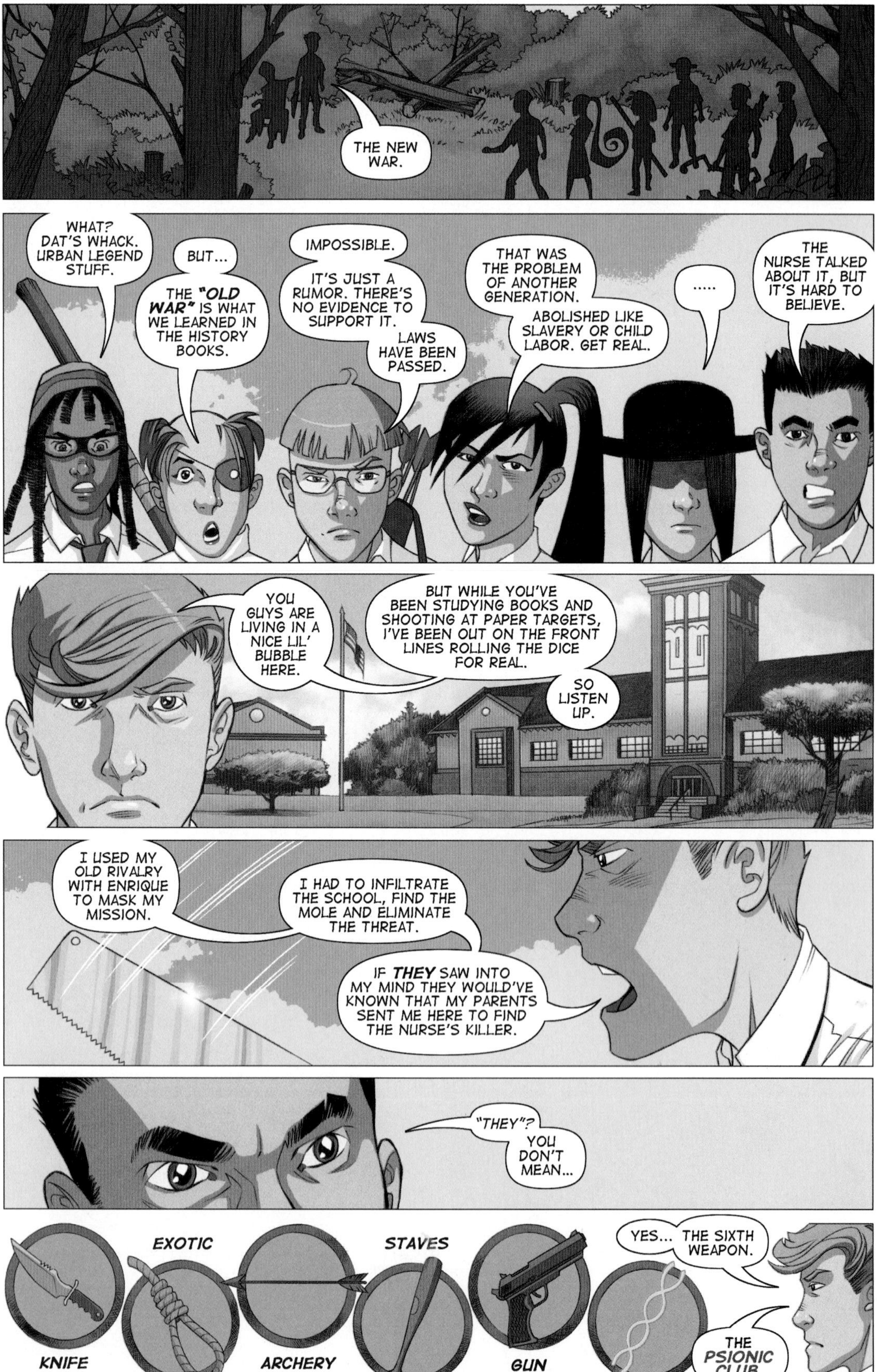
THE NEW WAR.
WHAT? DAT'S WHACK. URBAN LEGEND STUFF.
BUT...
THE "OLD WAR" IS WHAT WE LEARNED IN THE HISTORY BOOKS.
IMPOSSIBLE.
IT'S JUST A RUMOR. THERE'S NO EVIDENCE TO SUPPORT IT.
LAWS HAVE BEEN PASSED.
THAT WAS THE PROBLEM OF ANOTHER GENERATION.
ABOLISHED LIKE SLAVERY OR CHILD LABOR. GET REAL.
.....
THE NURSE TALKED ABOUT IT, BUT IT'S HARD TO BELIEVE.
YOU GUYS ARE LIVING IN A NICE LIL' BUBBLE HERE.
BUT WHILE YOU'VE BEEN STUDYING BOOKS AND SHOOTING AT PAPER TARGETS, I'VE BEEN OUT ON THE FRONT LINES ROLLING THE DICE FOR REAL.
SO LISTEN UP.
I USED MY OLD RIVALRY WITH ENRIQUE TO MASK MY MISSION.
I HAD TO INFILTRATE THE SCHOOL, FIND THE MOLE AND ELIMINATE THE THREAT.
IF THEY SAW INTO MY MIND THEY WOULD'VE KNOWN THAT MY PARENTS SENT ME HERE TO FIND THE NURSE'S KILLER.
"THEY"?
YOU DON'T MEAN...
EXOTIC
STAVES
KNIFE
ARCHERY
GUN
YES... THE SIXTH WEAPON.
THE PSIONIC CLUB.

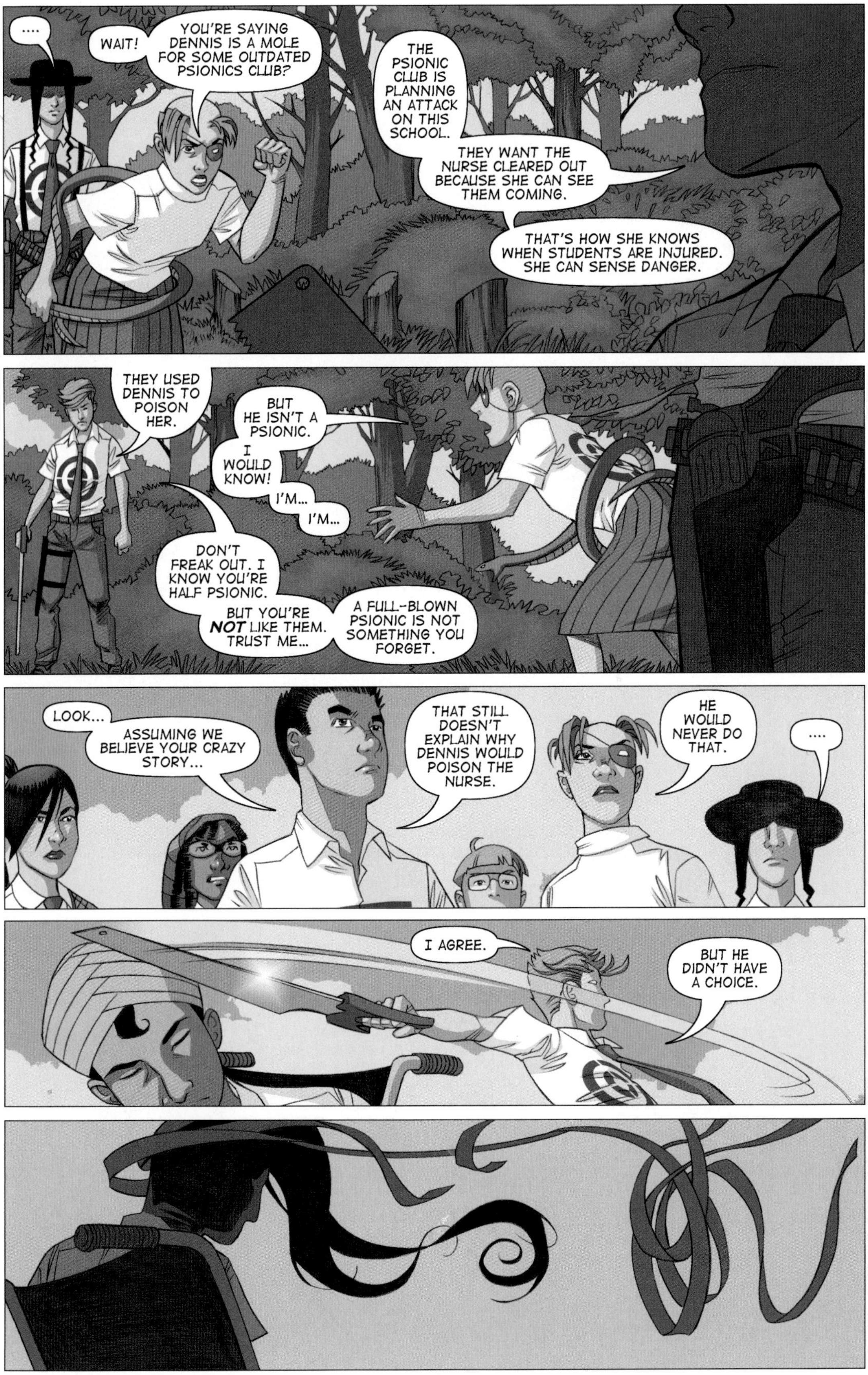
....
WAIT!
YOU'RE SAYING DENNIS IS A MOLE FOR SOME OUTDATED PSIONICS CLUB?
THE PSIONIC CLUB IS PLANNING AN ATTACK ON THIS SCHOOL.
THEY WANT THE NURSE CLEARED OUT BECAUSE SHE CAN SEE THEM COMING.
THAT'S HOW SHE KNOWS WHEN STUDENTS ARE INJURED. SHE CAN SENSE DANGER.
THEY USED DENNIS TO POISON HER.
BUT HE ISN'T A PSIONIC.
I WOULD KNOW!
I'M...
I'M...
DON'T FREAK OUT. I KNOW YOU'RE HALF PSIONIC.
BUT YOU'RE ***NOT*** LIKE THEM. TRUST ME...
A FULL-BLOWN PSIONIC IS NOT SOMETHING YOU FORGET.
LOOK...
ASSUMING WE BELIEVE YOUR CRAZY STORY...
THAT STILL DOESN'T EXPLAIN WHY DENNIS WOULD POISON THE NURSE.
HE WOULD NEVER DO THAT.
....
I AGREE.
BUT HE DIDN'T HAVE A CHOICE.

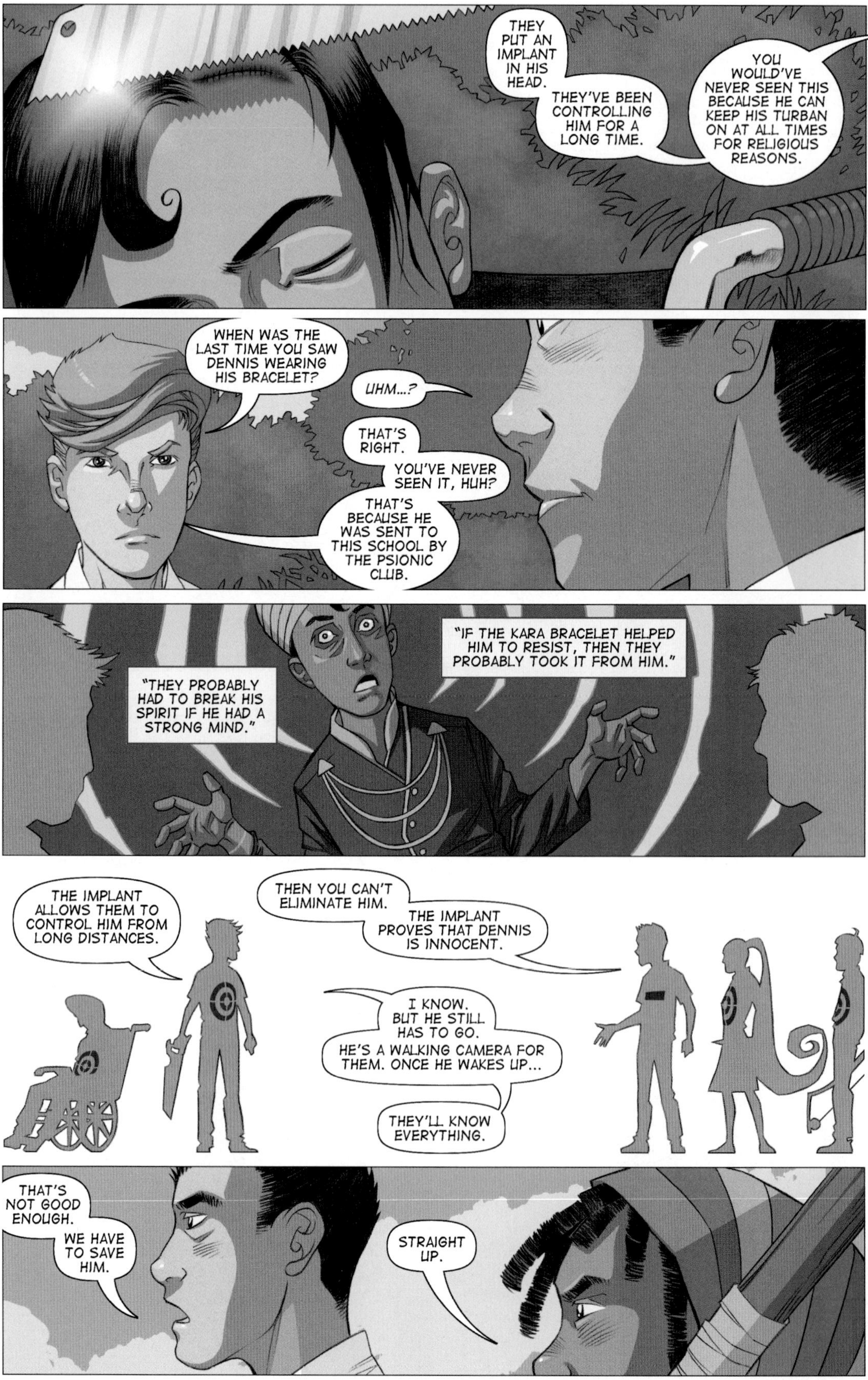
THEY PUT AN IMPLANT IN HIS HEAD.
THEY'VE BEEN CONTROLLING HIM FOR A LONG TIME.
YOU WOULD'VE NEVER SEEN THIS BECAUSE HE CAN KEEP HIS TURBAN ON AT ALL TIMES FOR RELIGIOUS REASONS.
WHEN WAS THE LAST TIME YOU SAW DENNIS WEARING HIS BRACELET?
UHM...?
THAT'S RIGHT.
YOU'VE NEVER SEEN IT, HUH?
THAT'S BECAUSE HE WAS SENT TO THIS SCHOOL BY THE PSIONIC CLUB.
"THEY PROBABLY HAD TO BREAK HIS SPIRIT IF HE HAD A STRONG MIND."
"IF THE KARA BRACELET HELPED HIM TO RESIST, THEN THEY PROBABLY TOOK IT FROM HIM."
THE IMPLANT ALLOWS THEM TO CONTROL HIM FROM LONG DISTANCES.
THEN YOU CAN'T ELIMINATE HIM.
THE IMPLANT PROVES THAT DENNIS IS INNOCENT.
I KNOW. BUT HE STILL HAS TO GO.
HE'S A WALKING CAMERA FOR THEM. ONCE HE WAKES UP...
THEY'LL KNOW EVERYTHING.
THAT'S NOT GOOD ENOUGH.
WE HAVE TO SAVE HIM.
STRAIGHT UP.

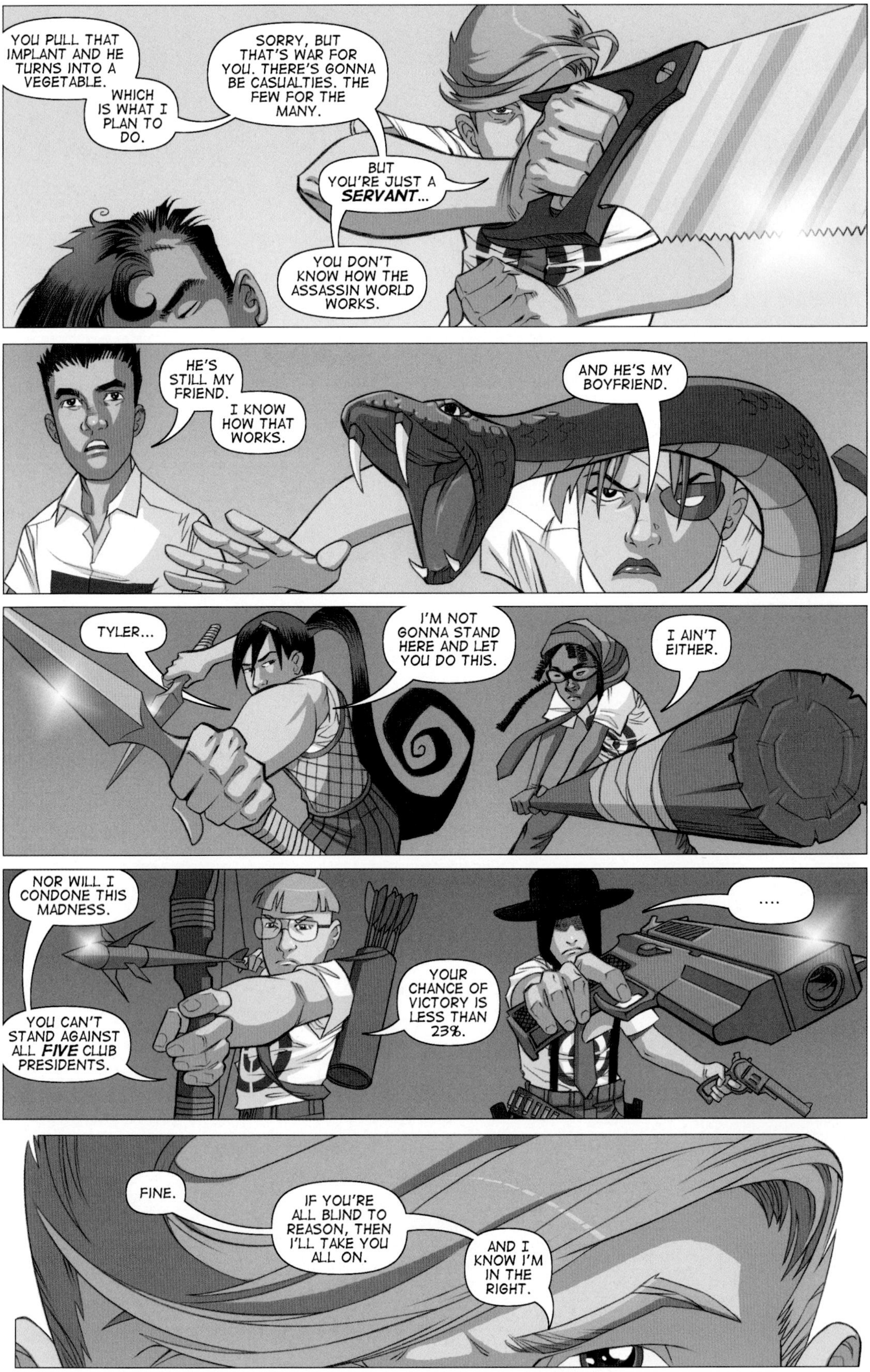
YOU PULL THAT IMPLANT AND HE TURNS INTO A VEGETABLE.
WHICH IS WHAT I PLAN TO DO.
SORRY, BUT THAT'S WAR FOR YOU. THERE'S GONNA BE CASUALTIES. THE FEW FOR THE MANY.
BUT YOU'RE JUST A **SERVANT**...
YOU DON'T KNOW HOW THE ASSASSIN WORLD WORKS.
HE'S STILL MY FRIEND.
I KNOW HOW THAT WORKS.
AND HE'S MY BOYFRIEND.
TYLER...
I'M NOT GONNA STAND HERE AND LET YOU DO THIS.
I AIN'T EITHER.
NOR WILL I CONDONE THIS MADNESS.
YOU CAN'T STAND AGAINST ALL ***FIVE*** CLUB PRESIDENTS.
YOUR CHANCE OF VICTORY IS LESS THAN 23%.
....
FINE.
IF YOU'RE ALL BLIND TO REASON, THEN I'LL TAKE YOU ALL ON.
AND I KNOW I'M IN THE RIGHT.

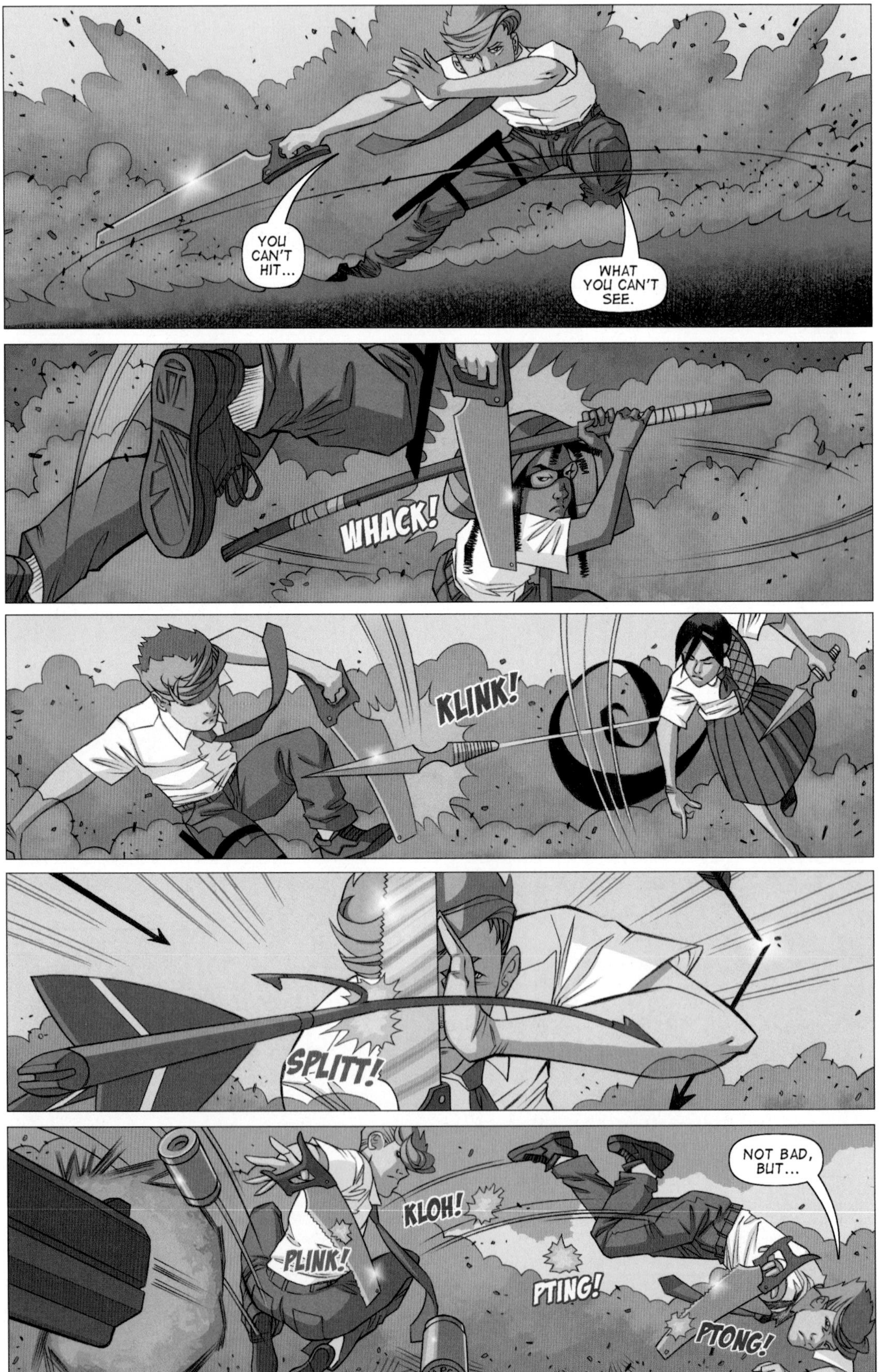
YOU CAN'T HIT...
WHAT YOU CAN'T SEE.
WHACK!
KLINK!
SPLITT!
PLINK!
KLOH!
PTING!
PTONG!
NOT BAD, BUT...

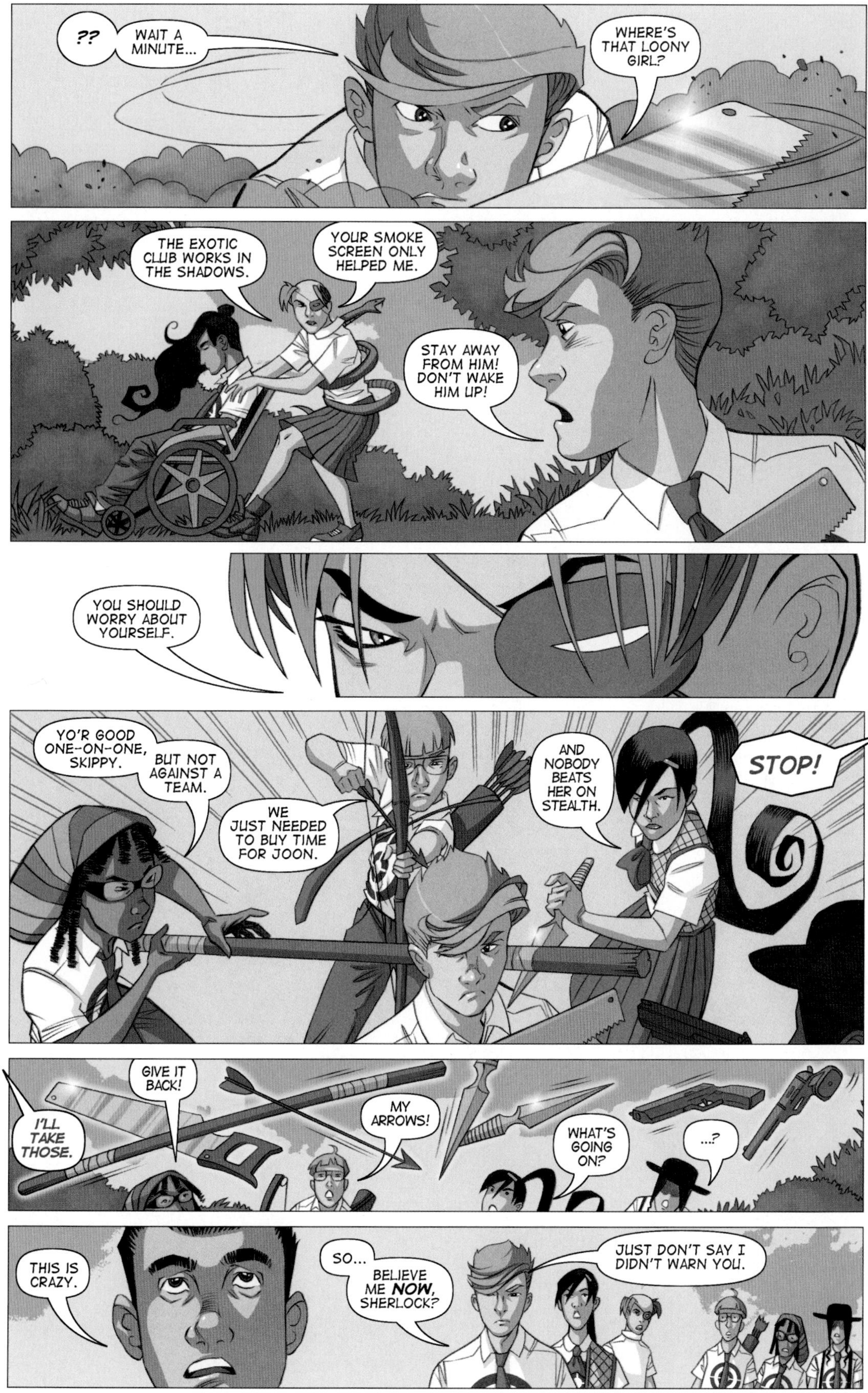
??
WAIT A MINUTE...
WHERE'S THAT LOONY GIRL?
THE EXOTIC CLUB WORKS IN THE SHADOWS.
YOUR SMOKE SCREEN ONLY HELPED ME.
STAY AWAY FROM HIM! DON'T WAKE HIM UP!
YOU SHOULD WORRY ABOUT YOURSELF.
YO'R GOOD ONE--ON-ONE, SKIPPY.
BUT NOT AGAINST A TEAM.
WE JUST NEEDED TO BUY TIME FOR JOON.
AND NOBODY BEATS HER ON STEALTH.
STOP!
I'LL TAKE THOSE.
GIVE IT BACK!
MY ARROWS!
WHAT'S GOING ON?
...?
THIS IS CRAZY.
SO... BELIEVE ME NOW, SHERLOCK?
JUST DON'T SAY I DIDN'T WARN YOU.

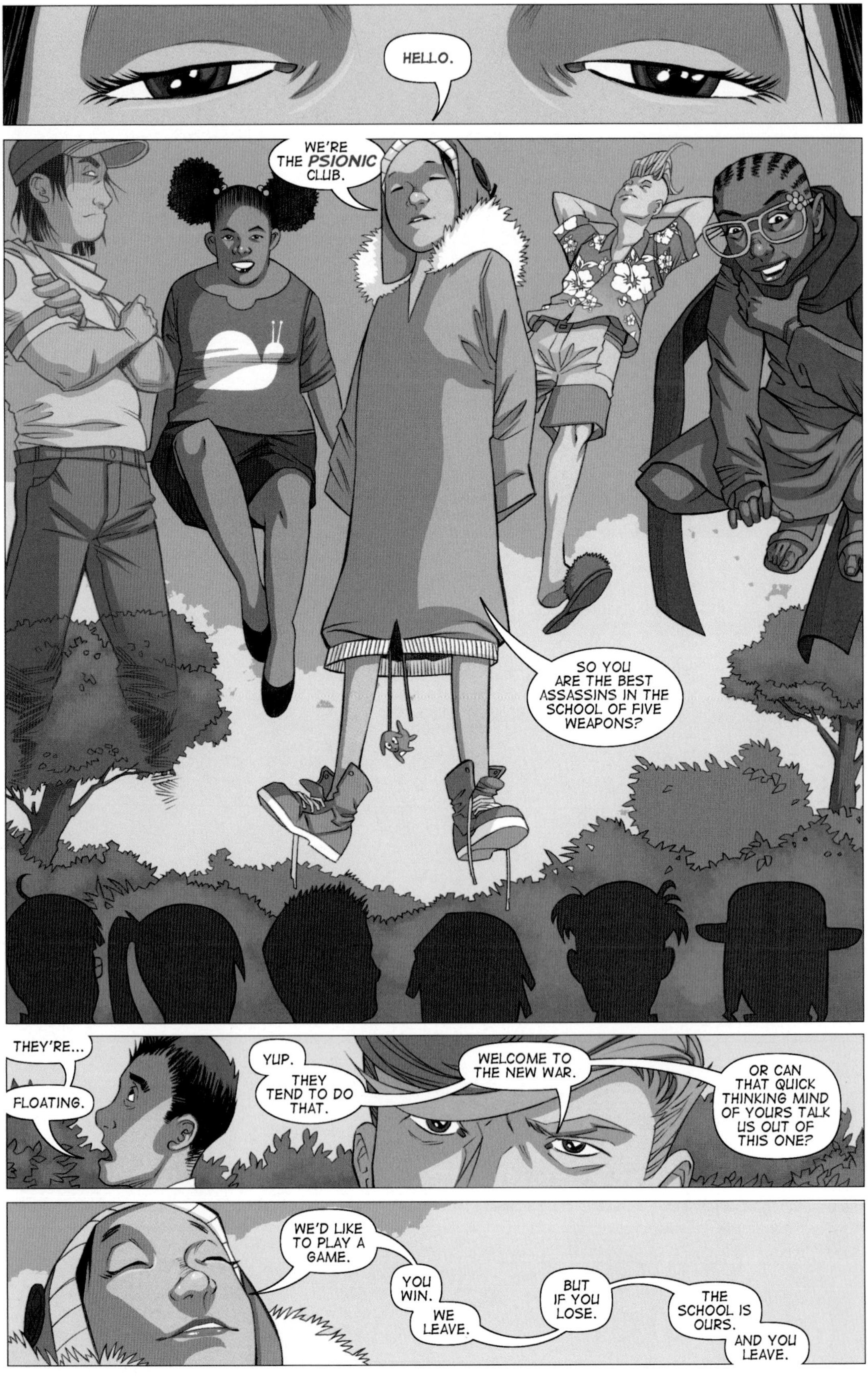
HELLO.
WE'RE THE *PSIONIC* CLUB.
SO YOU ARE THE BEST ASSASSINS IN THE SCHOOL OF FIVE WEAPONS?
THEY'RE...
FLOATING.
YUP.
THEY TEND TO DO THAT.
WELCOME TO THE NEW WAR.
OR CAN THAT QUICK THINKING MIND OF YOURS TALK US OUT OF THIS ONE?
WE'D LIKE TO PLAY A GAME.
YOU WIN.
WE LEAVE.
BUT IF YOU LOSE.
THE SCHOOL IS OURS.
AND YOU LEAVE.

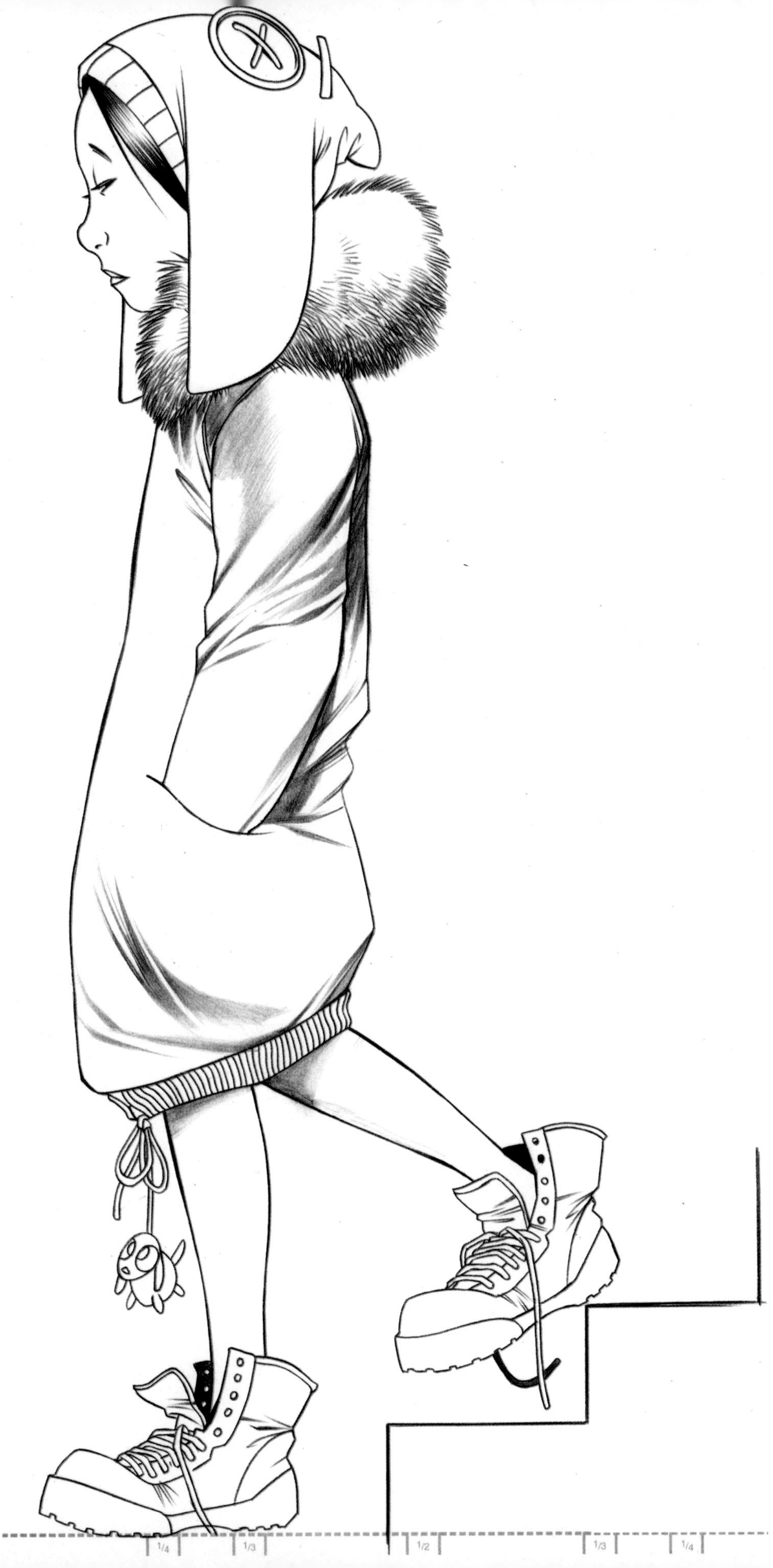
1/4
1/3
1/2
1/3
1/4

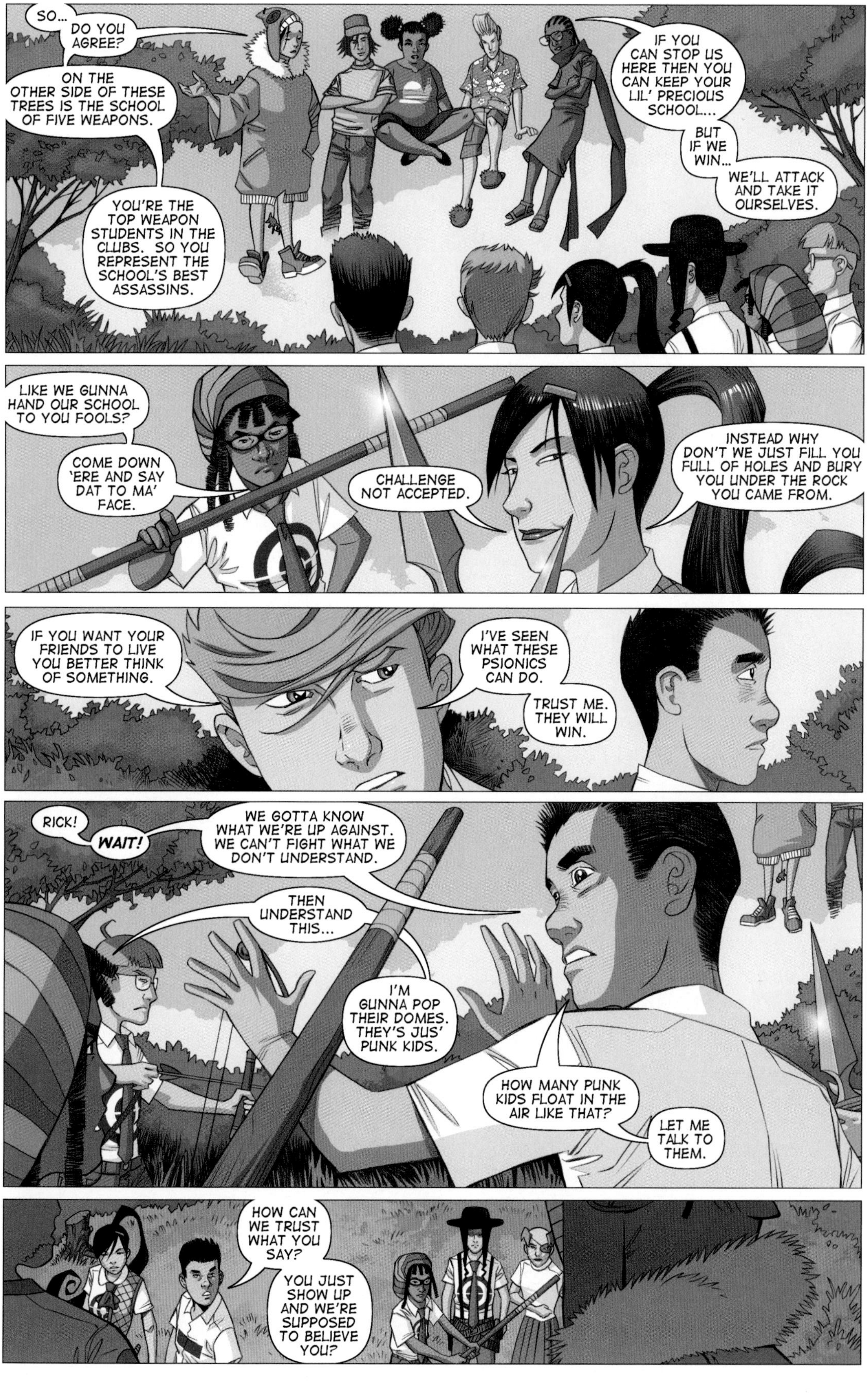
SO... DO YOU AGREE?
ON THE OTHER SIDE OF THESE TREES IS THE SCHOOL OF FIVE WEAPONS.
YOU'RE THE TOP WEAPON STUDENTS IN THE CLUBS. SO YOU REPRESENT THE SCHOOL'S BEST ASSASSINS.
IF YOU CAN STOP US HERE THEN YOU CAN KEEP YOUR LIL' PRECIOUS SCHOOL...
BUT IF WE WIN...
WE'LL ATTACK AND TAKE IT OURSELVES.
LIKE WE GUNNA HAND OUR SCHOOL TO YOU FOOLS?
COME DOWN 'ERE AND SAY DAT TO MA' FACE.
CHALLENGE NOT ACCEPTED.
INSTEAD WHY DON'T WE JUST FILL YOU FULL OF HOLES AND BURY YOU UNDER THE ROCK YOU CAME FROM.
IF YOU WANT YOUR FRIENDS TO LIVE YOU BETTER THINK OF SOMETHING.
I'VE SEEN WHAT THESE PSIONICS CAN DO.
TRUST ME. THEY WILL WIN.
RICK!
WAIT!
WE GOTTA KNOW WHAT WE'RE UP AGAINST. WE CAN'T FIGHT WHAT WE DON'T UNDERSTAND.
THEN UNDERSTAND THIS...
I'M GUNNA POP THEIR DOMES. THEY'S JUS' PUNK KIDS.
HOW MANY PUNK KIDS FLOAT IN THE AIR LIKE THAT?
LET ME TALK TO THEM.
HOW CAN WE TRUST WHAT YOU SAY?
YOU JUST SHOW UP AND WE'RE SUPPOSED TO BELIEVE YOU?

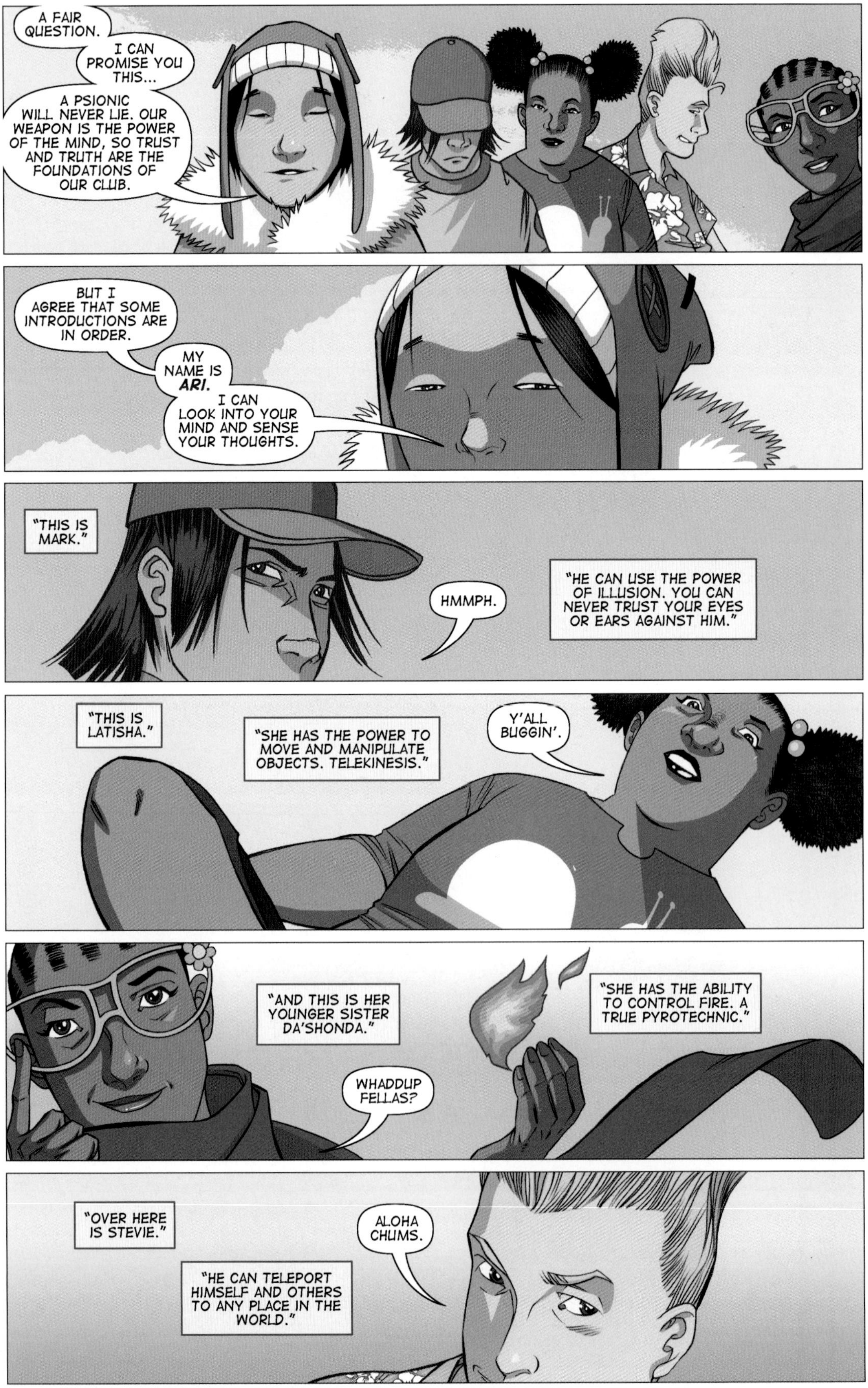
A FAIR QUESTION.
I CAN PROMISE YOU THIS...
A PSIONIC WILL NEVER LIE. OUR WEAPON IS THE POWER OF THE MIND, SO TRUST AND TRUTH ARE THE FOUNDATIONS OF OUR CLUB.
BUT I AGREE THAT SOME INTRODUCTIONS ARE IN ORDER.
MY NAME IS ARI.
I CAN LOOK INTO YOUR MIND AND SENSE YOUR THOUGHTS.
"THIS IS MARK."
HMMPH.
"HE CAN USE THE POWER OF ILLUSION. YOU CAN NEVER TRUST YOUR EYES OR EARS AGAINST HIM."
"THIS IS LATISHA."
"SHE HAS THE POWER TO MOVE AND MANIPULATE OBJECTS. TELEKINESIS."
Y'ALL BUGGIN'.
"AND THIS IS HER YOUNGER SISTER DA'SHONDA."
WHADDUP FELLAS?
"SHE HAS THE ABILITY TO CONTROL FIRE. A TRUE PYROTECHNIC."
"OVER HERE IS STEVIE."
ALOHA CHUMS.
"HE CAN TELEPORT HIMSELF AND OTHERS TO ANY PLACE IN THE WORLD."

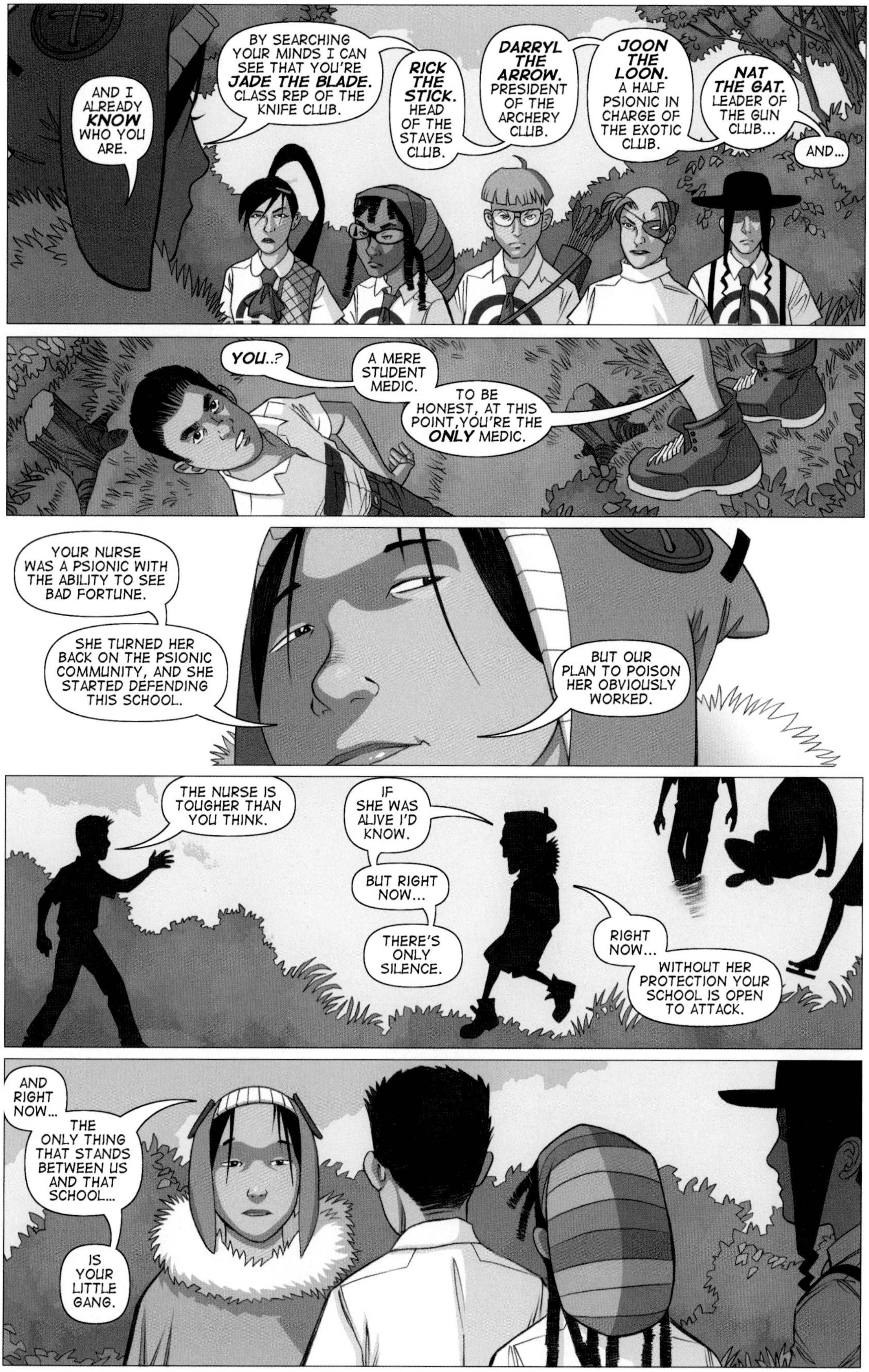
AND I ALREADY KNOW WHO YOU ARE.
BY SEARCHING YOUR MINDS I CAN SEE THAT YOU'RE JADE THE BLADE. CLASS REP OF THE KNIFE CLUB.
RICK THE STICK. HEAD OF THE STAVES CLUB.
DARRYL THE ARROW. PRESIDENT OF THE ARCHERY CLUB.
JOON THE LOON. A HALF PSIONIC IN CHARGE OF THE EXOTIC CLUB.
NAT THE GAT. LEADER OF THE GUN CLUB...
AND...
YOU..?
A MERE STUDENT MEDIC.
TO BE HONEST, AT THIS POINT,YOU'RE THE ONLY MEDIC.
YOUR NURSE WAS A PSIONIC WITH THE ABILITY TO SEE BAD FORTUNE.
SHE TURNED HER BACK ON THE PSIONIC COMMUNITY, AND SHE STARTED DEFENDING THIS SCHOOL.
BUT OUR PLAN TO POISON HER OBVIOUSLY WORKED.
THE NURSE IS TOUGHER THAN YOU THINK.
IF SHE WAS ALIVE I'D KNOW.
BUT RIGHT NOW...
THERE'S ONLY SILENCE.
RIGHT NOW...
WITHOUT HER PROTECTION YOUR SCHOOL IS OPEN TO ATTACK.
AND RIGHT NOW...
THE ONLY THING THAT STANDS BETWEEN US AND THAT SCHOOL...
IS YOUR LITTLE GANG.

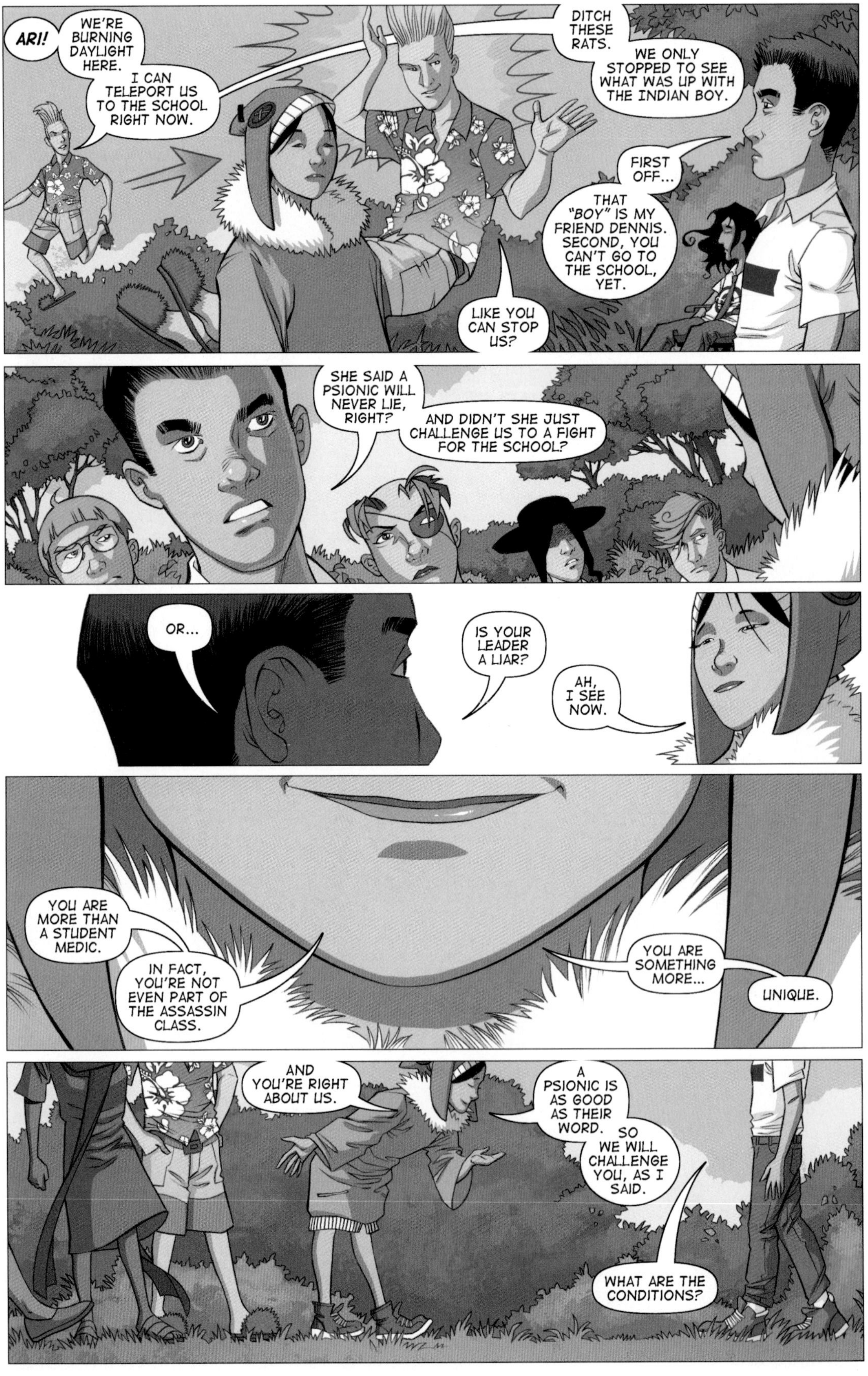
ARI!
WE'RE BURNING DAYLIGHT HERE.
I CAN TELEPORT US TO THE SCHOOL RIGHT NOW.
DITCH THESE RATS.
WE ONLY STOPPED TO SEE WHAT WAS UP WITH THE INDIAN BOY.
FIRST OFF...
THAT "BOY" IS MY FRIEND DENNIS. SECOND, YOU CAN'T GO TO THE SCHOOL, YET.
LIKE YOU CAN STOP US?
SHE SAID A PSIONIC WILL NEVER LIE, RIGHT?
AND DIDN'T SHE JUST CHALLENGE US TO A FIGHT FOR THE SCHOOL?
OR...
IS YOUR LEADER A LIAR?
AH, I SEE NOW.
YOU ARE MORE THAN A STUDENT MEDIC.
IN FACT, YOU'RE NOT EVEN PART OF THE ASSASSIN CLASS.
YOU ARE SOMETHING MORE...
UNIQUE.
AND YOU'RE RIGHT ABOUT US.
A PSIONIC IS AS GOOD AS THEIR WORD.
SO WE WILL CHALLENGE YOU, AS I SAID.
WHAT ARE THE CONDITIONS?

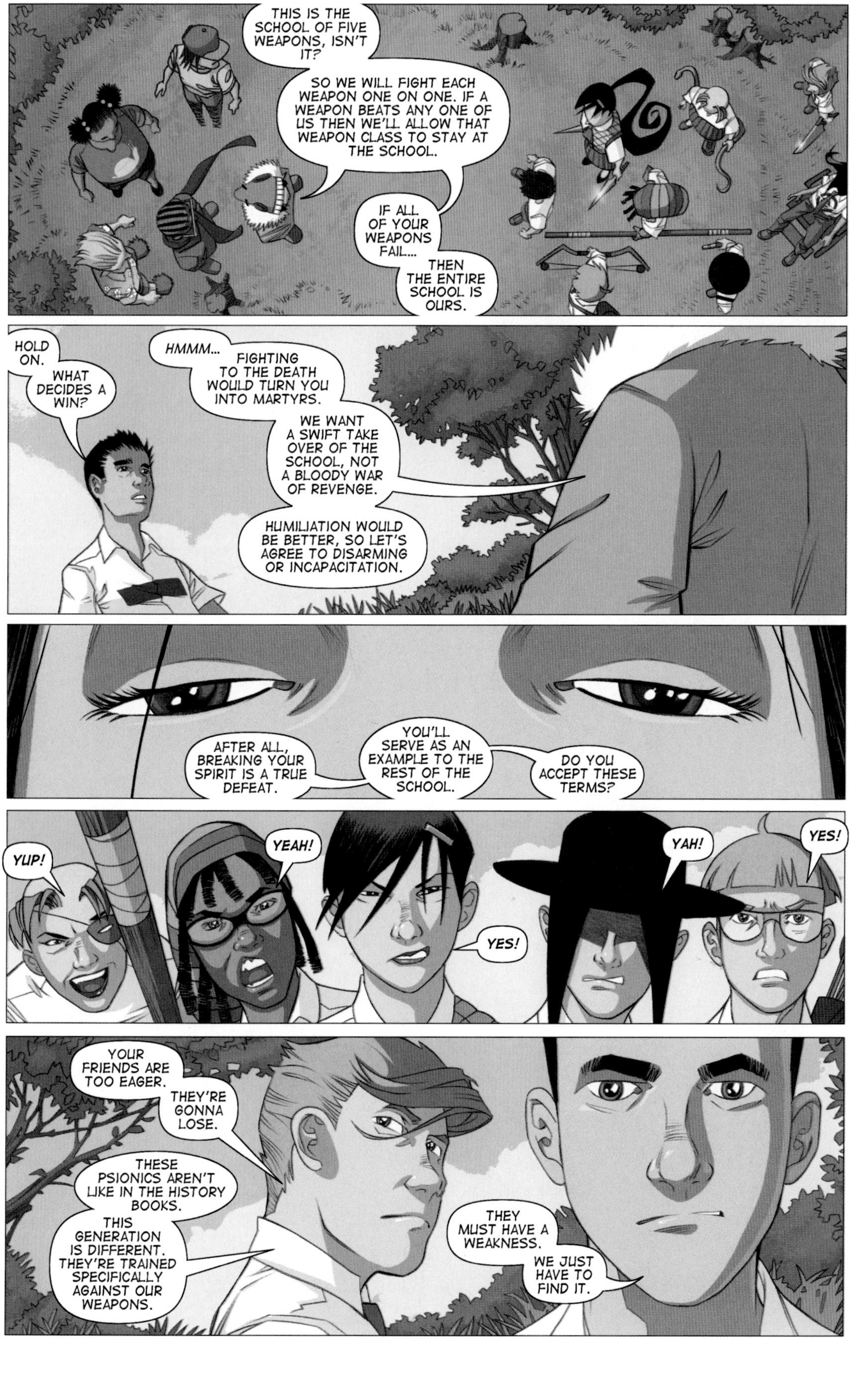
THIS IS THE SCHOOL OF FIVE WEAPONS, ISN'T IT?
SO WE WILL FIGHT EACH WEAPON ONE ON ONE. IF A WEAPON BEATS ANY ONE OF US THEN WE'LL ALLOW THAT WEAPON CLASS TO STAY AT THE SCHOOL.
IF ALL OF YOUR WEAPONS FAIL...
THEN THE ENTIRE SCHOOL IS OURS.
HOLD ON.
WHAT DECIDES A WIN?
HMMM... FIGHTING TO THE DEATH WOULD TURN YOU INTO MARTYRS.
WE WANT A SWIFT TAKE OVER OF THE SCHOOL, NOT A BLOODY WAR OF REVENGE.
HUMILIATION WOULD BE BETTER, SO LET'S AGREE TO DISARMING OR INCAPACITATION.
AFTER ALL, BREAKING YOUR SPIRIT IS A TRUE DEFEAT.
YOU'LL SERVE AS AN EXAMPLE TO THE REST OF THE SCHOOL.
DO YOU ACCEPT THESE TERMS?
YUP!
YEAH!
YES!
YAH!
YES!
YOUR FRIENDS ARE TOO EAGER.
THEY'RE GONNA LOSE.
THESE PSIONICS AREN'T LIKE IN THE HISTORY BOOKS.
THIS GENERATION IS DIFFERENT. THEY'RE TRAINED SPECIFICALLY AGAINST OUR WEAPONS.
THEY MUST HAVE A WEAKNESS.
WE JUST HAVE TO FIND IT.

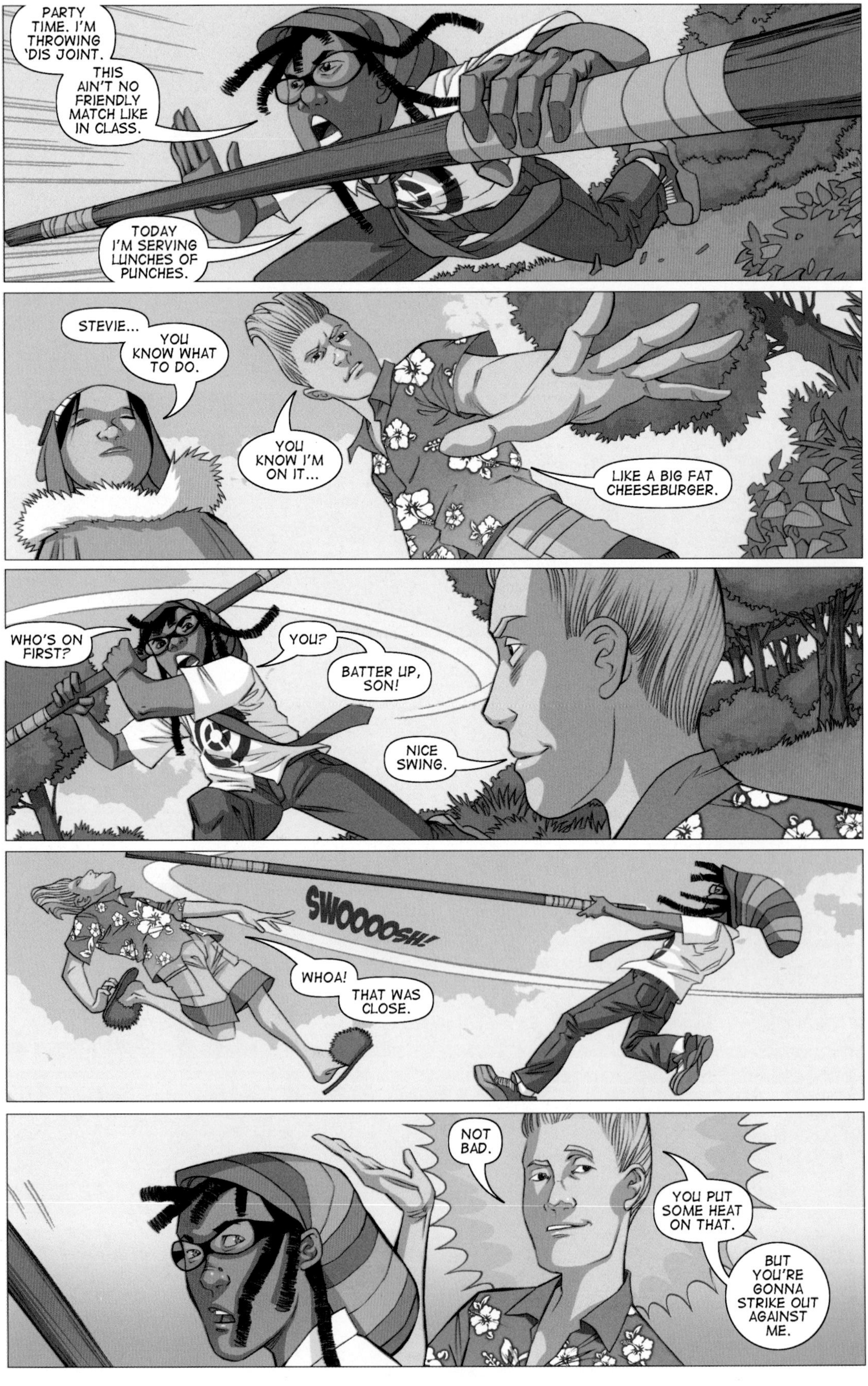
PARTY TIME. I'M THROWING 'DIS JOINT.
THIS AIN'T NO FRIENDLY MATCH LIKE IN CLASS.
TODAY I'M SERVING LUNCHES OF PUNCHES.
STEVIE...
YOU KNOW WHAT TO DO.
YOU KNOW I'M ON IT...
LIKE A BIG FAT CHEESEBURGER.
WHO'S ON FIRST?
YOU?
BATTER UP, SON!
NICE SWING.
SWOOOOSH!
WHOA!
THAT WAS CLOSE.
NOT BAD.
YOU PUT SOME HEAT ON THAT.
BUT YOU'RE GONNA STRIKE OUT AGAINST ME.

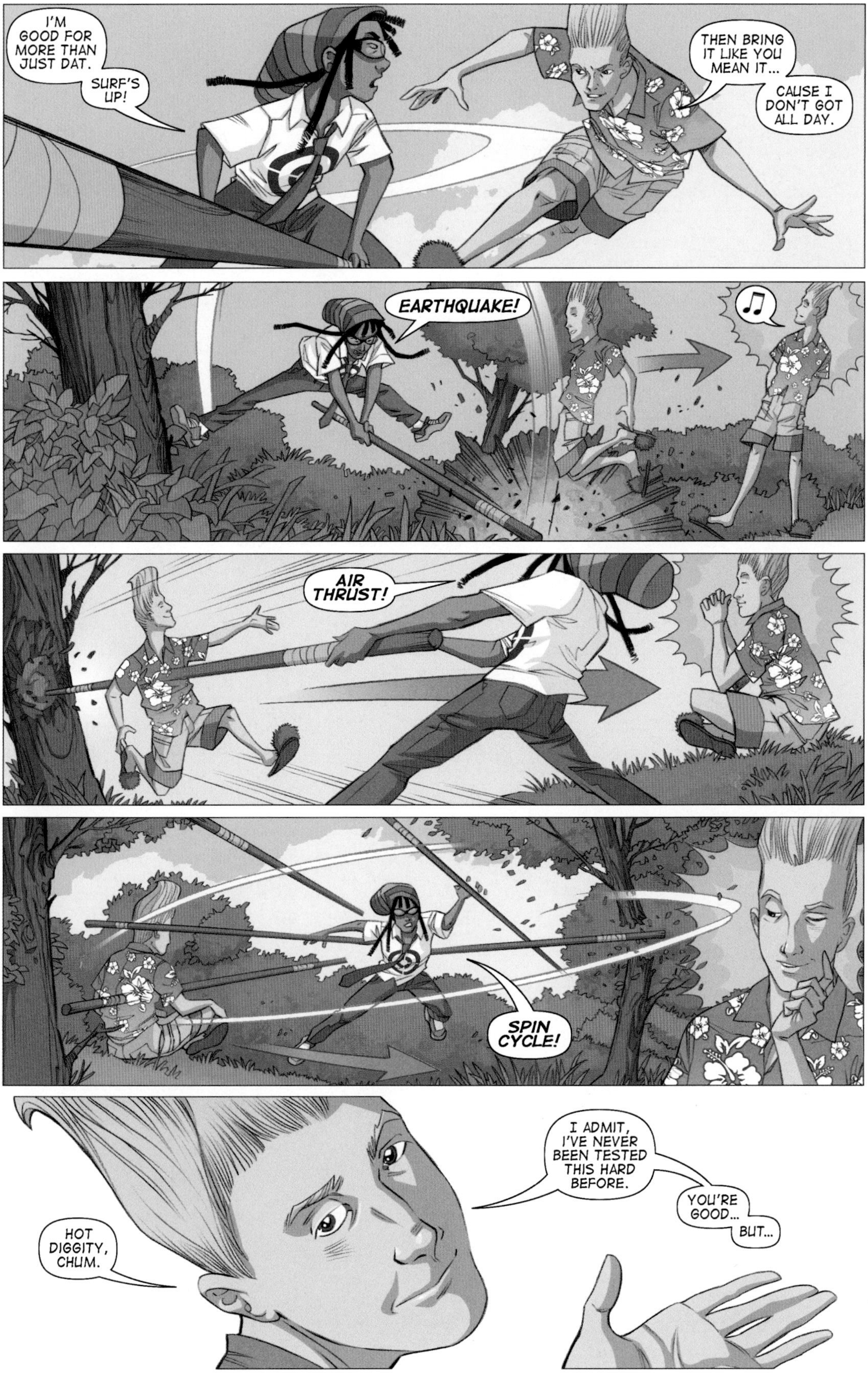
I'M GOOD FOR MORE THAN JUST DAT.
SURF'S UP!
THEN BRING IT LIKE YOU MEAN IT...
CAUSE I DON'T GOT ALL DAY.
EARTHQUAKE!
♪
AIR THRUST!
SPIN CYCLE!
I ADMIT, I'VE NEVER BEEN TESTED THIS HARD BEFORE.
YOU'RE GOOD...
BUT...
HOT DIGGITY, CHUM.

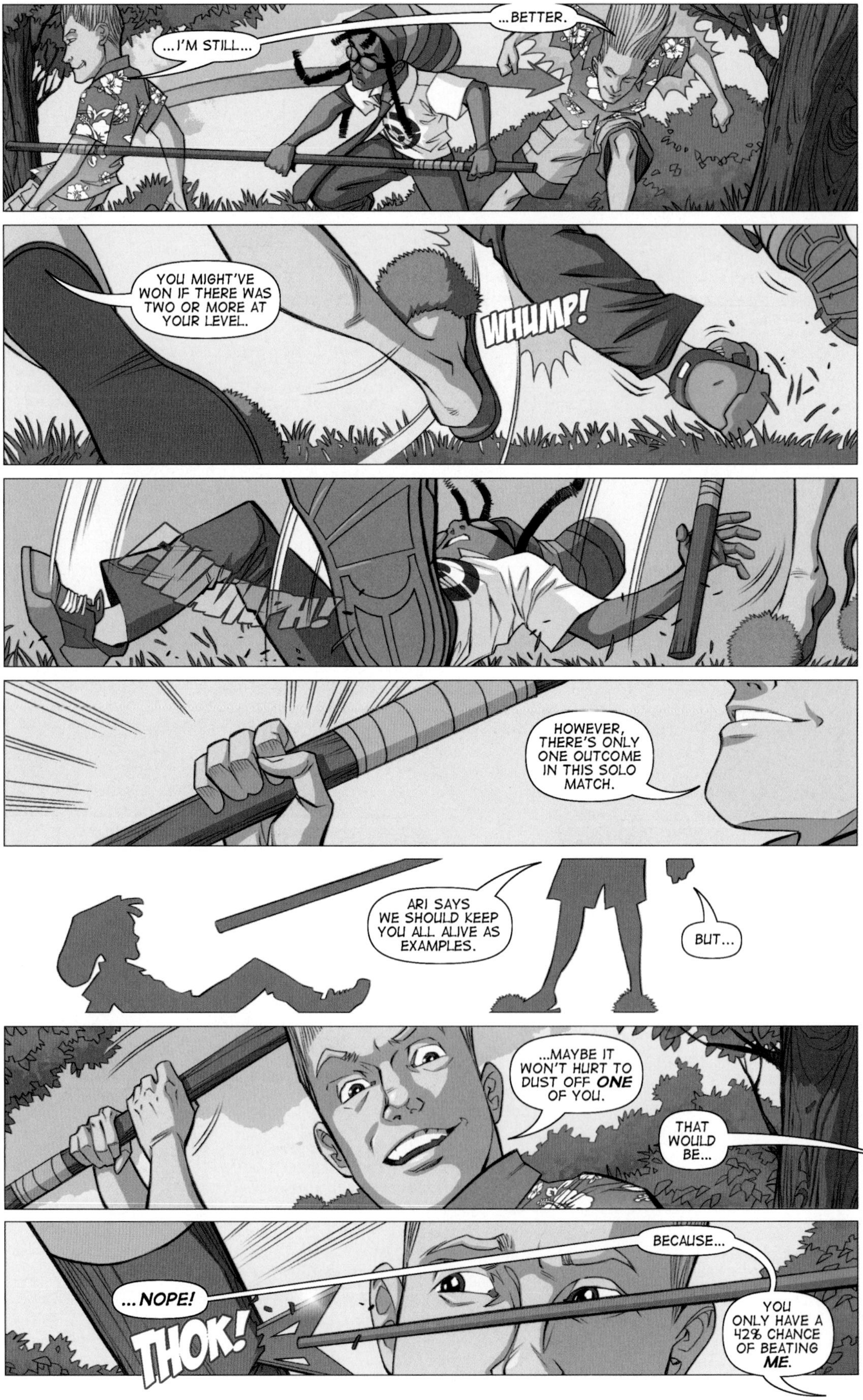
...I'M STILL...
...BETTER.
YOU MIGHT'VE WON IF THERE WAS TWO OR MORE AT YOUR LEVEL.
WHUMP!
WHAMPH!
HOWEVER, THERE'S ONLY ONE OUTCOME IN THIS SOLO MATCH.
ARI SAYS WE SHOULD KEEP YOU ALL ALIVE AS EXAMPLES.
BUT...
...MAYBE IT WON'T HURT TO DUST OFF ONE OF YOU.
THAT WOULD BE...
BECAUSE...
...NOPE!
THOK!
YOU ONLY HAVE A 42% CHANCE OF BEATING ME.

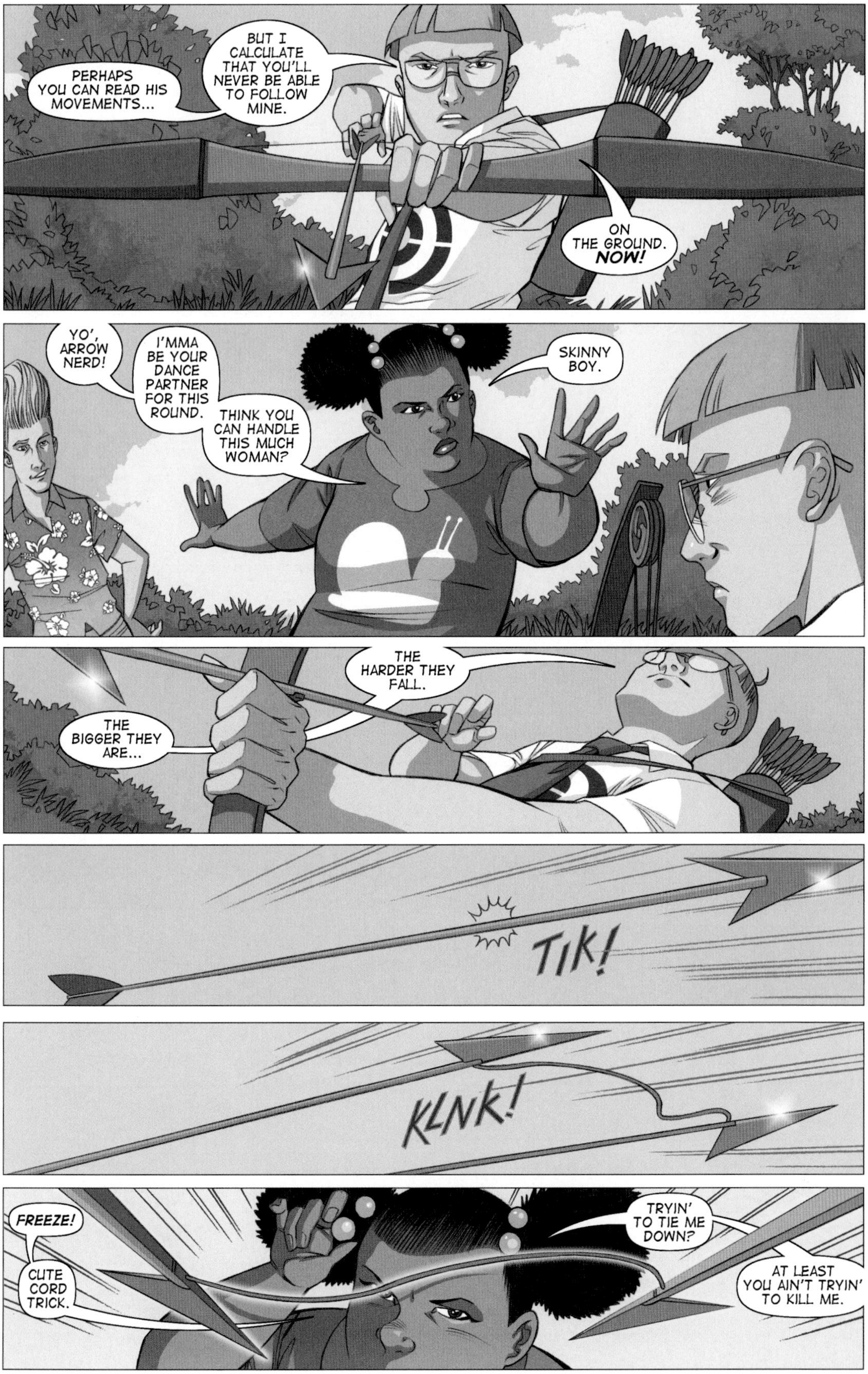
PERHAPS YOU CAN READ HIS MOVEMENTS...
BUT I CALCULATE THAT YOU'LL NEVER BE ABLE TO FOLLOW MINE.
ON THE GROUND. NOW!
YO', ARROW NERD!
I'MMA BE YOUR DANCE PARTNER FOR THIS ROUND.
THINK YOU CAN HANDLE THIS MUCH WOMAN?
SKINNY BOY.
THE BIGGER THEY ARE...
THE HARDER THEY FALL.
TIK!
KLNK!
FREEZE!
CUTE CORD TRICK.
TRYIN' TO TIE ME DOWN?
AT LEAST YOU AIN'T TRYIN' TO KILL ME.

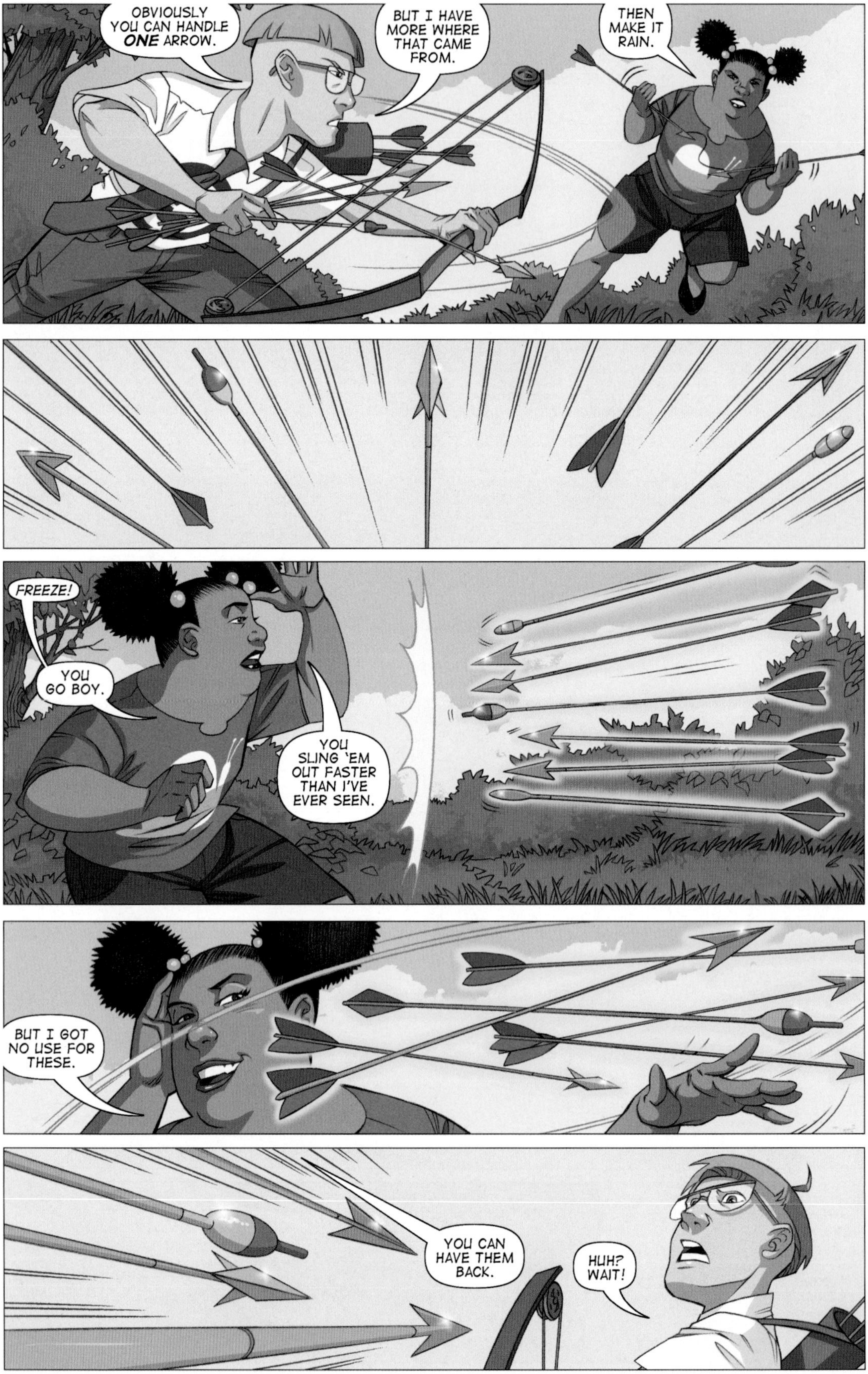
OBVIOUSLY YOU CAN HANDLE ONE ARROW.
BUT I HAVE MORE WHERE THAT CAME FROM.
THEN MAKE IT RAIN.
FREEZE!
YOU GO BOY.
YOU SLING 'EM OUT FASTER THAN I'VE EVER SEEN.
BUT I GOT NO USE FOR THESE.
YOU CAN HAVE THEM BACK.
HUH? WAIT!

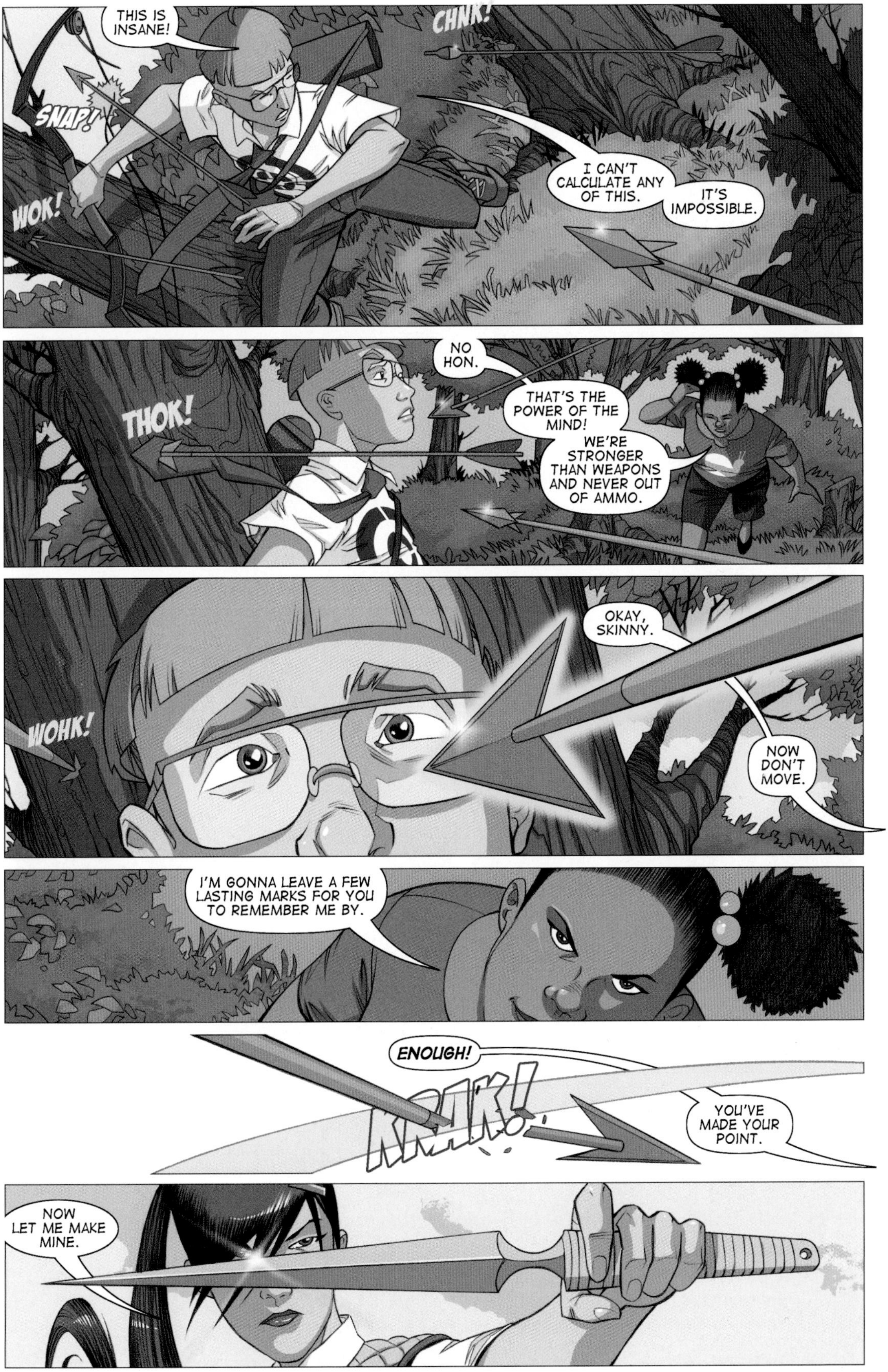
CHNK!
THIS IS INSANE!
SNAP!
WOK!
I CAN'T CALCULATE ANY OF THIS.
IT'S IMPOSSIBLE.
THOK!
NO HON.
THAT'S THE POWER OF THE MIND!
WE'RE STRONGER THAN WEAPONS AND NEVER OUT OF AMMO.
WOHK!
OKAY, SKINNY.
NOW DON'T MOVE.
I'M GONNA LEAVE A FEW LASTING MARKS FOR YOU TO REMEMBER ME BY.
ENOUGH!
KRAK!
YOU'VE MADE YOUR POINT.
NOW LET ME MAKE MINE.

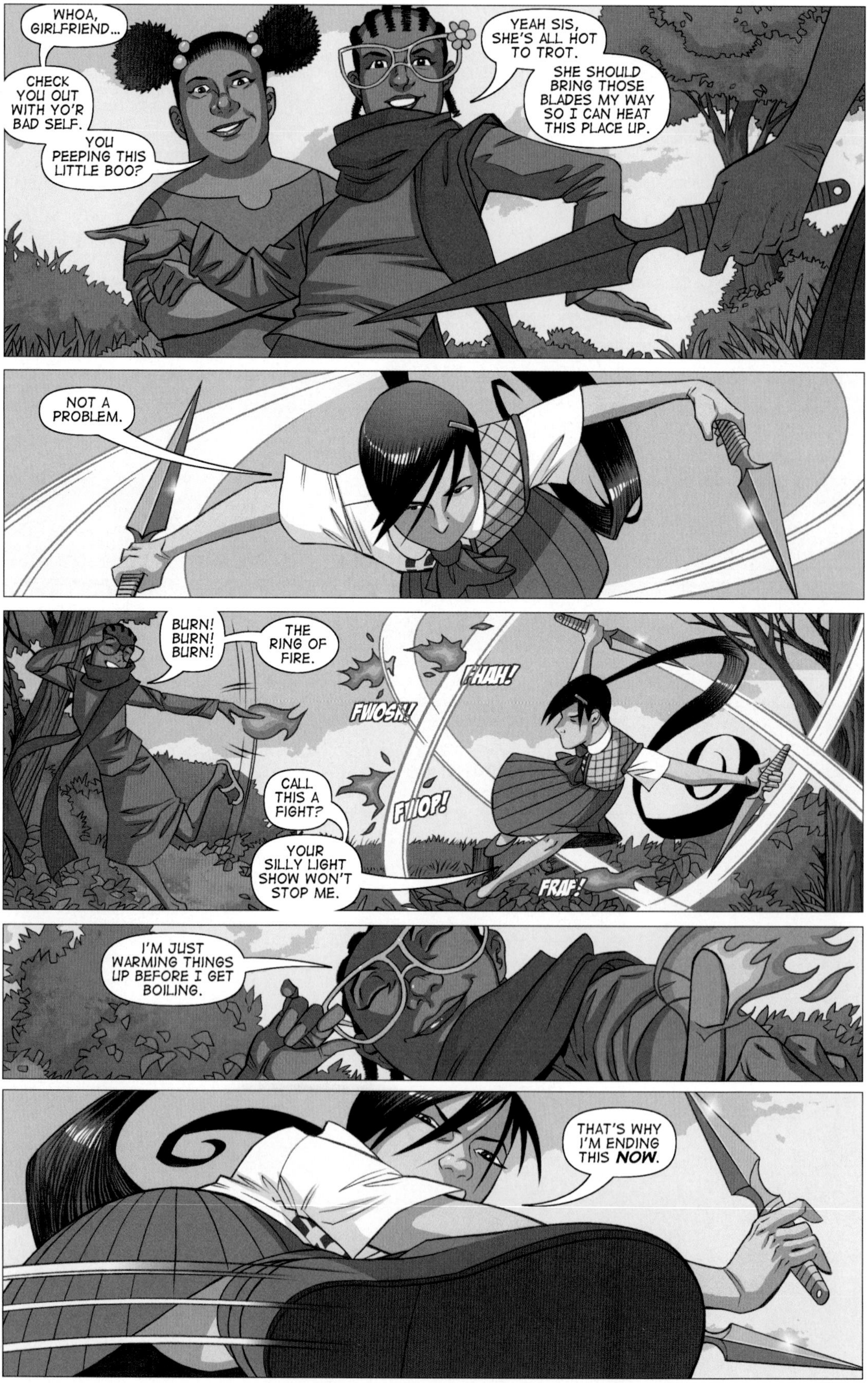
WHOA, GIRLFRIEND...
CHECK YOU OUT WITH YO'R BAD SELF.
YOU PEEPING THIS LITTLE BOO?
YEAH SIS, SHE'S ALL HOT TO TROT.
SHE SHOULD BRING THOSE BLADES MY WAY SO I CAN HEAT THIS PLACE UP.
NOT A PROBLEM.
BURN! BURN! BURN!
THE RING OF FIRE.
FHAH!
FWOSH!
CALL THIS A FIGHT?
FWOP!
YOUR SILLY LIGHT SHOW WON'T STOP ME.
FRAF!
I'M JUST WARMING THINGS UP BEFORE I GET BOILING.
THAT'S WHY I'M ENDING THIS **NOW**.

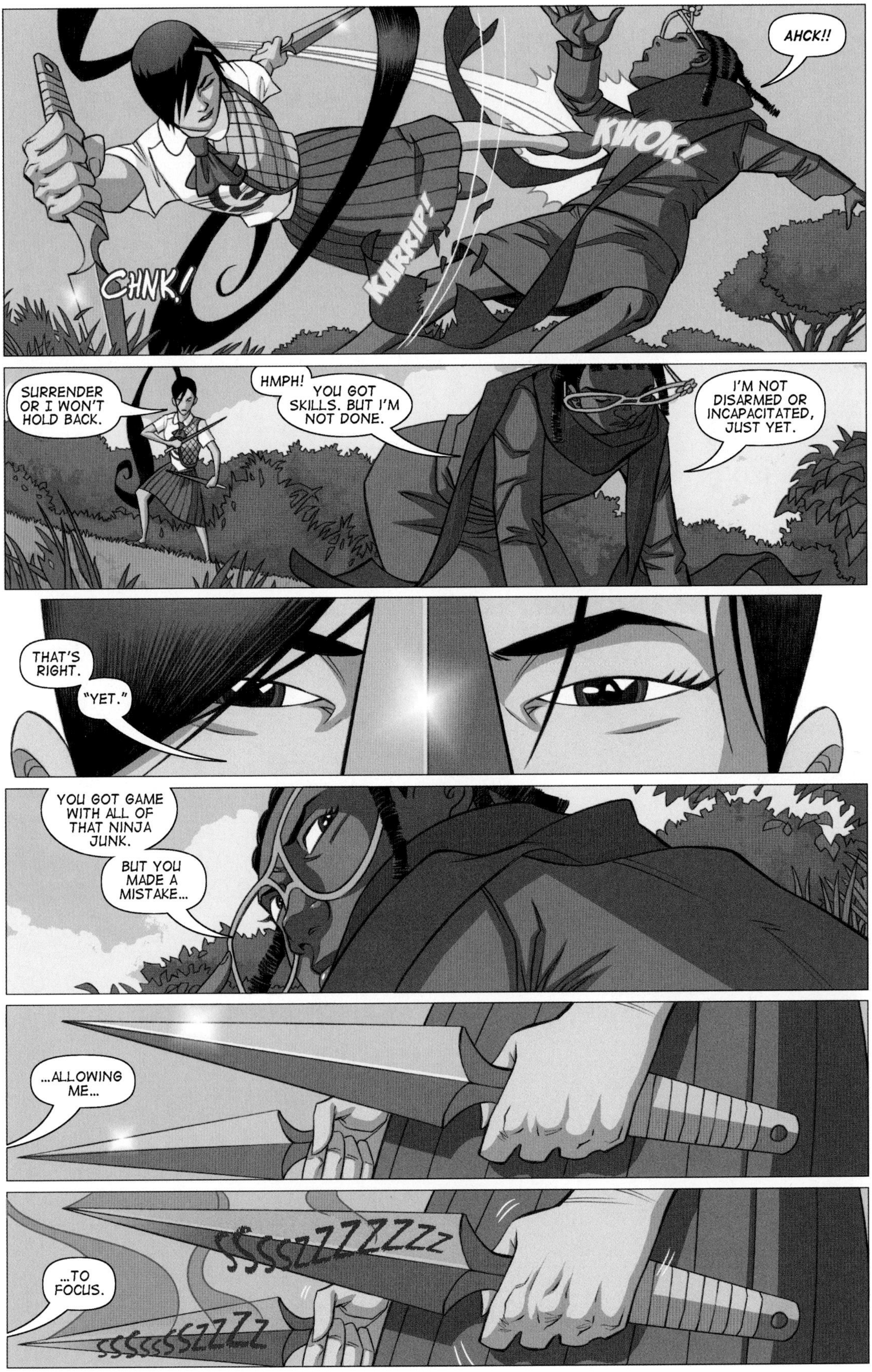
AHCK!!
KWOK!
KARRIP!
CHNK!
SURRENDER OR I WON'T HOLD BACK.
HMPH!
YOU GOT SKILLS. BUT I'M NOT DONE.
I'M NOT DISARMED OR INCAPACITATED, JUST YET.
THAT'S RIGHT.
"YET."
YOU GOT GAME WITH ALL OF THAT NINJA JUNK.
BUT YOU MADE A MISTAKE...
...ALLOWING ME...
...TO FOCUS.
SSSSZZZZZZZZ
SSSSSSSZZZZZ

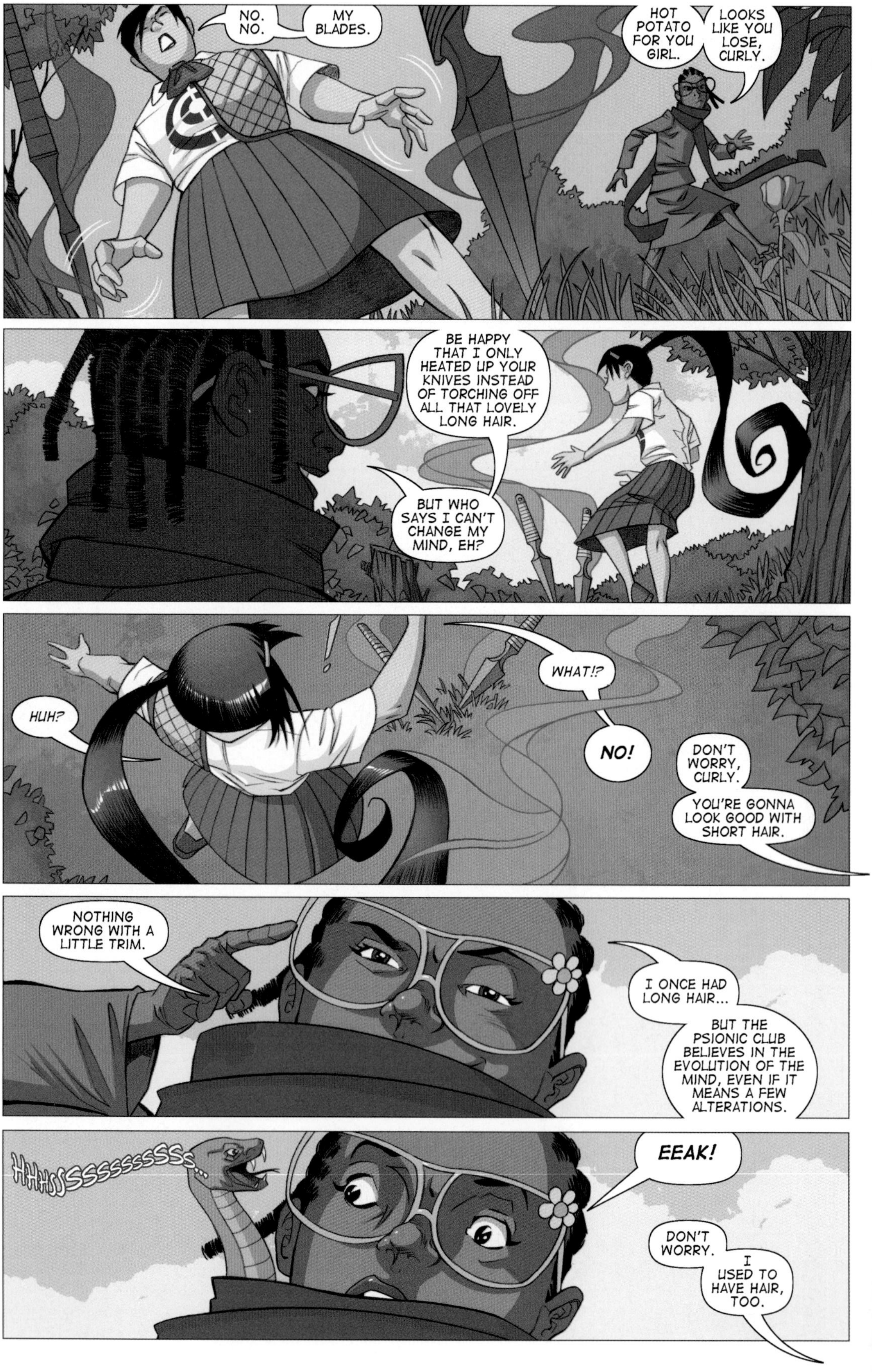
NO. NO.
MY BLADES.
HOT POTATO FOR YOU GIRL.
LOOKS LIKE YOU LOSE, CURLY.
BE HAPPY THAT I ONLY HEATED UP YOUR KNIVES INSTEAD OF TORCHING OFF ALL THAT LOVELY LONG HAIR.
BUT WHO SAYS I CAN'T CHANGE MY MIND, EH?
HUH?
WHAT!?
NO!
DON'T WORRY, CURLY.
YOU'RE GONNA LOOK GOOD WITH SHORT HAIR.
NOTHING WRONG WITH A LITTLE TRIM.
I ONCE HAD LONG HAIR...
BUT THE PSIONIC CLUB BELIEVES IN THE EVOLUTION OF THE MIND, EVEN IF IT MEANS A FEW ALTERATIONS.
HHHSSSSSSSSSSSS...
EEAK!
DON'T WORRY.
I USED TO HAVE HAIR, TOO.

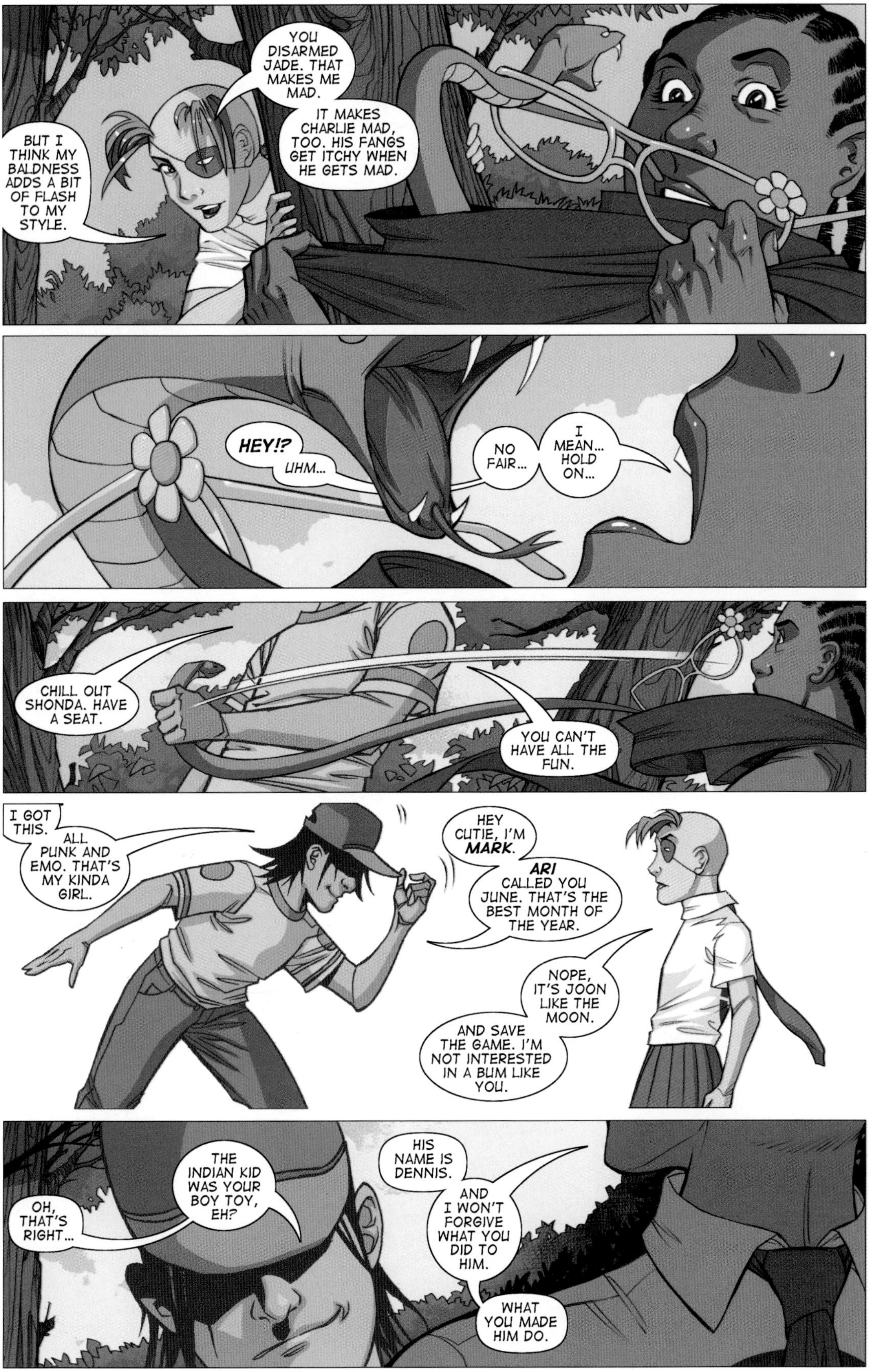
YOU DISARMED JADE. THAT MAKES ME MAD.
IT MAKES CHARLIE MAD, TOO. HIS FANGS GET ITCHY WHEN HE GETS MAD.
BUT I THINK MY BALDNESS ADDS A BIT OF FLASH TO MY STYLE.
HEY!? UHM...
NO FAIR...
I MEAN... HOLD ON...
CHILL OUT SHONDA. HAVE A SEAT.
YOU CAN'T HAVE ALL THE FUN.
I GOT THIS.
ALL PUNK AND EMO. THAT'S MY KINDA GIRL.
HEY CUTIE, I'M MARK.
ARI CALLED YOU JUNE. THAT'S THE BEST MONTH OF THE YEAR.
NOPE, IT'S JOON LIKE THE MOON.
AND SAVE THE GAME. I'M NOT INTERESTED IN A BUM LIKE YOU.
OH, THAT'S RIGHT...
THE INDIAN KID WAS YOUR BOY TOY, EH?
HIS NAME IS DENNIS.
AND I WON'T FORGIVE WHAT YOU DID TO HIM.
WHAT YOU MADE HIM DO.

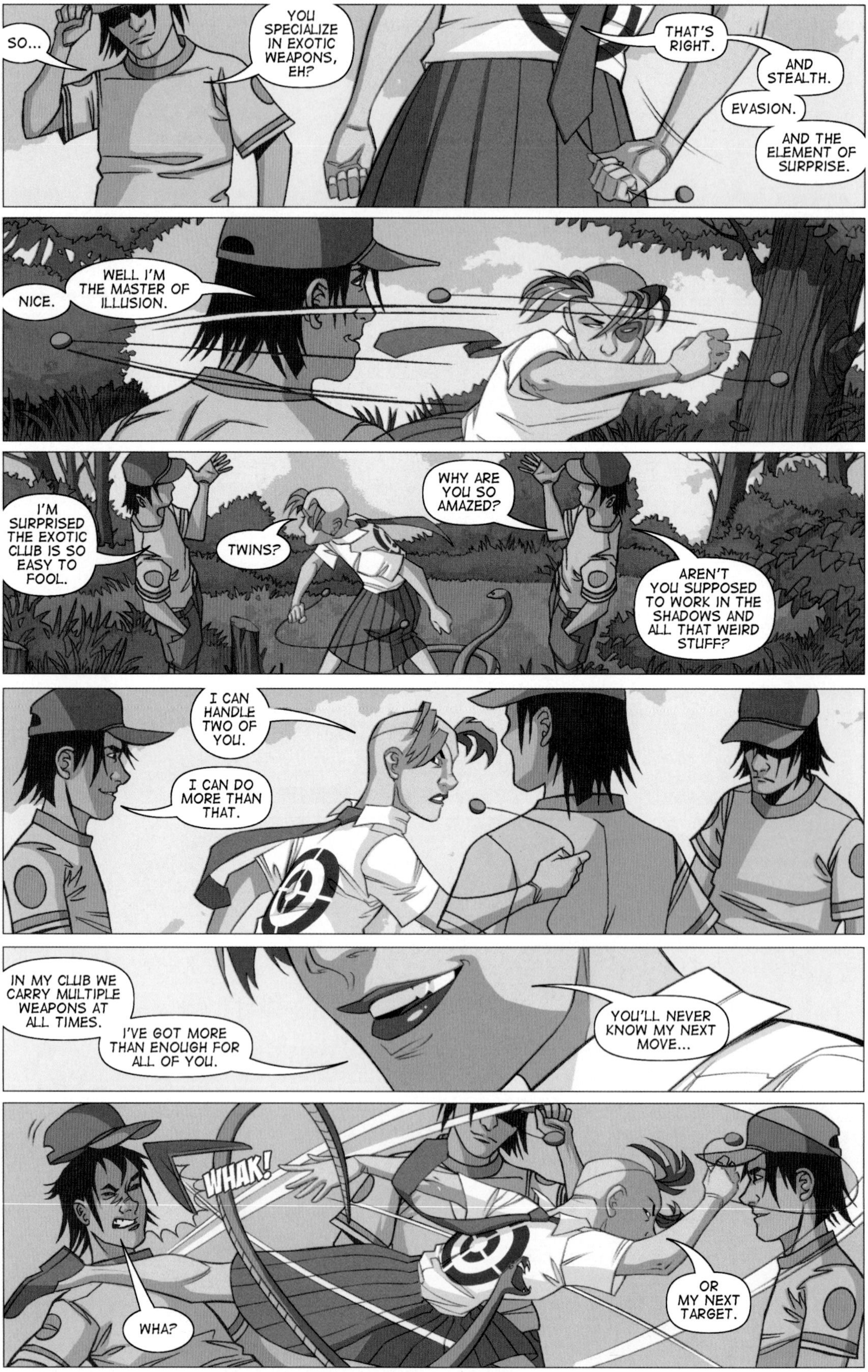
SO...
YOU SPECIALIZE IN EXOTIC WEAPONS, EH?
THAT'S RIGHT.
AND STEALTH.
EVASION.
AND THE ELEMENT OF SURPRISE.
NICE.
WELL I'M THE MASTER OF ILLUSION.
I'M SURPRISED THE EXOTIC CLUB IS SO EASY TO FOOL.
TWINS?
WHY ARE YOU SO AMAZED?
AREN'T YOU SUPPOSED TO WORK IN THE SHADOWS AND ALL THAT WEIRD STUFF?
I CAN HANDLE TWO OF YOU.
I CAN DO MORE THAN THAT.
IN MY CLUB WE CARRY MULTIPLE WEAPONS AT ALL TIMES.
I'VE GOT MORE THAN ENOUGH FOR ALL OF YOU.
YOU'LL NEVER KNOW MY NEXT MOVE...
WHAK!
WHA?
OR MY NEXT TARGET.

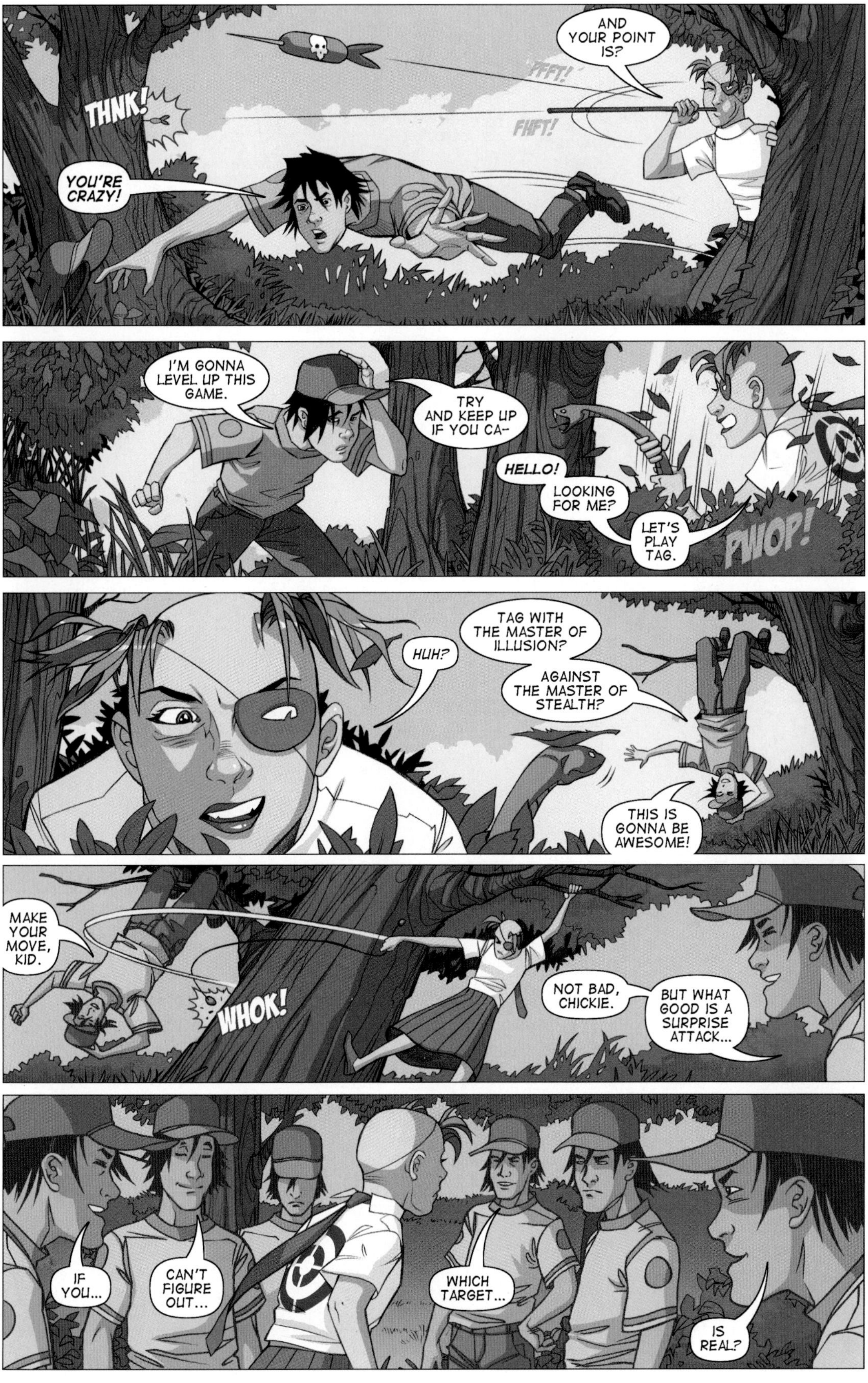
AND YOUR POINT IS?
PFFT!
FHFT!
THNK!
YOU'RE CRAZY!
I'M GONNA LEVEL UP THIS GAME.
TRY AND KEEP UP IF YOU CA-
HELLO!
LOOKING FOR ME?
LET'S PLAY TAG.
PWOP!
HUH?
TAG WITH THE MASTER OF ILLUSION?
AGAINST THE MASTER OF STEALTH?
THIS IS GONNA BE AWESOME!
MAKE YOUR MOVE, KID.
WHOK!
NOT BAD, CHICKIE.
BUT WHAT GOOD IS A SURPRISE ATTACK...
IF YOU...
CAN'T FIGURE OUT...
WHICH TARGET...
IS REAL?

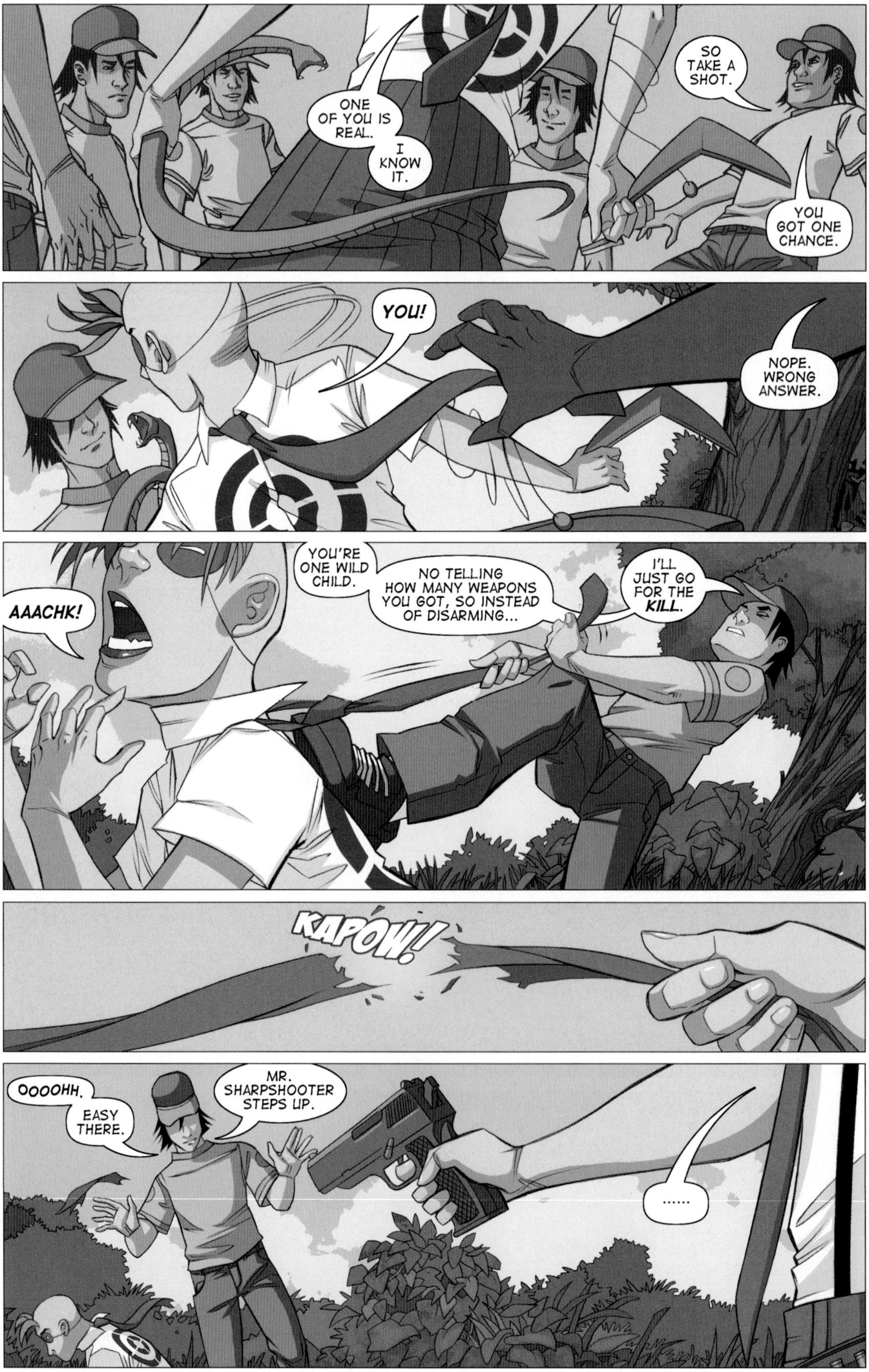
ONE OF YOU IS REAL.
I KNOW IT.
SO TAKE A SHOT.
YOU GOT ONE CHANCE.
YOU!
NOPE. WRONG ANSWER.
AAACHK!
YOU'RE ONE WILD CHILD.
NO TELLING HOW MANY WEAPONS YOU GOT, SO INSTEAD OF DISARMING...
I'LL JUST GO FOR THE KILL.
KAPOW!
OOOOHH.
EASY THERE.
MR. SHARPSHOOTER STEPS UP.
......

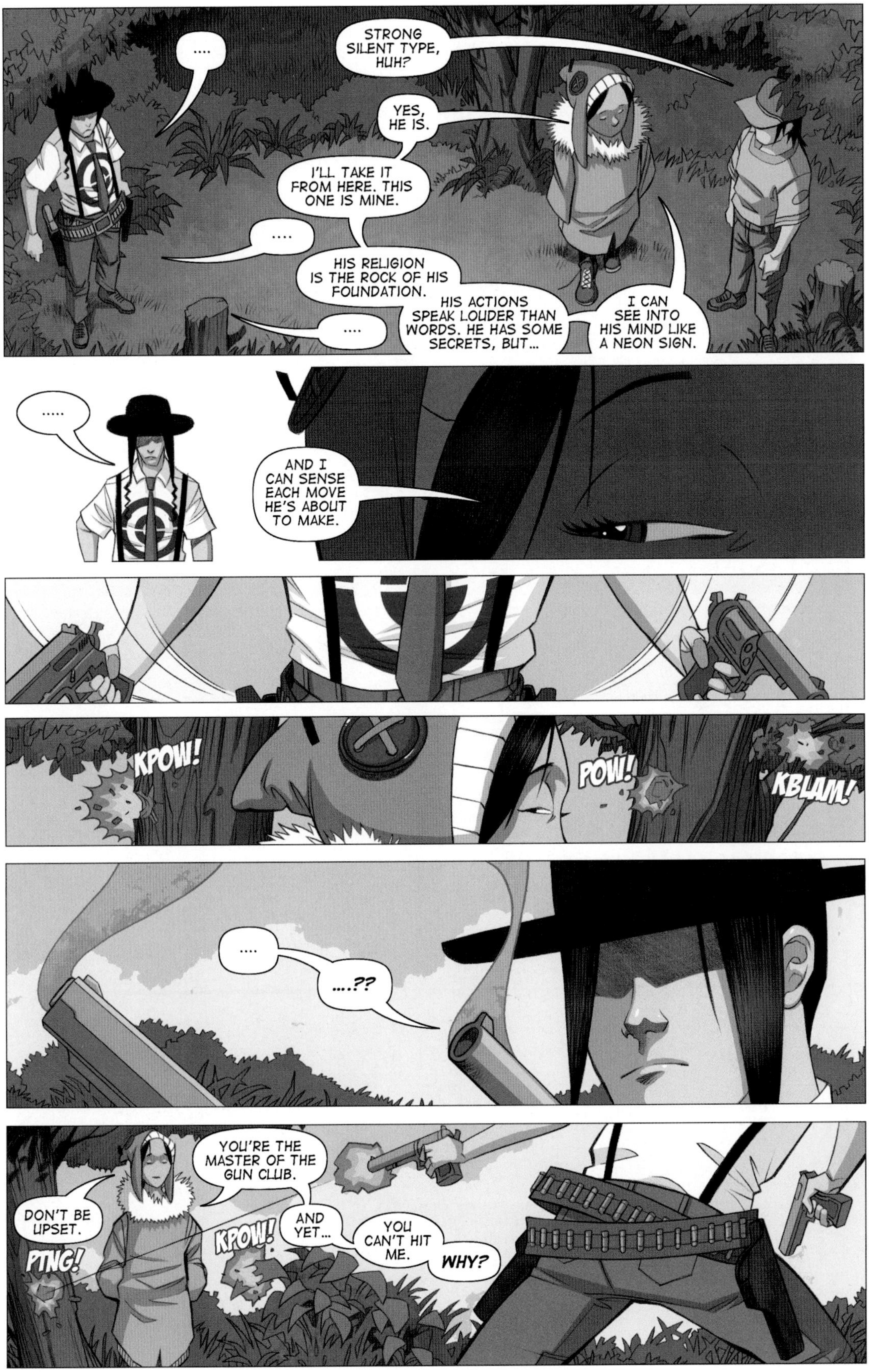
....
STRONG SILENT TYPE, HUH?
YES, HE IS.
I'LL TAKE IT FROM HERE. THIS ONE IS MINE.
....
HIS RELIGION IS THE ROCK OF HIS FOUNDATION.
....
HIS ACTIONS SPEAK LOUDER THAN WORDS. HE HAS SOME SECRETS, BUT...
I CAN SEE INTO HIS MIND LIKE A NEON SIGN.
.....
AND I CAN SENSE EACH MOVE HE'S ABOUT TO MAKE.
KPOW!
POW!
KBLAM!
....
....??
DON'T BE UPSET.
YOU'RE THE MASTER OF THE GUN CLUB.
AND YET...
YOU CAN'T HIT ME.
WHY?
KPOW!
PTNG!

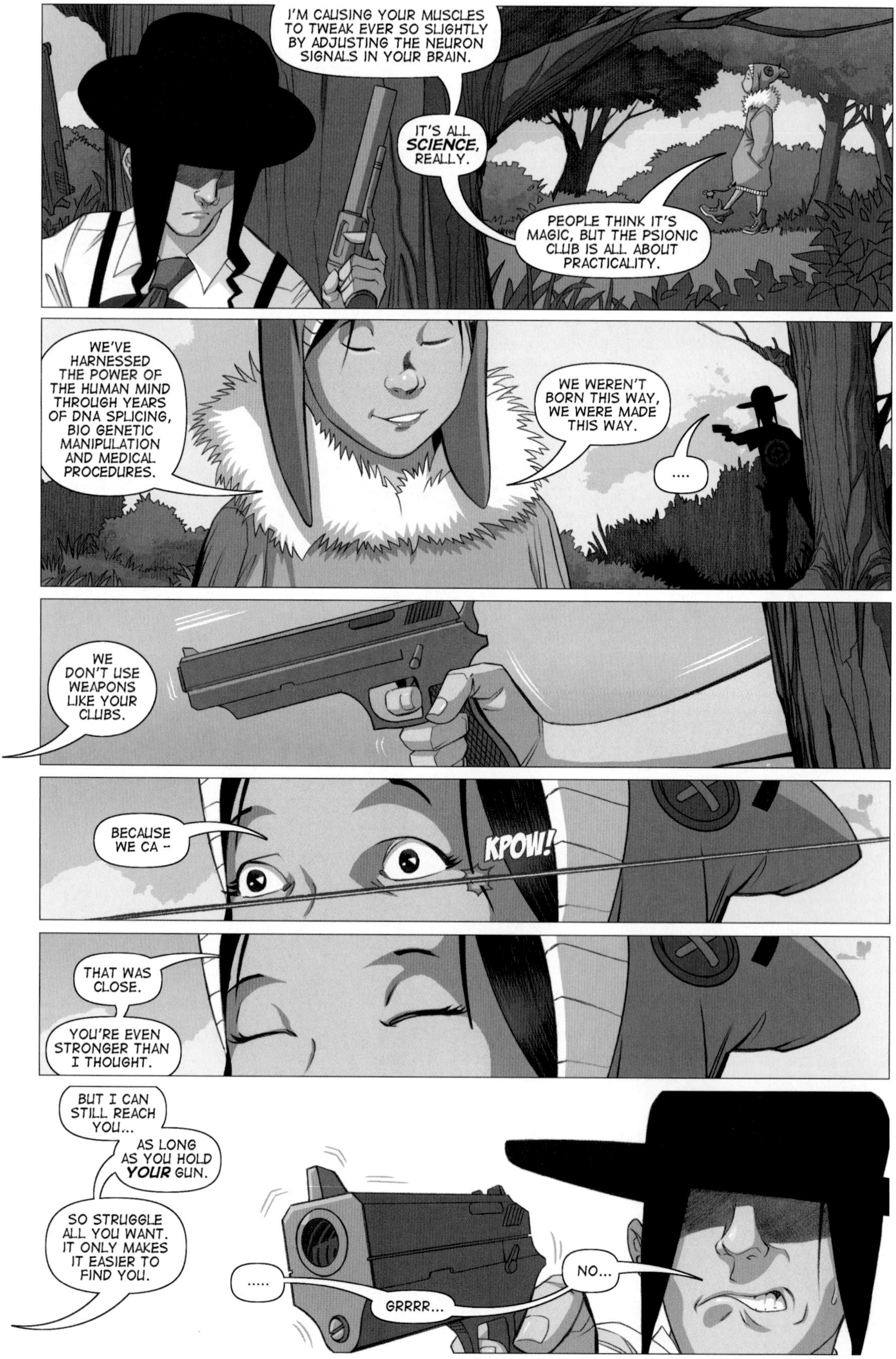
I'M CAUSING YOUR MUSCLES TO TWEAK EVER SO SLIGHTLY BY ADJUSTING THE NEURON SIGNALS IN YOUR BRAIN.
IT'S ALL *SCIENCE,* REALLY.
PEOPLE THINK IT'S MAGIC, BUT THE PSIONIC CLUB IS ALL ABOUT PRACTICALITY.
WE'VE HARNESSED THE POWER OF THE HUMAN MIND THROUGH YEARS OF DNA SPLICING, BIO GENETIC MANIPULATION AND MEDICAL PROCEDURES.
WE WEREN'T BORN THIS WAY, WE WERE MADE THIS WAY.
....
WE DON'T USE WEAPONS LIKE YOUR CLUBS.
BECAUSE WE CA –
KPOW!
THAT WAS CLOSE.
YOU'RE EVEN STRONGER THAN I THOUGHT.
BUT I CAN STILL REACH YOU...
AS LONG AS YOU HOLD *YOUR* GUN.
SO STRUGGLE ALL YOU WANT. IT ONLY MAKES IT EASIER TO FIND YOU.
.....
NO...
GRRRR...

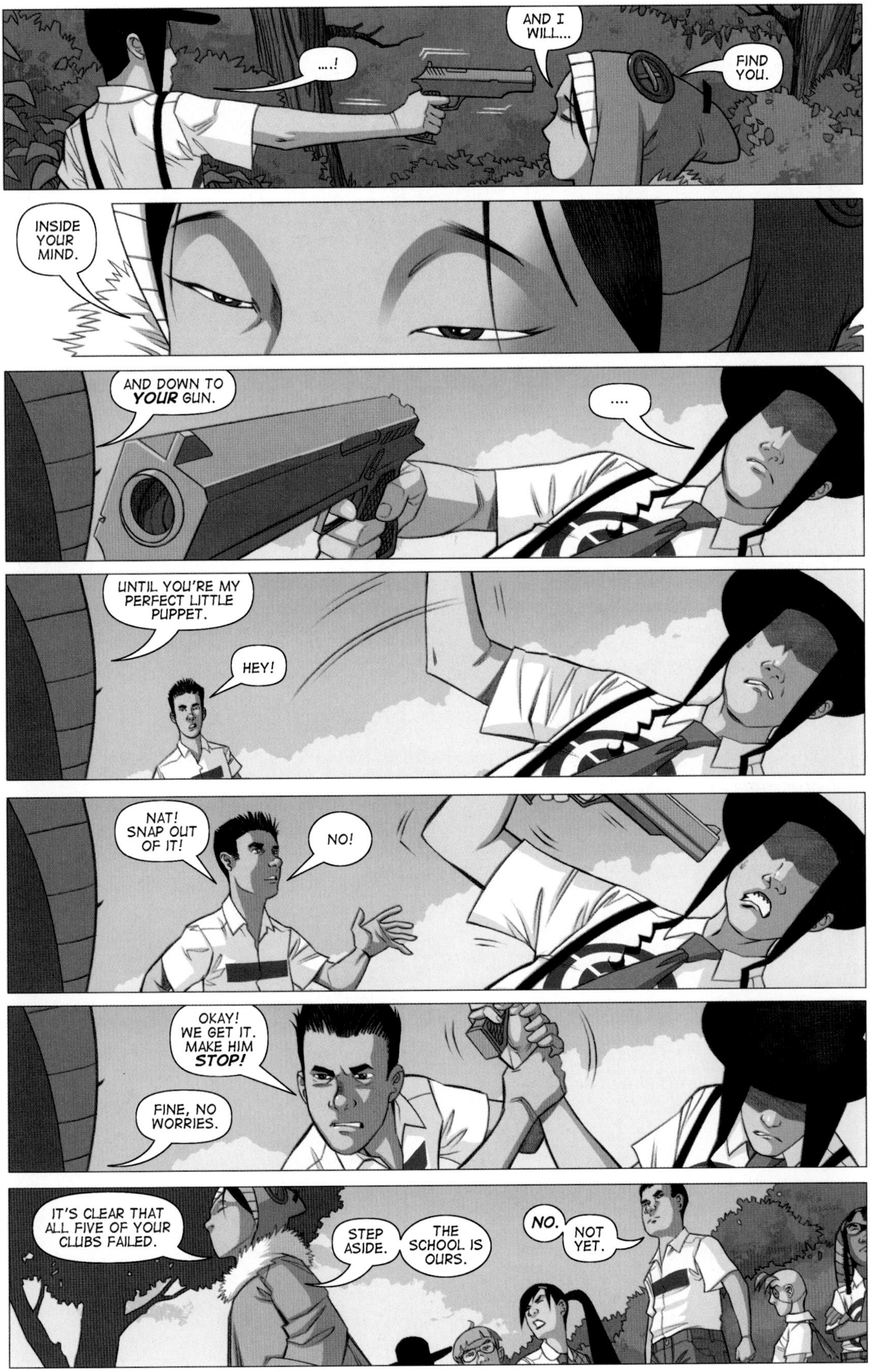
....!
AND I WILL...
FIND YOU.
INSIDE YOUR MIND.
AND DOWN TO YOUR GUN.
....
UNTIL YOU'RE MY PERFECT LITTLE PUPPET.
HEY!
NAT! SNAP OUT OF IT!
NO!
OKAY! WE GET IT. MAKE HIM STOP!
FINE, NO WORRIES.
IT'S CLEAR THAT ALL FIVE OF YOUR CLUBS FAILED.
STEP ASIDE.
THE SCHOOL IS OURS.
NO.
NOT YET.

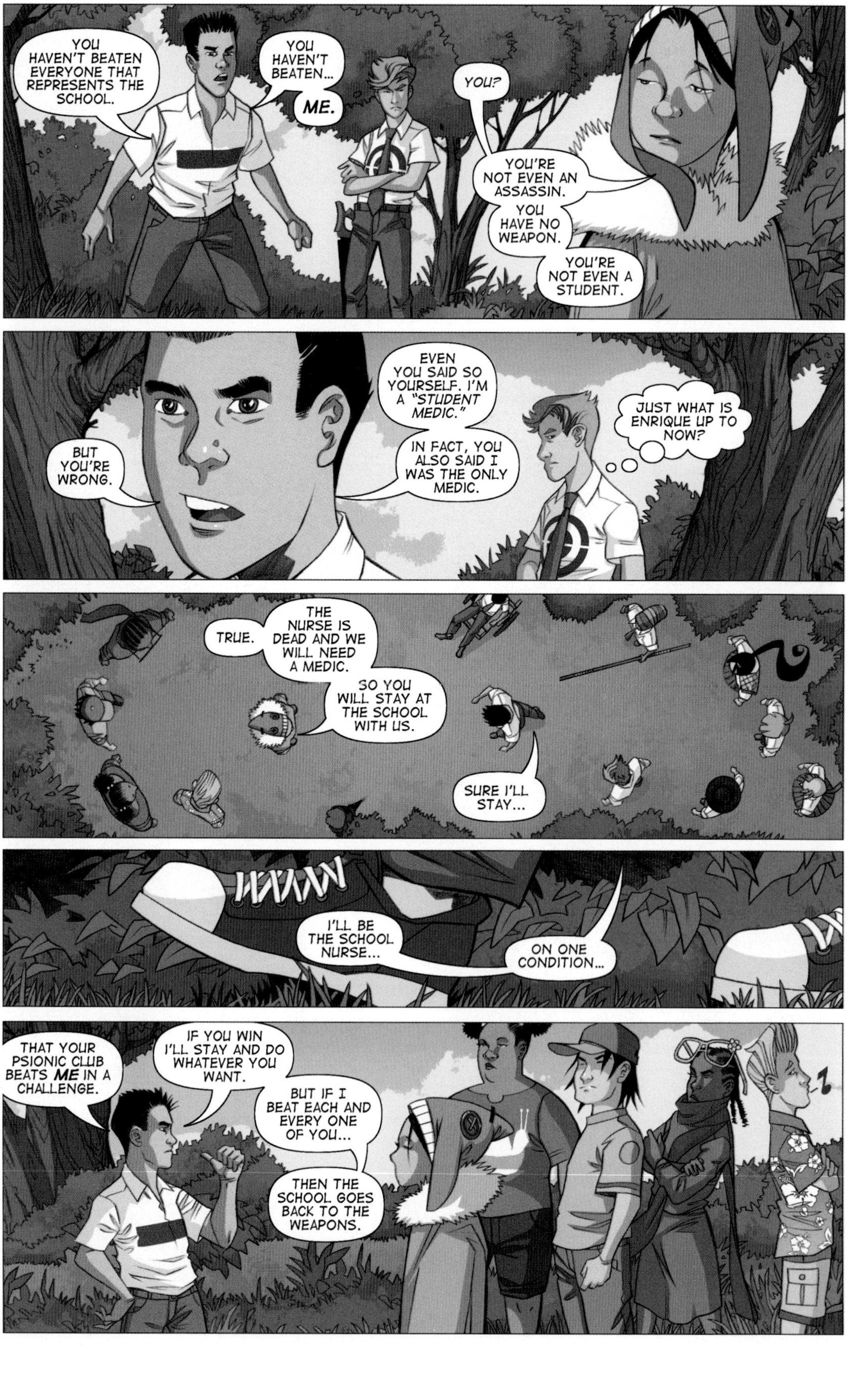
YOU HAVEN'T BEATEN EVERYONE THAT REPRESENTS THE SCHOOL.
YOU HAVEN'T BEATEN...
ME.
YOU?
YOU'RE NOT EVEN AN ASSASSIN.
YOU HAVE NO WEAPON.
YOU'RE NOT EVEN A STUDENT.
BUT YOU'RE WRONG.
EVEN YOU SAID SO YOURSELF. I'M A "STUDENT MEDIC."
IN FACT, YOU ALSO SAID I WAS THE ONLY MEDIC.
JUST WHAT IS ENRIQUE UP TO NOW?
TRUE.
THE NURSE IS DEAD AND WE WILL NEED A MEDIC.
SO YOU WILL STAY AT THE SCHOOL WITH US.
SURE I'LL STAY...
I'LL BE THE SCHOOL NURSE...
ON ONE CONDITION...
THAT YOUR PSIONIC CLUB BEATS ME IN A CHALLENGE.
IF YOU WIN I'LL STAY AND DO WHATEVER YOU WANT.
BUT IF I BEAT EACH AND EVERY ONE OF YOU...
THEN THE SCHOOL GOES BACK TO THE WEAPONS.

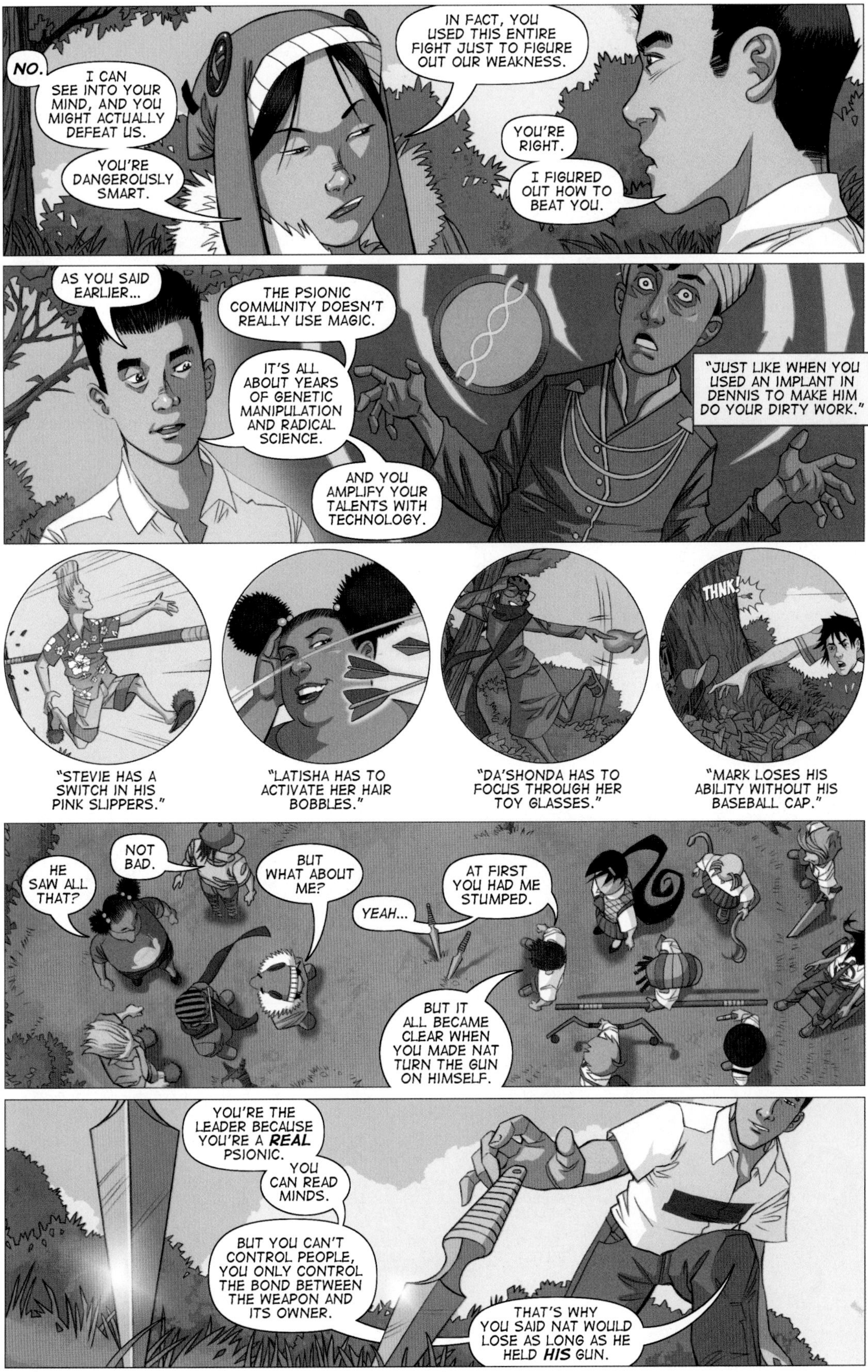
NO.
I CAN SEE INTO YOUR MIND, AND YOU MIGHT ACTUALLY DEFEAT US.
YOU'RE DANGEROUSLY SMART.
IN FACT, YOU USED THIS ENTIRE FIGHT JUST TO FIGURE OUT OUR WEAKNESS.
YOU'RE RIGHT.
I FIGURED OUT HOW TO BEAT YOU.
AS YOU SAID EARLIER...
THE PSIONIC COMMUNITY DOESN'T REALLY USE MAGIC.
IT'S ALL ABOUT YEARS OF GENETIC MANIPULATION AND RADICAL SCIENCE.
AND YOU AMPLIFY YOUR TALENTS WITH TECHNOLOGY.
"JUST LIKE WHEN YOU USED AN IMPLANT IN DENNIS TO MAKE HIM DO YOUR DIRTY WORK."
"STEVIE HAS A SWITCH IN HIS PINK SLIPPERS."
"LATISHA HAS TO ACTIVATE HER HAIR BOBBLES."
"DA'SHONDA HAS TO FOCUS THROUGH HER TOY GLASSES."
THNK!
"MARK LOSES HIS ABILITY WITHOUT HIS BASEBALL CAP."
HE SAW ALL THAT?
NOT BAD.
BUT WHAT ABOUT ME?
YEAH...
AT FIRST YOU HAD ME STUMPED.
BUT IT ALL BECAME CLEAR WHEN YOU MADE NAT TURN THE GUN ON HIMSELF.
YOU'RE THE LEADER BECAUSE YOU'RE A REAL PSIONIC.
YOU CAN READ MINDS.
BUT YOU CAN'T CONTROL PEOPLE, YOU ONLY CONTROL THE BOND BETWEEN THE WEAPON AND ITS OWNER.
THAT'S WHY YOU SAID NAT WOULD LOSE AS LONG AS HE HELD HIS GUN.

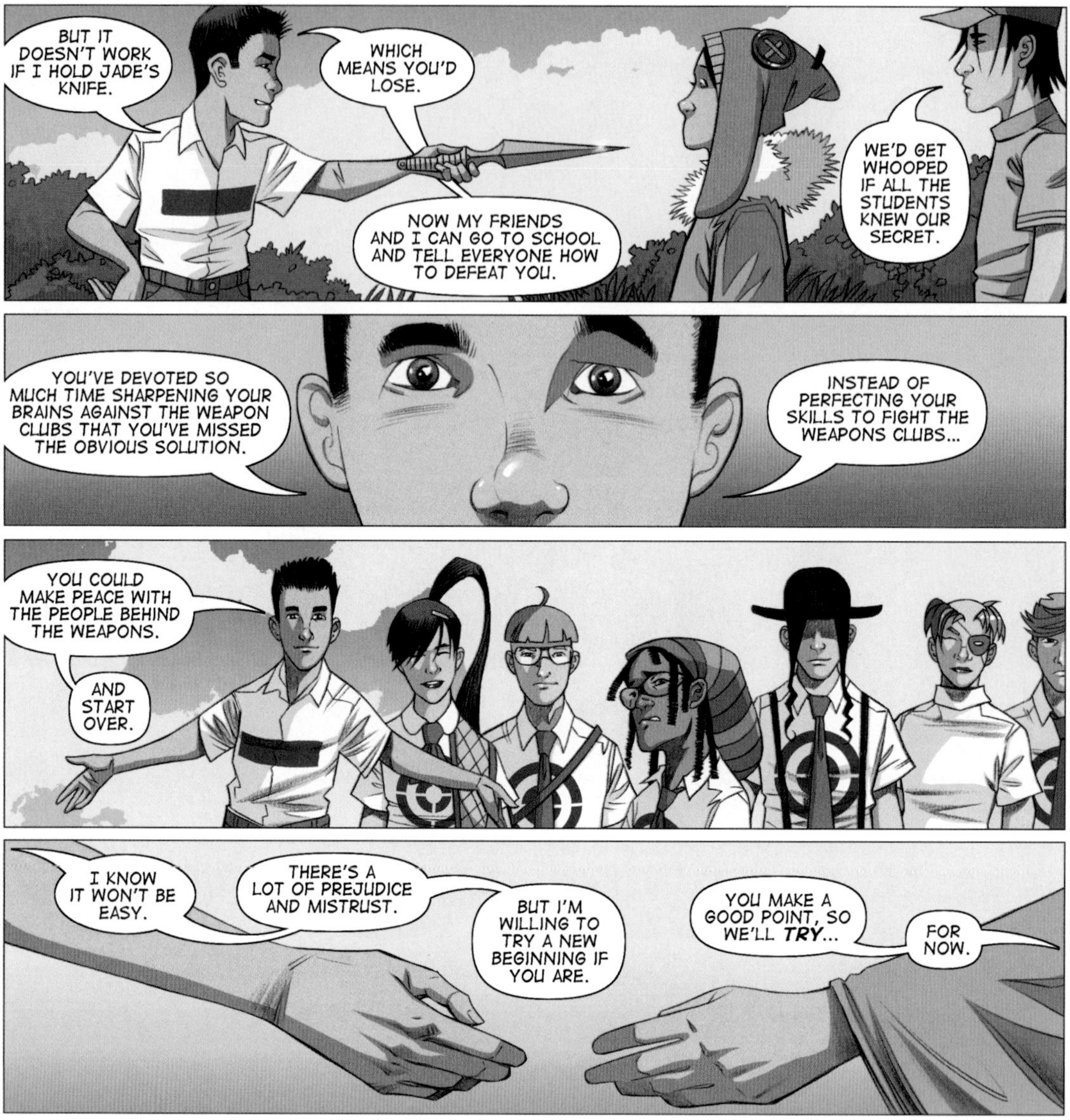

BUT IT DOESN'T WORK IF I HOLD JADE'S KNIFE.
WHICH MEANS YOU'D LOSE.
NOW MY FRIENDS AND I CAN GO TO SCHOOL AND TELL EVERYONE HOW TO DEFEAT YOU.
WE'D GET WHOOPED IF ALL THE STUDENTS KNEW OUR SECRET.
YOU'VE DEVOTED SO MUCH TIME SHARPENING YOUR BRAINS AGAINST THE WEAPON CLUBS THAT YOU'VE MISSED THE OBVIOUS SOLUTION.
INSTEAD OF PERFECTING YOUR SKILLS TO FIGHT THE WEAPONS CLUBS...
YOU COULD MAKE PEACE WITH THE PEOPLE BEHIND THE WEAPONS.
AND START OVER.
I KNOW IT WON'T BE EASY.
THERE'S A LOT OF PREJUDICE AND MISTRUST.
BUT I'M WILLING TO TRY A NEW BEGINNING IF YOU ARE.
YOU MAKE A GOOD POINT, SO WE'LL ***TRY***...
FOR NOW.

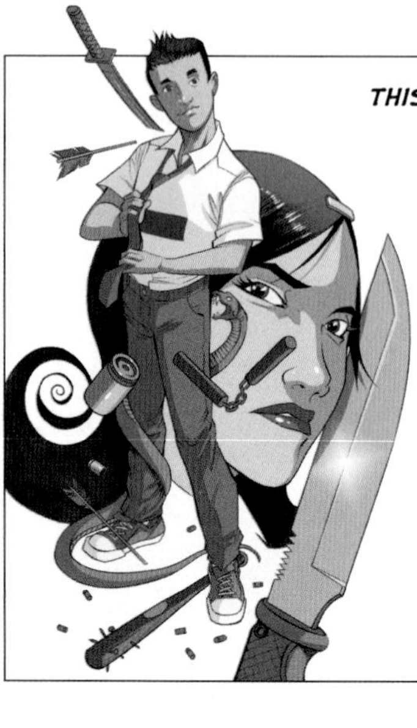

THIS WAS THE BEGINNING OF A NEW ERA FOR ASSASSIN EDUCATION.

EVENTUALLY, THE PSIONIC CLUB WAS INTEGRATED INTO THE SYSTEM, AND EVERYONE AGREED THAT THE INSTITUTION SHOULD BE RENAMED AS THE *SCHOOL OF SIX WEAPONS*.

THIS WASN'T ACCEPTED BY THE ENTIRE PSIONIC COMMUNITY, MANY WHO WANTED TO REMAIN HIDDEN. HOWEVER, ***ARI'S*** BREAKOUT GROUP CREATED A BRIDGE BETWEEN THE PSIONICS AND THE WEAPON CLASSES, AND IT EVEN SPARKED POSSIBLE CHANGES IN THE ASSASSIN AND SERVANT CLASSES.

ENRIQUE STAYED ON AS STUDENT MEDIC, UNDER THE SUPERVISION OF THE NURSE, AND GRADUATED WITH FULL HONORS.

TYLER ALSO RETURNED TO SCHOOL AS A LEGITIMATE STUDENT. THIS HELPED ENRIQUE AND TYLER REBUILD THEIR CHILDHOOD FRIENDSHIP AS THEY ENCOUNTERED OTHER ADVENTURES IN THE WORLD OF ASSASSINS.

BUT ONE THING THAT NEVER CHANGED WAS ENRIQUE'S SHARP MIND, HIS TRUST IN FRIENDSHIP, AND THE IDEA THAT PROBLEMS CAN BE SOLVED BY USING YOUR HEAD... INSTEAD OF YOUR FISTS.

THANKS FOR READING.

JIMMIE ROBINSON!

EXTRAS FROM JIMMIE'S SKETCHBOOK

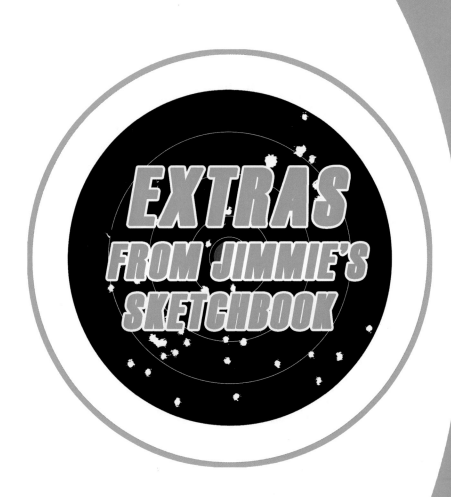

Issue 6, page 6 layouts.

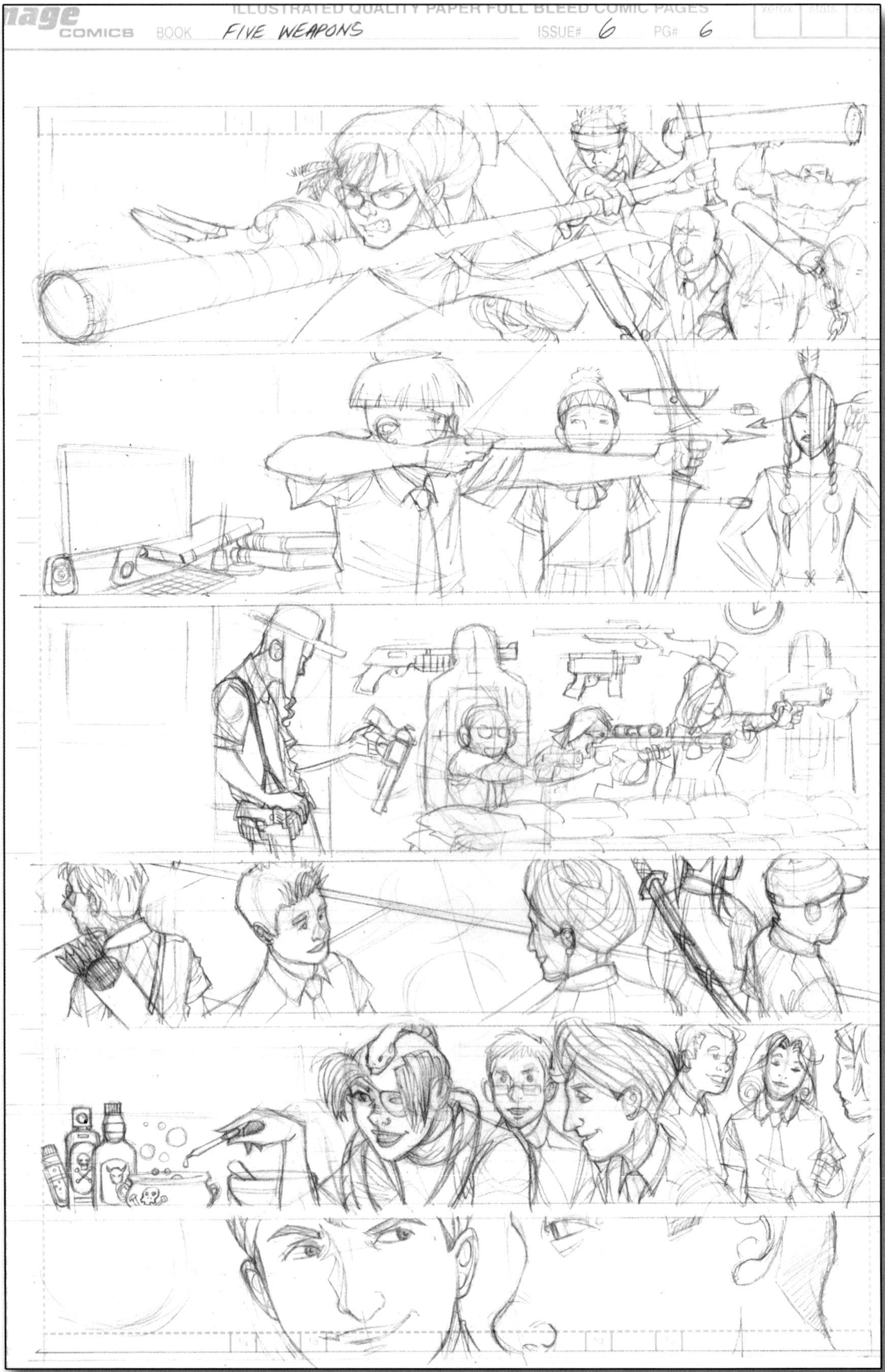
ILLUSTRATED QUALITY PAPER FULL BLEED COMIC PAGES
COMICS BOOK FIVE WEAPONS ISSUE# 6 PG# 6

Issue 6, page 6 pencils.

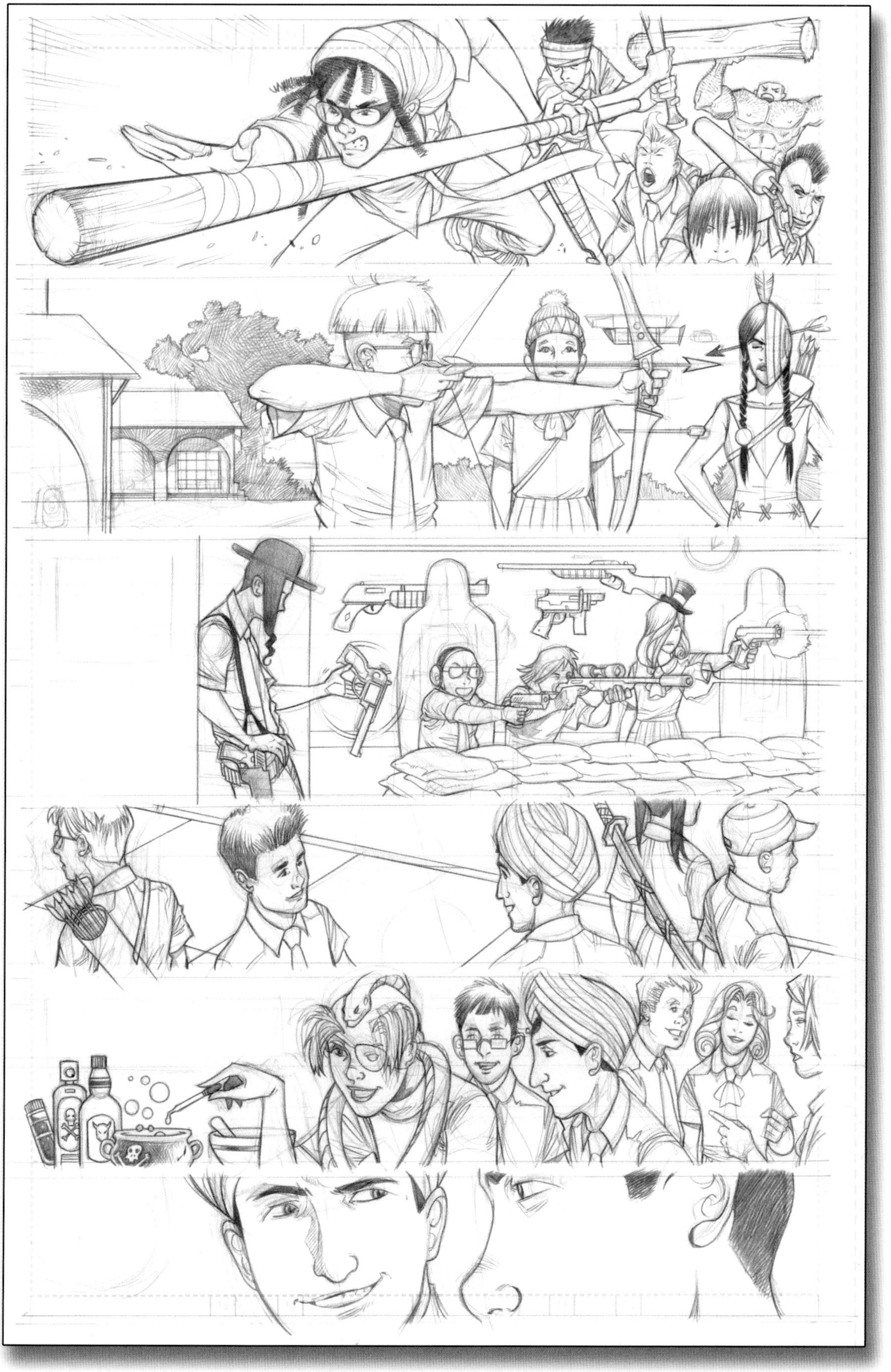

Issue 9 cover--from initial sketch to finished pencils.

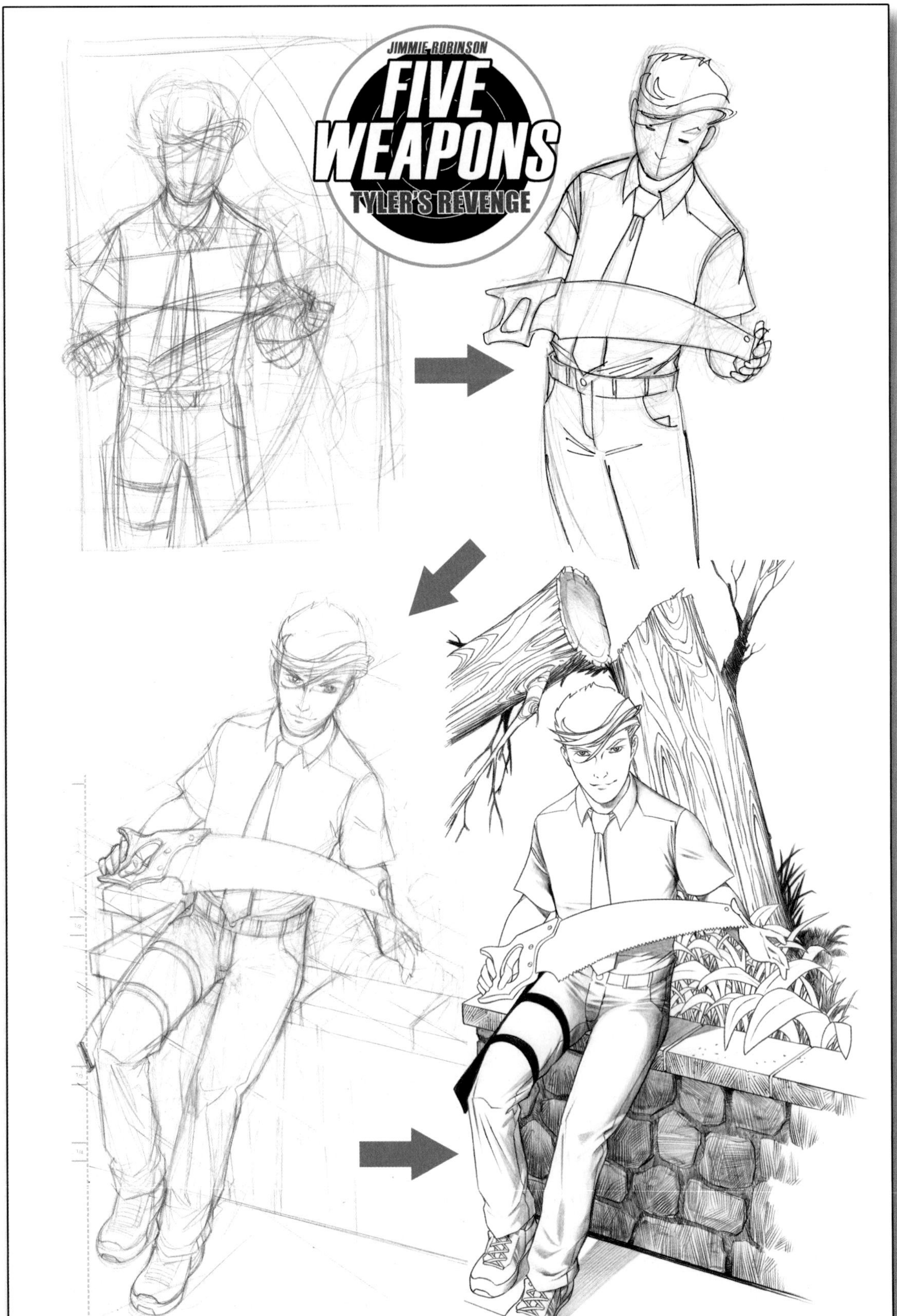
JIMMIE ROBINSON
FIVE WEAPONS
TYLER'S REVENGE

Issue 6, page 13 pencils.

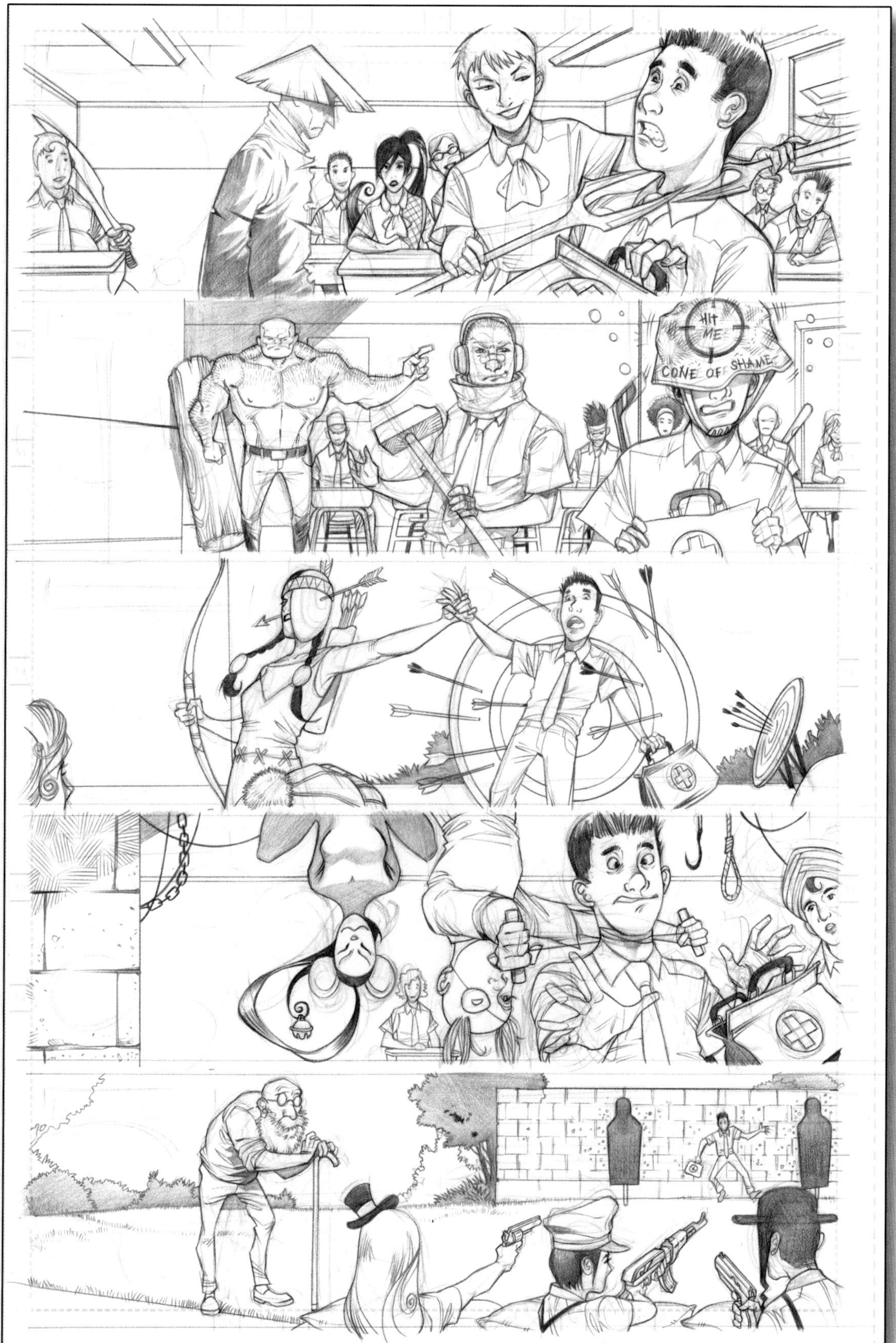
HIT ME
CONE OF SHAME

Issue 8, page 6 pencils.

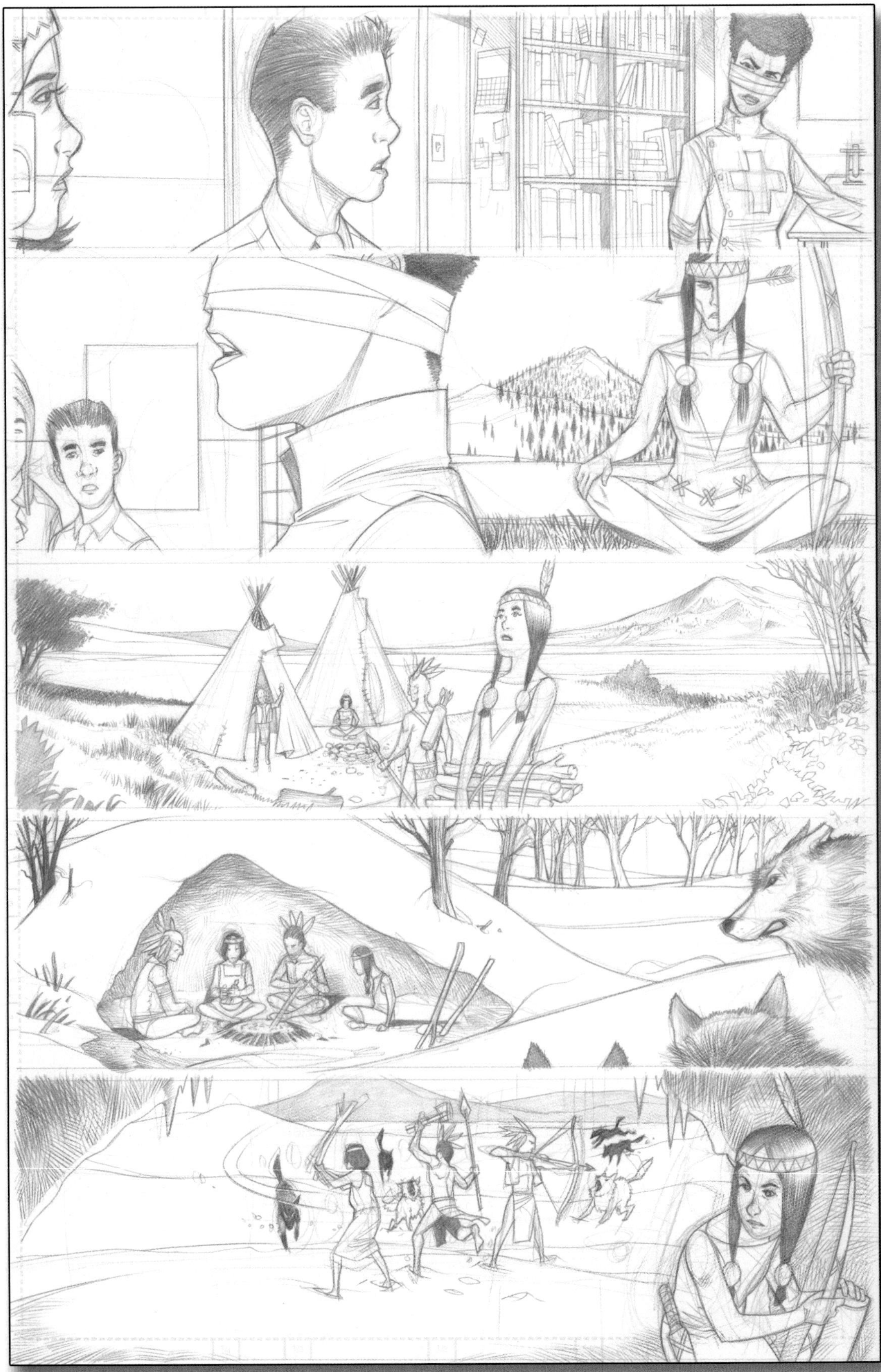

Issue 10, page 1 pencils.

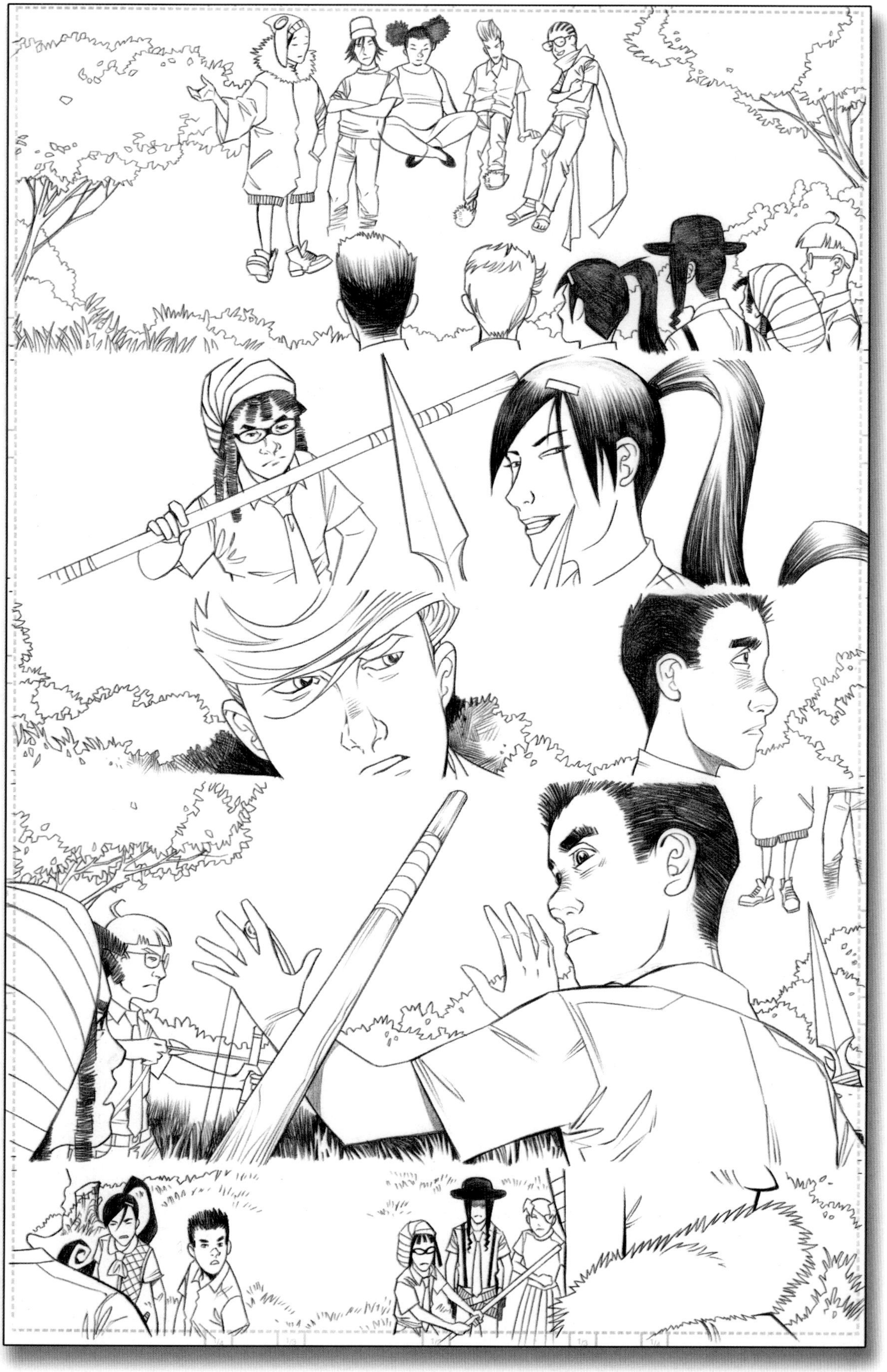

Rob Guillory's alternate cover for issue 6.

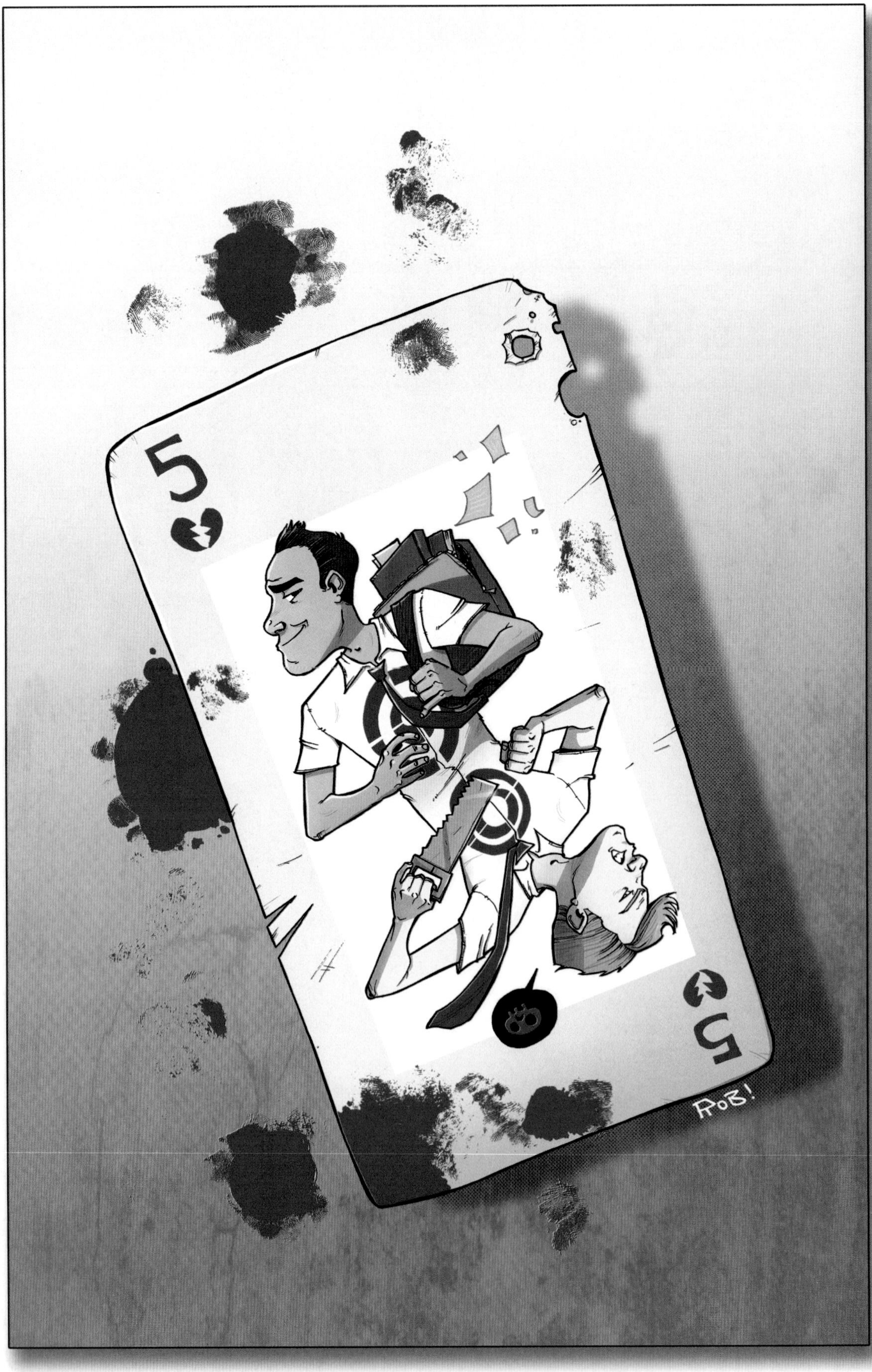

5
5
ROB!

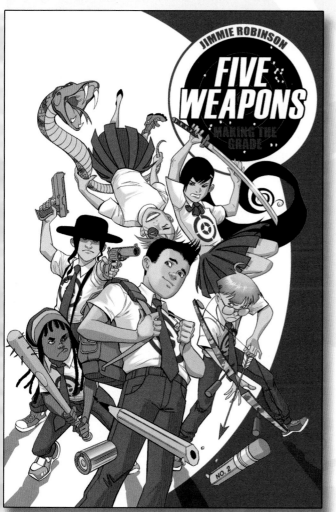

THIS is diversity! Graphic Novels For the Discriminating Reader

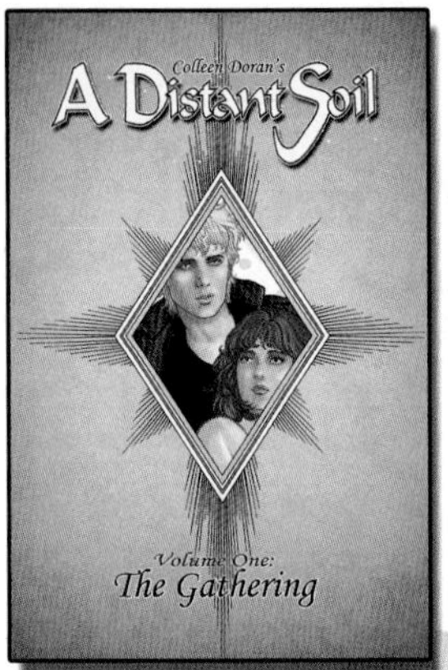
Colleen Doran's
A Distant Soil
Volume One:
The Gathering

A DISTANT SOIL

Colleen Doran's legendary magnum opus completely remastered and re-edited with beautiful new die-cut covers. Five volumes.

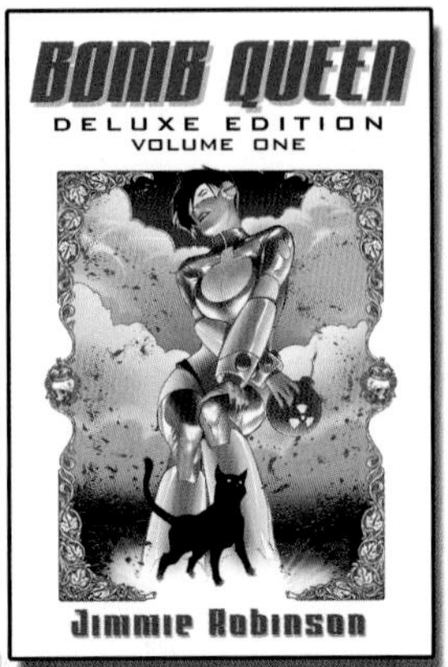
BOMB QUEEN
DELUXE EDITION
VOLUME ONE
Jimmie Robinson

BOMB QUEEN DELUXE

Jimmie Robinson's adults only satire of politics, sex and social mores. Not for the easily offended! Four Over-size hardcover volumes.

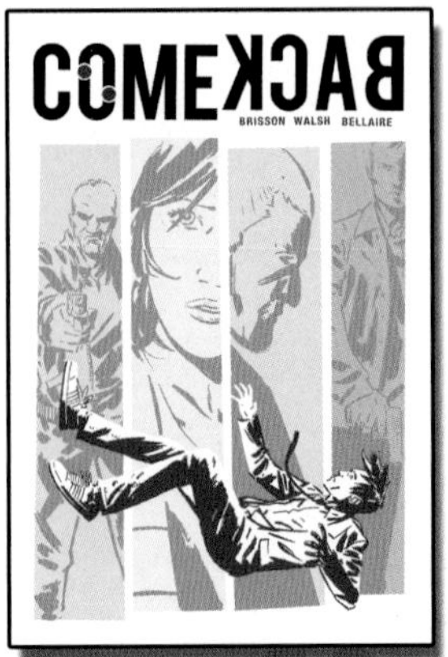
COMEBACK
BRISSON WALSH BELLAIRE

COMEBACK

Comeback is more than a company--we will bring your loved ones back moments before their untimely deaths...for a price.

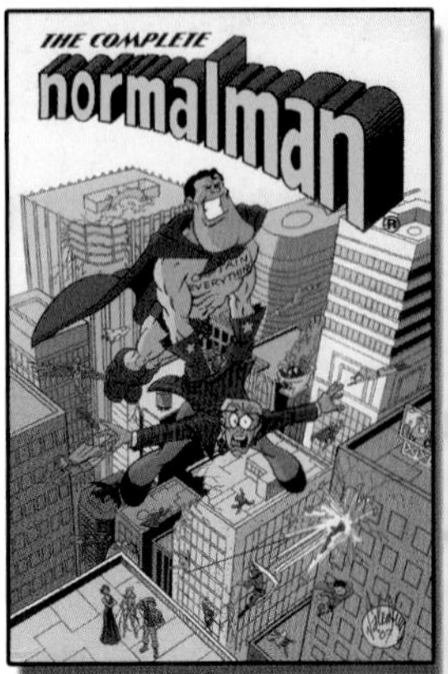
THE COMPLETE
normalman

COMPLETE normalman

The legendary classic parody series collected in one gigantic volume for the first time!

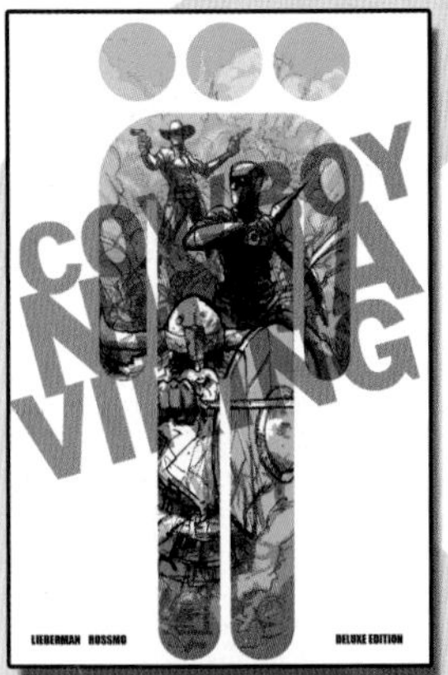
COWBOY
NINJA
VIKING
LIEBERMAN ROSSMO
DELUXE EDITION

COWBOY NINJA VIKING

Now in a Deluxe Oversize hardcover edition! Duncan has three distinct personalities...of course he's a government agent.

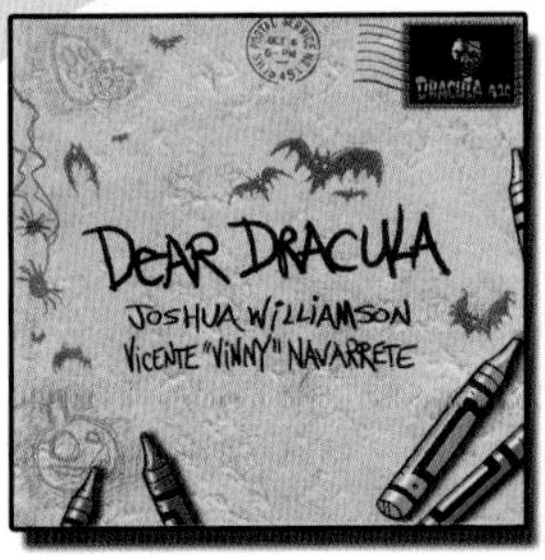
DEAR DRACULA
JOSHUA WILLIAMSON
VICENTE "VINNY" NAVARRETE

DEAR DRACULA

All Sam wants this Halloween is to become a real vampire! So he writes a letter to his hero, Count Dracula...who pays him a visit!

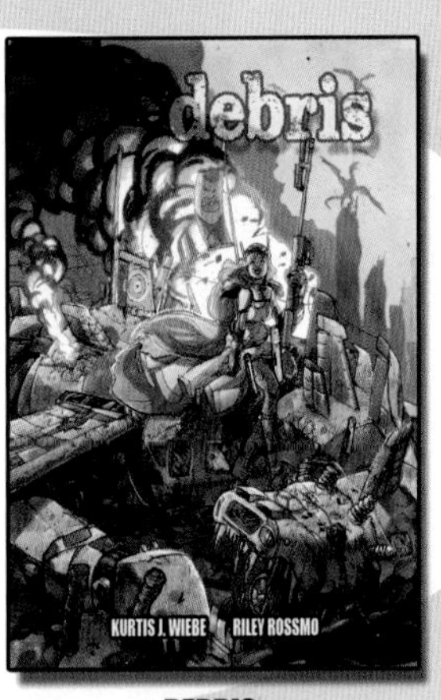
debris
KURTIS J. WIEBE
RILEY ROSSMO

DEBRIS

Maya must find a source of pure water to save the world before the garbage monsters bring it all to an end.

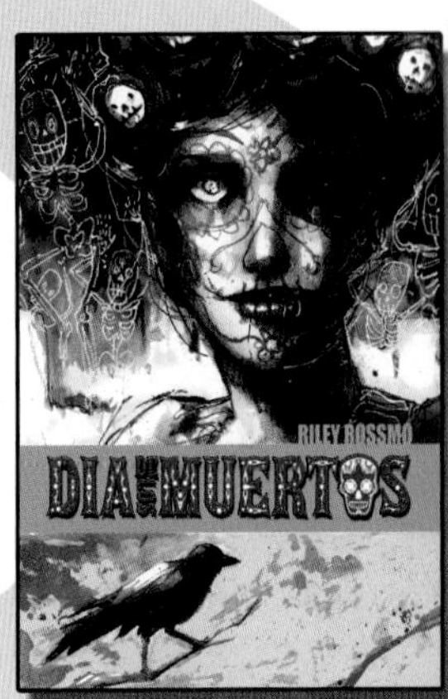
RILEY ROSSMO
DIA DE LOS MUERTOS

DIA DE LOS MUERTOS

Nine acclaimed writers and one amazing artist, Riley Rossmo, tell tales from the Mexican Day of the Dead.

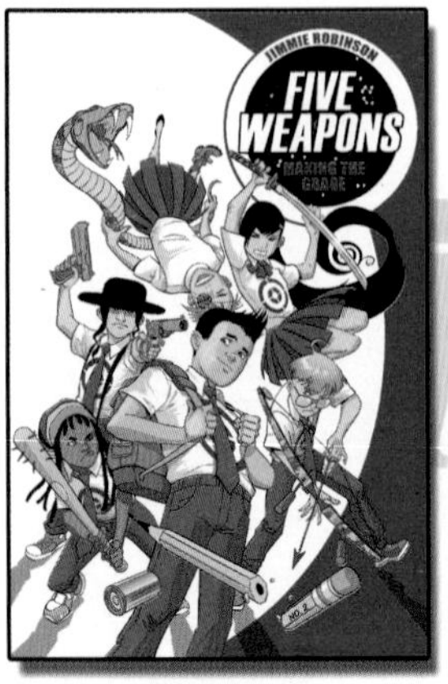
JIMMIE ROBINSON
FIVE WEAPONS
MAKING THE GRADE

FIVE WEAPONS

In a school for assassins, Tyler has the greatest of them all going for him...his mind! Jimmie Robinson's latest epic makes the grade.

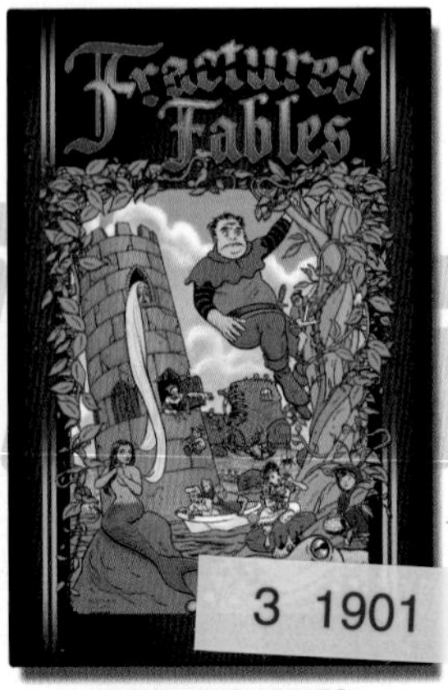
Fractured Fables

FRACTURED FABLES

Award winning cartoonists put a wicked but hilarious spin on well worn Fairy tales in this not-to-be-missed anthology.

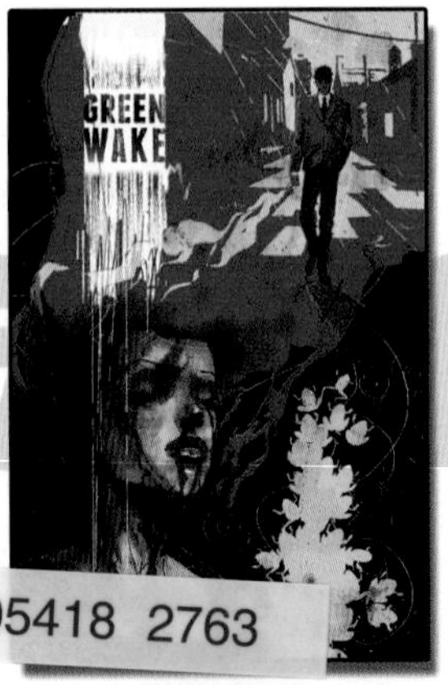
GREEN WAKE

GREEN WAKE

A riveting tale of loss and horror that blends mystery and otherworldly eccentricity in two unforgettable, critically acclaimed volumes.

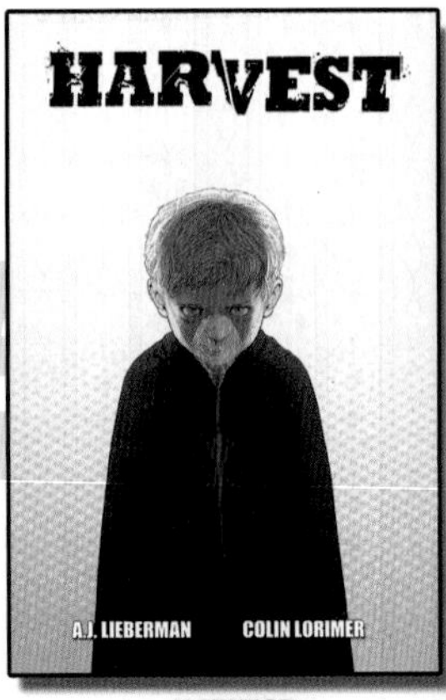
HARVEST
A.J. LIEBERMAN
COLIN LORIMER

HARVEST

Welcome to Dr. Benjamin Dane's nightmare. His only way out is to bring down the man who set him up harvesting organs.